Blake Snyder would be so proud of *Save the Cat! Writes for TV* because like all his books, it cuts straight to the truth: No matter where you are in your TV writing career, a newbie or a 25+ year veteran (me), you need to write a fresh, new pilot. Author Jamie Nash uses Blake's life-changing beat sheet and adjusts it for TV's "wonkiness." Whether you're writing a comedy or drama for network, cable, or streaming, this book with its thought-provoking exercises, sage advice, and beat sheets from successful TV shows will definitely get you closer to FADE OUT... and quite possibly your own TV show!

> — Kriss Turner Towner, Executive Producer, *Greenleaf*;
> Consulting Producer, *Black Monday*, *The Soul Man*; Co-Executive
> Producer, *The Romanoffs*, *Everybody Loves Chris*, *The Bernie Mac Show*

While I wish it were called *Save the Dog!*, I believe *Save the Cat!* can open eyes and demystify some of the biggest challenges TV writers face on that daunting blank page.

> — Steven Levitan, Co-Creator, *Modern Family*

Save the Cat! Writes for TV will help you wrap your arms around the process of turning inspiration into a script and more importantly, a series. Highly recommended.

> — Nick Bakay, Executive Producer, *Mom*; Consulting Producer,
> *Bob Hearts Abishola*, *The Kominsky Method*, *'Til Death*, *The King of Queens*

There's joy in TV Land! As a longtime user and fan of *Save the Cat!*, I've found Jamie Nash has shifted the focus (without losing the principles) of Blake Snyder's groundbreaking work, creating a whole new way to look at developing television series that's filled with insight, ingenuity, and a generous sprinkling of humor. A new must-read for newcomers to the field and veterans looking to shake up their process.

> — Paris Barclay, Director/Producer/Writer, *Sons of Anarchy*, *Glee*,
> *House*, *The Good Wife*, *In Treatment*, *Scandal*, *Empire*, *CSI*, *Lost*, *The
> West Wing*, *ER*, *NYPD Blue*

This book should be required reading not only for writers, but for all the film producers out there who are looking to branch out into TV. It breaks down the fundamental tenets of television storytelling in such a delightfully entertaining way that you often forget how much you're actually learning!

> — Juliet Berman, Producer/Head of Development, Treehouse Pictures (*Set It Up*, *Sand Castle*, *That Awkward Moment*)

This book will be by my side the next time I'm staring at a blank screen and wondering, "How do I do this again?" Eye-opening and inspirational, *Save the Cat Writes for TV* is an invaluable tool for anyone—from first-time writers to pros like me.

> — Lilla Zuckerman, Co-Executive Producer, *Prodigal Son*, *Agents of S.H.I.E.L.D.*; Supervising Producer, *Suits*; Consulting Producer, *Haven*

The opportunities to write for television have exploded in the last few years and *Save the Cat! Writes for TV* is the book TV writers have been waiting for. Beyond formulas and restrictive templates, this great new book provides the guidance we all need to shape and organize our ideas into well-structured scripts. I have been writing TV for decades—if only this book was around when I started! Just like Blake Snyder's original, this new member of the *Cat!* family will become a go-to industry standard.

> — Rick Drew, Producer/Story Editor/Writer of over 100 episodes of television, including *MacGyver*, *Airwolf*, *Goosebumps*, *Lonesome Dove*; Screenwriting Teacher, Vancouver Film School

Da Cat makes the leap from film to TV and *definitely* sticks the landing! This easy-to-read book is a must for writers in search of a well-structured TV script. It scores a perfect 10 from me.

> — Geoff Harris, TV Writer and Consultant, Former Network Development Executive

SAVE THE CAT!®
WRITES
FOR TV

The Last Book on Creating Binge-Worthy Content You'll Ever Need

JAMIE NASH
BASED ON THE BOOKS BY
BLAKE SNYDER

Published in the United States by *Save the Cat!*® Press, Los Angeles, CA

www.savethecat.com

Cover Design: Shadow Works Ltd.
Interior Design: Gina Mansfield Design

Library of Congress Control Number: 2020946914
Trade Paperback ISBN: 978-0-9841576-9-3
ebook ISBN: 978-0-9841576-2-4

Printed in the United States of America

TABLE
OF
CONTENTS

THE COLD OPEN

I've been using *Save the Cat!* longer than anybody on planet Earth.

Anybody.

I think.

I'm 90% sure.

I'd bet a dollar on it.

Back in the early 'aughts (2000s not 1900s), I cyber-met this ultra-friendly screenwriting dude named Blake Snyder. He was by far the most successful screenwriter person I had ever met. Which made me suspicious. Why was he talking to me? Some wannabe screenwriter-goof living in Maryland and writing quirky scripts, trying to be the next John Waters or Lloyd Kaufman or Roger Corman.

Blake checked out a few of my screenplays—the ones I didn't think I could pull off on my $500-to-feed-the-crew budgets. He liked what he read. He saw something. And not too long after, Blake enlisted me to co-write a script with him that we'll call *Untitled Fast & the Furious-Style Talking Car Movie*. (Call me Disney+. I'll send the PDF.) I was a baby-screenwriter and this was the guy who wrote the Disney hit *Blank Check* and sold a big spec script to Steven Spielberg and bagged a blind-script deal (whatever the heck that meant). Blake had everything I didn't: IMDB credits, a fancy agent, and Spielberg's home phone number. He was also a screenwriting Jedi Master. A Yoda of parentheticals and sluglines. The Mr. Miyagi of three-act structure and character arcs. He made me "wax his car " and "paint his fence," somehow magically teaching me how to write good scene descriptions and less "on the nose" dialogue.

I was still struggling to understand how Joseph Campbell and Robert McKee applied to my Farrelly-Brothers-rip-off-gross-out comedies when Blake started dropping brain bombs about putting trailer moments into my "Fun & Games" and how the Magical Midpoint's "false victory" upped the stakes on my "Bad Guys Close In."

This pre-dated Blake's writing of *Save the Cat!®: The Last Book on Screenwriting You'll Ever Need* by a few years. He was just an experienced co-writer/mentor spewing hard-learned techniques that helped make all that high-minded Campbell and Mckee stuff more palatable.

I assumed Blake's nuggets of wisdom were all "common industry" rigamarole. I didn't realize I was some guinea pig in his lab experiment. I figured if I stepped into CAA or Universal Studios, they'd all be talking about "Dark Night of the Soul" moments and asking about my hero's "shard of glass." Blake had a bunch of different wrinkles too—the good stuff you discover through years of experience. His generous sharing allowed me to level up and fast-forward from a clueless newbie... to a slightly clued-in newbie.

I was ahead of the game.

I had an edge.

I knew all the valuable secrets.

Then he gave them all away.

Save the Cat! is Blake in a book. It's that experienced Steven Spielberg on speed dial Obi-Wan for everyone to share. The book allows the reader to live my experience. It's an invisible co-writer/mentor/showrunner challenging you, asking, "But what's the Midpoint?" or "Is the All Is Lost coming too early?" or "Why is this paced so slowly?"

The questions *Save the Cat!* plants in your psyche will be the ones you'll hear in writers' rooms and ask of co-writers. Sometimes, you'll ignore them. Sometimes, they'll cause you to go back to the drawing board. But there will always be a strong reason to ask the question, a note-behind-the-note. And having that co-writer there to always have your back...will make you better. It'll level you up.

For those of you who have read *Save the Cat!* or picked up the other books in the series, the key tenets have stayed mostly the same. All of the books in the *Save the Cat!* oeuvre continue to forward Blake's basic principles.

But a word of warning....

TV gets wonky.

TV requires some new stuff.

Wonkier stuff.

Save the Cat! teaches writers how to develop a well-crafted story. But TV shows are more than just stories. They're story engines, story brands. Shows, of course, contain stories and stories always hit all the standard beats laid out in *Save the Cat!*.

But what is a story? Is it an episode? A season? Or an entire series?

See!

Wonky.

In this book, we'll put an emphasis on the most important thing you'll need to start: TV pilots (aka first episodes of shows). TV pilots must do all the duty of a great standalone story while also providing a launchpad to an entire series. They also happen to be one of the single hardest things to write.

If you're familiar with *the Cat!,* you'll recognize lots of the basics, the beats, the genres.

But there'll be other stuff.

New stuff.

Stuff I've learned the hard way.

Stuff I've done, studied, and taught over the years.

Stuff I'm giving away.

I hope it can be your co-writer.

I hope it can be your Blake.

INTRODUCTION

SO YOU WANNA BE A TV WRITER?

A long time ago, in a Hollywood far far away, film was the cool kid. Directors were Gleaming Rock Gods. They were emperors conquering summer box office and lording over the most anticipated blockbusters and franchises in the entertainment landscape. They also were making serious art and important stories—killing it at Sundance and claiming Oscar® glory. In short, films were kicking serious butt.

TV was sitting at the un-cool table. It was safe. It sold soap. Its lukewarm shows were designed for the masses aka your grandma, your lame brother, your boring square parents. It was bland, episodic, formulaic, and unadventurous. Poor TV actors were stigmatized and stuck in the television gutter. No serious director wanted to touch it. TV writers were well-paid lame-os. Sell-outs even.

Then came the HBO. Then Netflix. Then the Peacock.

Now, everyone wants to Netflix & Chill. Cool kids wanna be binge-watched. Movie stars can't wait to headline their own limited series. Wunderkind directors are signing massive overall deals. And even film franchises can't wait to jump on the Disney+ and Amazon Prime and HBO Max bandwagons.

It was a few years ago that I sensed the change. I was pitching my usual "weirdo" stuff to the movie folks. They were digging the takes but looking for something safe, similar, samey-same. It was frustrating. The movie game had gone cookie-cutter. What happened to the fresh voices and bold ideas? What happened to risk? Where were the Gleaming Rock Gods?!

Apparently, they had all moved over to the small screen.

My TV peeps were the ones asking for the fun freaky stuff—like *Bojack Horseman* and *Russian Doll* and *End of the F**king World.* I particularly remember a week of meetings where two different producers gave the same bonkers idea as an example of the out-of-the-box pitch they were seeking: a show about cars that used human blood for gasoline. (It's called *Blood Drive*—it got made—go binge it!)

Cars.

That drank blood.

On TV?!!!

Welcome to the upside-down world.

Even the prestige Oscar® content and independent-minded Sundance fare seemed to be sliding over to the small screen. *The Crown*, *Mad Men*, *Atlanta*, *The Marvelous Mrs. Maisel*, *Fleabag* all stream right into your living room, while movie theaters are mostly dominated by $300-million budgeted extravaganzas built to entertain the entire world.

(Of course, TV's also been "drinking film's milkshake" with its own blockbuster IP swings—things like *The Mandalorian*, *The Lord of the Rings*, and numerous shows featuring DC & Marvel Superheroes.)

Equally as important to you, dear reader, who just plunked down hard cash for a book about writing: in TV the writer is king. These kings are called **showrunners** and instead of crowns and scepters, they wield index cards and dry-erase boards. Unlike film, where writers are hired and fired at a whim and rarely spend time on sets or get their pictures on the cover of *Variety*, the TV Writer has more control, more respect, and more Gleaming Rock God glory.

TV IS A TEAM SPORT

TV writing is typically an office gig where a group of 5-10 (or sometimes even more on big network shows) sit in a comfy conference room and brainstorm season arcs, outline episodes, post copious note cards, order Chinese food, trash-talk studio notes, and occasionally break to actually go type things on their laptops like "FADE IN:" and "INT. CENTRAL PERK - DAY"

The showrunner is sort of the player-coach of these writing teams. They write and lead writers and guide story decisions but also hire and fire people, get yelled at by studio chiefs, stress over budgets and schedules, coax disgruntled actors out of trailers, and make tough decisions about Mrs. Maisel's shoes and Tyrion Lannister's Starbucks cups. On any given day, they're rewriting scripts, schmoozing fancy actors, or pulling their hair out in the edit bay. Oftentimes they do all three in a day plus take Zoom meetings about marketing strategy or bad ratings or adding an extra commercial break to their already pressed-for-time show.

It's hard, all-encompassing work. It might be one of the most taxing jobs in film and television. It's also the polar opposite of what most of us want from a writing job: boardroom politics, payrolls, constant compromise, and big bad ulcers.

Ultimately, it's the showrunner's voice that flavors a series. They're like old-school auteur writer-directors. From Shonda Rhimes to Aaron Sorkin to Amy Sherman-Palladino, you can feel their uber-talented fingerprints all over the shows they run.

But nobody is handed the showrunner crown and scepter on their first day.

You need to work your way up.

You need to get into one of these rooms.

How do you do it?

Read on...

WHO IS THIS BOOK FOR?

This book is specifically designed for people creating original TV stories and those trying to break into television by writing original TV stories or spec scripts for established TV shows.

Or Aaron Sorkin.

Because I'm sure Aaron Sorkin randomly picks up books on TV writing to sharpen his skills before he dives into his next season of award-winning TV.

The chapters ahead give you the tools to come up with show ideas, develop season arcs, and most importantly, write pilot episodes.

Great pilot scripts are what you need to land one of those coveted writers' room gigs. And that's what *Save the Cat!*® *Writes for TV* is all about.

TV SCRIPTS DON'T SELL SHOWS, TV SCRIPTS SELL YOU

Much like in feature writing, the way to break into TV is to write an original script that is pure fyre. Here's the wonky thing: these scripts hardly ever sell. Why? Because shows are a big investment across multiple seasons, and the powers-that-be are suspicious of the unwashed masses strutting into their office with wild new ideas. They prefer to turn to proven entities with big track records and experience—people who not only have great writing skills but also the ability to play nice with others and can manage stressful moving trains and crippling pressure and last-minute studio notes that pull the rug out from under everyone. And these showrunners are writers who, like all writers, have their own ideas that they're passionate about. It's quite a commitment to jump on board a show, and the showrunners that TV trusts most are reluctant to give up weeks and hours and years of their lives to work on things that they're not burning to create. Those passion projects, more often than not, originate from their own brains—not yours.

It's not completely unheard of for outsiders to sell an original TV show. But it's rare. It's like Bigfoot-sighting rare. It's like Bigfoot-riding-on-a-unicorn rare. Of course, with the ever-increasing hunger for content, maybe we'll see a lot more Bigfoots and unicorns.

For now, the best advice is to set your sights on one of those coveted TV writers' room seats, learn and work your way up the ladder, then become king (err... showrunner)! To take the first step, you're gonna need script samples, show ideas, and pilots that demonstrate your cleverness, unique voice, and chutzpah!

YOUR SCRIPT PORTFOLIO

No one cares if you have a fancy degree or if you worked as a summer intern for *Celebrity Big Brother* Season 3. Those things might be valuable to get contacts who can share your work with people in the know... but to get hired in TV, you're going to need scripts! Great ones!

This book focuses on the four most important things you'll need in your portfolio:

1. **SHOWS** — Coming up with a unique show that has the potential to run for many seasons. These shows have distinctive worlds, hero-worthy characters, timely themes, and story engines that provide motivations and conflicts week-after-week.

2. **SEASON ARCS** — While new writers are not asked to crank out entire seasons of television just to sell their show, they're often asked to pitch the overall vibe of the series. This is where knowing how to write a high-level season arc is key. The emphasis here is "high-level" because your real energy needs to be saved for the pilots.

3. **PILOTS** — First episodes of your original series. These stories demonstrate your voice, your knack for creating original ideas, and your abilities to craft first episodes. They also introduce and sell your unique show to prospective buyers and potential viewers. Original pilots are the most common things writers are asked to submit as a working sample when applying for TV jobs.

4. **TV PITCHES** — 5- to 10-page pitches of everything a studio or network would ever need to know about your cool new TV series idea.

In television, they're looking to staff rooms filled with unique voices. Strive for stories that are "you on a plate" (as the great screenwriting guru Chef Gordon Ramsay would say). Start by writing stories you would actually want to see. Create the type of shows you'd want to add to your DVR or binge-watch on a lonely Saturday night. **Don't try to guess what they want—write what you want.**

LET'S TALK TV TALK

TV has its own jargon. I'll be throwing around a bunch of TV terms that you'll need to know.

This is a good time to introduce the first: **breaking story**. That's the act of creating the beats of a story. Breaking story usually happens during those first days of a writers' room where the writing team has to figure out the trajectory of a season and/or the individual episodes within the season. You can break a season, a character arc, or a single episode.

Okay, now that you know what it means… let's break some story.

PART 1

THE SHOW

🐾 WHAT'S THE SHOW?

Ten or 15 years ago, would-be Vince Gilligans were forced to write standalone episodes of shows already on the air. Young Vinny G would crank out a 30-page *Happy Days* spec where Fonzie got attacked by a land shark or an episode of *Love Boat* where the Pacific Princess hit an iceberg and only had a life raft big enough for either Captain Stubing or Isaac the bartender.

These were known as spec scripts. Unlike feature films, where specs are typically your original concepts, TV writers picked a currently existing show and write a standalone episode to demonstrate they could "write in a show's voice."

Things have changed.

These days, showrunners and staffers ask their prospective writers' room candidates to submit 100% original material. While some TV muckety-mucks will hire newbie scribes based on feature scripts or plays or other materials, the vast majority are asking for pilots, i.e., first episodes of original shows.

So instead of coming up with a fun Season 5 predicament for Jerry and Kramer to get mixed up in, nowadays you need to conceive your own show, its world, its people, and write an amazing first episode which both launches the show and demonstrates its promise.

There's a chicken/egg problem here. Before you write a great pilot, you must first have a great idea for a show. You don't need an entire 10 seasons mapped out or anything—let's keep it one episode at a time for now—but you need enough to know what you're setting up, who your characters are, what the tone is, and what you need to seed in the first episode for the ongoing series. A pilot must propose a promise of greatness for the episodes and seasons ahead. But it takes more than just a snazzy cliffhanger to make a viewer click "Record Series."

Your pilot must deliver enough information for the audience to grasp the show's broader potential and hook them to make the longer commitment for the rest of the season(s).

Movie concepts tend to be big and flashy with dollops of irony. New twists on old ideas. Premises that promise splashy trailers and immediately inspire set pieces and pitchable gags. While it's great for television shows to have all those things, the priority is on delivering strong characters we want to invite into our living rooms week after week or binge after binge

Movies are a fling... TV shows are a relationship.

And like any relationship, they need to be built to last. They must go beyond quick sizzle or spectacle that burns out after the third episode or the first season.

YOUR FIRST FIVE QUESTIONS

How do you create a show? And where do you start?

Here are 5 key questions you need to answer when creating your show:

1. **What's your world?**
2. **What's your franchise type?**
3. **Who are your characters?**
4. **What's your format?**
5. **Who's your audience?**

In this chapter, we're going to tackle world, franchise type, format and audience. In the next chapter, we'll focus entirely on character.

WHAT'S YOUR WORLD?

While the occasional comedy show is "about nothing" (I'm looking at you, *Seinfeld*), they're often created by comedians with years of stand-up experience who have honed a specific and hilarious POV. The rest of us need to make shows about unique and fresh worlds... the New Jersey mob, women's wrestling in the '80s, high-school glee clubs, the West Wing, TV newsrooms, the Baltimore City drug economy, high-stakes high-school football, etc. If you deliver a peek behind the curtain on something fresh, it'll draw attention.

Worlds are more than just locations (though they can be that too), they're story arenas. They can be about groups of people, ways of thinking, even historical periods.

You've heard that old lame writing advice, "write what you know."

Worlds are the things you know... or things you wanna know. What are you expert in? What do you want to be an expert in? You're curating a peek behind the curtain, a secret knowledge, a tour. So... what's your expertise?

There are three places to find your worlds:

1. Worlds you've lived in.
2. Worlds you want to live in.
3. Worlds you create.

Worlds you've lived in. These are the worlds you've been immersed in and know all the gritty details. Most of us have a fresh world or two in our backstories. Have you worked at an unusual place (or tragically mundane, like Dunder Mifflin) or maybe you have an offbeat hobby? Do you run in unique social circles or suffer through a bizarre or unbelievable family dynamic? Maybe you have a strange marriage or living situation or psychological profile?

For example, on the whole, I'm a really boring dude, but still, I've accumulated some worlds. I've worked in Computer Gaming (*Mythic Quest* beat me to that one already); I adjunct teach at an art college (the same one *Broad City* talks about!); I used to be a high-school basketball ref ("Refs!" starring Danny McBride coming your way on HBO), I grew up LARPing (Live Action Role-Playing games—don't make fun, or I'll hit you with my foam sword). On the personal front, I have a son with autism; his school, support, and other families in like situations are unique worlds I've lived (shows like *Atypical* and *Little Voice* and *The Good Doctor* are doing awesome jobs in this space). Back in college, I was a street performer (juggling and magic), hung out at Renaissance festivals, performed with an improvisational murder mystery company, and spent way too much time and money in comic-book stores and hustling ping-pong.

Nowadays, I do podcasting, shoot independent films, have season tickets to the NFL (go Ravens!), play poker with a crew of poker weirdos, and meet regularly with a gang of novel writers.

That's just off the top of my head. Any of these worlds could be the stuff of a TV show. I'm sure if I dig deeper, I could get weirder and fresher. So can you.

Worlds you want to live in. These are the worlds you don't have experience with but you'd love to research. Think of the things you gravitate toward. What non-fiction books are on your Kindle? Mine tend to be behind-the-scenes exposès of sports teams, pro wrestlers, dotcom-era businesses, and tell-all Hollywood stories. Lots of worlds to explore there. Ones I already explore for fun. And that's the money. Try to dive into something you'd love to go all-in with. You've got an excuse now!

What do you always find yourself talking about? What websites do you visit or stories do you click on? What keeps you up at night and gets you going early in the morning? Pick one world and go for it!

There are other worlds lurking out there. One morning you'll read an article about competitive eating contests and say, "That would make a great show!" I remember an article about the cut-throat world of ice cream men in NYC. That's a world. I saw another idea about *Dungeons & Dragons*' Dungeon Masters who hire themselves out to run games for non-gamers. Keep your eyes and ears open and worlds will appear in your social media, on the news, and in the wild.

Worlds you create. These are for the world-builders. All the budding JK Rowlings or George Lucases or George R.R. Martins. These are the scribes who will invent science fiction, fantasy, and horror realms that may be analogous to our world in some way but require heaps of imagination. You'll churn up the politics, the science, and the magic. Or maybe you're just an expert on some subgenre: vampires, cyberpunk, fantasy worlds, etc. Perhaps you want to mix elements of these genres with one of the worlds you actually know and have lived in, or a real world you want to research. Mixing in genre tropes with your worlds can be a great way to freshen up things that might otherwise be "been there, done that."

WHAT ARE YOUR WORLDS?

Okay, enough talk, bust out your story notebook, and make a list. Try your hand at each of the three world types.

What are the worlds you've collected? Were you a waiter at Olive Garden? A giant rat at Chucky Cheese? Did you teach kung fu at the YMCA? Did you win a trophy for competitive Pictionary? Are you a professional coloring book artist? Do you and your terrier compete in dog shows?

Think of worlds at home, at work, and at play. Think of the past and right now. Even a deep dive into your seemingly mundane worlds can be interesting. List *everything* without censoring yourself. Challenge yourself to come up with 20 potential worlds. Then when you have 20, come up with 20 more. You don't have to be an expert in any of them—even if you spent an hour or a week in one of these worlds, you probably have some insight or opinion on it.

Next, dive into the worlds you'd love to know more about. Career paths you didn't go down. College courses you wish you had taken. Books or articles that sparked your interest. Cold cases of unsolved mysteries. Things you find yourself gravitating toward but have never lived. Again, go for 20 or more.

Last, if you're inclined, invent some worlds. Maybe they're riffs on ones you wrote above. Apply a dose of sci-fi or fantasy to a world you've lived in or are intrigued by. If you're the type that wants to be a world-builder, you may already have universes you've dabbled with or thought about. Write 'em down.

To help you brainstorm, here are some types of worlds commonly seen in TV:

- **9-TO-5'S** — Probably the most common world types on television are peeks behind the curtains of industries, careers, or workplaces. Oftentimes, these worlds are simply where the lead character works, whether it's for money, fame, personal drive, or even illegal. Examples: *The Office*, *Billions*, *Homeland*, *GLOW*, *The Sopranos*, *Six Feet Under*, *The Americans*, *Weeds*, *CSI*.

- **FAMILY MATTERS** — The second most common world types focus on unique families, crews, gangs, and situationships. Examples: *What We Do in the Shadows*, *Sons of Anarchy*, *This Is Us*, *Modern Family*, *Big Love*.

- **LOCATIONS, LOCATIONS, LOCATIONS** — These worlds are defined by geography or physical spaces where people live (that aren't necessarily jobs or workplaces). A space station, a fantasy world, a state, a city. Examples: *Deep Space 9*, *Northern Exposure*, *Picket Fences*.

- **GROWING PAINS** — These worlds focus on life-phases such as adolescence, teenage years, having children, mid-life crisis, divorce, death, etc. Examples: *Parenthood*, *Divorce*, *Better Things*, *Freaks & Geeks*, *Grace and Frankie*, *The Kominsky Method*.

- **BLAST FROM THE PAST** — These worlds feature historical periods or eras or even nostalgia. The week-to-week is flavored from the norms, ideas, and events particular to that era. (This is not to say all shows set in the past are Blast from the Past shows. *Better Call Saul* is set in the past but really doesn't exist to highlight that world.) Examples: *The Goldbergs*, *Mad Men*, *Happy Days*, *That '70s Show*.

- **LIFESTYLES** — These worlds delve into a "way of life" that goes beyond how someone works, where they live, or who they live with. These worlds are about style, attitudes, world views, and philosophies. Examples: *Sex and the City* (dating in NYC), *The Big Bang Theory* (all things Geek), *Ramy*, *Insecure*.

- **MAKE-BELIEVE** — These worlds are created from imagination and inhabited by zombies or dragons and wizards. These are for the world-builders. If you grew up loving these kinds of stories, you probably want to live in these worlds! Examples include *Game of Thrones*, *Gotham*, *Westworld*, *Lost*, *The Walking Dead*, *Carnival Row*.

For each of the world types, try listing out all the worlds you've lived in, studied, or you'd want to live in. At this stage, even an appetite for something that fascinates you belongs on the list. You might even be able to think of more world types. Good! This list isn't an attempt to categorize all the possible worlds, it's just meant to guide your thinking. The more world types, the better!

Something new… but different. Again, take care to find something fresh. *Mad Men* has been done. So has *GLOW*. But there are other stories set in the 1960s or ones about professional wrestling or maybe just women taking over a male-dominated sport.

The easiest way to make it fresh is to make it specific. *Very specific.* Don't just turn up with a show about a woman in the causally misogynistic 1960s. Show up with a show about a young Jewish mom who wants to be a Lenny Bruce-style comic in the 1960s. That's a world we haven't seen.

Okay, I hear ya… you're shouting… but what about medical shows? Or cops? Or lawyers? Those shows are evergreen, right?

Well, yes… and no.

You need to find your spin. Most great ideas don't come out of the blue. They're Reese's Peanut Butter Cups… a mix of two great tastes. Or pumpkin spice and lattes!

If Doctors are your latte... what's your pumpkin spice? Is it Doctors... the Musical (*Doc Rock!!*)? Or location... *NYMD*? Or maybe it's exorcist doctors? Or pet doctors? Or doctors who work in a Walmart Health Clinic?

Here are successful examples of worlds with the extra flavor infusion—old models (lattes) and added spice (pumpkin):

Grey's Anatomy = Sex & the Surgery

Sons of Anarchy = Hamlet with bikers

What We Do in the Shadows = The Office with vampires

Breaking Bad was pitched as "Mr. Chips to Scarface." That was fresh! That was spicy.

It's difficult to find the freshness in shows about family. Sometimes what's fresh is the telling. When *Modern Family* debuted, the special sauce was Mockumentary. Giving that *The Office* magic to a family show made it new and shiny. *The Goldbergs* is a straight-forward family show sprinkled with nostalgia dust. *This Is Us* is a soapy family drama that uses non-linear storytelling to keep us off balance and deliver mystery and plot twists in addition to its heartstring-plucking.

Your world must feel fresh and new—the type of thing viewers see advertised and must tune into.

WHAT'S THE FRANCHISE?

One of the first questions I ever got pitching television was "What's the franchise?"

This was a stumper.

Um... McDonald's? LeBron James? Marvel Superheroes?

Nope, nope, maybe.

Franchise in this context means **story engine**. Your show needs to inspire years' worth of stories.

Shows aren't stories.

Sure, shows provide the springboard for stories. Lots of them. If done right, it's the gift that keeps on giving.

Worlds alone aren't stories either. But they'll hint at stories. Funny ones, scary ones, very special ones guest-starring Tom Hanks.

Let's say your world is Defense Attorneys (*Court Rock* for the win!), maybe a procedural that presents a new case every week like *Boston Legal* or *LA Law*. Or perhaps it's a show like Amazon's *Goliath* that focuses on one main legal case a season or a show like *Better Call Saul* that is focused on fractured relationships and problems that surface in the life of a shady lawyer. Each of these potential series presents very different expectations in the way of storytelling, even if they share a very general world. This is what your franchise type or story engine is all about.

When coupled with a world, your franchise type will suggest recurring heroes and problems and imply situations ripe with conflict (hero's goals vs. the obstacles blocking them).

THE 8 *SAVE THE CAT!* FRANCHISE TYPES

These franchises have some crossover with the *Save the Cat!* genres that we'll be talking about later. While those genres suggest patterns found in a single story with a definitive ending, franchise types are the engines that inspire many stories. Franchise types contain the seeds of generating episode ideas for seasons and years to come.

Here are the 8 *Save the Cat!* franchise types:

1. TRAPPED TOGETHER — Families, either by blood or by circumstance, who are forced to live, work, or deal with each other and usually get on each other's last nerve.

Elements of a Trapped Together franchise include:
- **A situation.** Your main characters are stuck together. The situation is the reason why. Be it family (domestic trap), a shared office (workplace trap), roommates, or some unchangeable situationship, your characters can't escape and are forced to deal with one another.

- **The inmates are the problem.** These stories are focused on tension derived from "those you know" as opposed to the group or family solving external problems. For example, the story engine of *The Big Bang Theory* is about really, really smart but socially challenged astrophysicists who work and live together. Their stories derive from interpersonal conflicts and not about saving the world from science disasters or trying to build the world's greatest physics department or putting the first human on Mars. Non-Trapped shows like *House* and *Law & Order* have some tension within their "family" (as do all good shows), but their stories derive from tackling external problems, often as a team, that come at them week to week or season to season.

- **Situational Stories**. Storylines often revolve around the trap itself. Families might have stories about sharing DVR space, chores, or holiday gatherings. Workplaces might have stories about training sessions, office parties, happy hours, surprise inspections. Whatever the situational story, it should cause an increase of tension among those who are trapped together.

Trapped Togethers are traditionally one of the most prevalent franchise types.

Examples: *Modern Family*, *All in the Family*, *The Office*, *What We Do in the Shadows*, *The Simpsons*, *The West Wing*, *The Big Bang Theory*, *Orange Is the New Black*

2. BLANK OF THE WEEK — A hero or group of heroes must deal with a new external problem each episode. It could be a case to solve, a monster to slay, a patient to cure. The blank is clearly identifiable or nameable, i.e., it's a crime or a client or a patient. These are often procedurals like cop shows, lawyer shows, and medical dramas.

Elements of a Blank of the Week franchise include:
- **A job (or duty)** that forces the heroes to deal with certain types of new problems every week.
- **A new blank every week**. Every episode is focused on solving a new problem relating to their job. The problems are

commonly easy to label: Monster of the Week, Case of the Week, Mystery of the Week, Client of the Week.

Though Blank of the Weeks are by their very nature episodic, they often have light serialized arcs running across their seasons (Will they/won't they type love stories, *The X-Files* Cigarette Smoking Man mythology, a mysterious killer who needs to be caught, etc). Blank of the Weeks need an endless amount of blanks that you can list at the outset, so that your show can go for seasons before it ever comes close to repeating itself.

Examples: *House, CSI, Supernatural, The Flash, Law & Order, Elementary, Lucifer, Hawaii Five-O, Fringe, Evil, The X-Files, Buffy the Vampire Slayer*

3. (WO)MAN WITH A PLAN — An individual hero or team works together to accomplish a season-long mission or plan: to take down the bad guys, slay the dragon, win the trophy, travel to a destination, etc.

Elements of a (Wo)Man with a Plan franchise include:
- **A goal**, be it to win an award, slay a villain, better their life, or conquer a world.
- **A goal-minded team or an individual** with a season-long pursuit.

These stories often feel like extended movie plots. Unlike movies, they're given breathing room to deep-dive into various plot elements and side stories.

Examples: *The Great, Mr. Robot, Battlestar Galactica, Billions, MindHunter, Preacher, Revenge, Prison Break*

4. DUDE WITH A SEASON-LONG PROBLEM — An innocent hero is dragged into a problem that's not of their own doing and must strive to deal with it through an entire season (or seasons!). A (Wo)Man with a Plan is bringing the action. A Dude with a Season-Long Problem is trying to *survive* the action.

Elements of a Dude With a Season-Long Problem franchise include:
- **An innocent hero** who is swept into a problem that isn't their doing.
- **A problem** that lasts a season or longer.

Examples: *Stranger Things, 24, Homeland, The Watchmen, Prison Break, Jack Ryan, The Handmaid's Tale, The Walking Dead*

5. WHYDUNIT — A detective on a season-long or series-long case finds out not only "who done it," but the more important question: *why*? Starting with shows like *Murder One*, procedurals went to a model where they had a single season-long mystery.

Elements of a Whydunit franchise include:
- **A detective**. It could be an amateur gumshoe, a cop, a private eye, a security guard, a doctor, or anyone who might engage in a season-long investigation.
- **A season-long mystery**, as opposed to mysteries that are solved week-to-week, which are the stuff of Blank of the Weeks.
- **Every week we get closer** to the answer with twists and reveals along the way.

Examples: *Homecoming, How to Get Away with Murder, The Alienist, True Detective, Twin Peaks, The Killing, Broadchurch, Veronica Mars, Riverdale*

6. I'M NO FOOL — An underestimated hero causes conflict in the way they approach a world that doesn't understand them. They can never completely triumph—that would change the franchise type or bring about the end of the show.

Elements of an I'm No Fool franchise include:
- **A fool**. They can be the smartest person in the room, but the world they exist in does not see them that way.
- **A world** that doesn't understand them.

Examples: *New Girl, I Love Lucy, The Unbreakable Kimmy Schmidt, Broad City, Crazy Ex-Girlfriend, Jane the Virgin, Better Things, Ramy*

7. BUDDY LOVE — Two people share a series-long relationship. While a common genre in feature films and a prevalent B Story thread that runs through many TV shows, it's difficult to maintain a single love story throughout an entire season, let alone an entire show run. Often these are shorter-season half-hour shows that stretch out the love story for 5-10 episodes.

Elements of a Buddy Love franchise include:
- **A match made in heaven/hell** between two buddies, be they lovers, mother-daughter, etc.
- **A complicated relationship** that evolves from episode to episode with ups and downs and blow-ups and turmoil.

Examples: *Catastrophe, Love, Gilmore Girls, Grace & Frankie, Run, You're the Worst*

8. MAD, MAD WORLD — The world takes center stage with a large scope and big casts, where important characters may never even meet each other. These stories have facets that often blend other franchise types in service of a larger world.

Elements of a Mad, Mad World franchise include:
- **World-first** stories that take precedence over any individual character or group of characters.
- **Many storylines** that show various facets of how the world works.
- **Who are you again?** Main characters that never meet or even know another character exists.

Examples: *Game of Thrones, The Wire, Deadwood, Westworld*

FRANCHISE FINDING

Choose your world and then try on a few franchises like new bathing suits. See if they fit. Do the twirl in the mirror. Then pick the one that feels right.

For example, I love the world of professional wrestling (old school Rowdy Roddy Piper fan here with a Hot Rod T-shirt to prove it). With my knowledge of the larger-than-life characters that live in that world and the general way that business works, I can start randomly thinking of shows for that world in different franchise types. Let's try some on!

WHYDUNIT — There's a murder in a "traveling wrestling show" and the dead wrestler's tag team partner must figure out who did it. Not bad. It's a detective show in the world of pro wrestling.

TRAPPED TOGETHER — A workplace show seems like the obvious choice for this unique "career." Maybe to get away from drawing comparisons to *GLOW*, we spin it into a mockumentary comedy. *What We Do in the Shadows* meets WWE. A documentary crew following around a group of low-level professional wrestlers who live and travel together and are trying to make it in the business. It's *Flight of the Concordes* with powerbombs. Oh, I'd so watch that. Maybe I need to write it!

FOOL TRIUMPHANT — A crazy Danny McBride type gets banned from the big WWE-style show and becomes the headliner in some rinky-dink small-scale promotion... but still thinks he's a gleaming god. The Scranton Wrestling Association.

Okay, I want this show. Someone get me Danny McBride on the phone stat!

Anyway, you can see what I'm doing here. Grab your world, dress it up in your franchise-type pants, and take it for a spin. Use the franchise types as your co-writer. How about Blank of the Week? Easy! A wrestling tag-team moonlights as bounty hunters. They're saying, "What about Dude with a Problem?" Then you'll answer, "What if John Cena got bit by a werewolf?!" That's a problem—a monster problem.

Some of these pairings won't work at all. Some require you to approach them from different angles. If you don't like your first Trapped Together, spin it another way—a family of wrestlers! A family of wrestling trainers! A family of wrestling super fans! Go for quantity, not quality, until you strike gold.

Okay, do that.

I've gotta put some calls into Cena and McBride... wait... a Buddy Love!

OH YEAH, THERE'S WIGGLE ROOM

Shows are messy. They don't all fit 100%. Sometimes franchises even change across time. An example is *Breaking Bad*. It starts with a dying chemist who is trying to give his family a life and a legacy by making some cash through the crystal meth biz (all the while creating heaps of trouble with the law and cartels). It's clear Dude With a Season-Long Problem stuff. But by the time we get to Season 6, we've gone from a guy fearing "the one who knocks" to *being* "the one who knocks." The one who knocks is closer to (Wo)Man with a Plan stuff.

Additionally, shows mix it up week-to-week. The franchise type is the primary focus but not the final say.

Pick a primary franchise type to start. It's helpful to have clarity when you're deciding what your show actually is. So choose one. After you start figuring out what your episodes are, you might go back and decide if you're dealing with a sub-franchise situation. Almost every show has elements of Trapped Together. For example, medical dramas have defined families (the medical professionals and hospital staff) but also often have Blank of the Week storylines directly related to the workplace.

A word of warning: Mad, Mad Worlds are hard to pin down. And if you're not disciplined, they can be catchalls. You'll notice these types of shows are pretty rare and tend to be prestige plays from masters of the television game. They might be one franchise type to avoid early on.

WHAT'S YOUR FORMAT?

Now that you know your world and franchise type, it's time to find some comp shows (ones whose story worlds or story types are roughly comparable to yours). Find a few. Some that if your show immediately proceeded or followed would make sense. Like in the salad days of *Cheers* followed by *Night Court* or *Friends* followed *Seinfeld*. Or how Friday nights are often the place to find network procedurals. Or Sundays might have cool HBO shows. Program your own night of television. Make an all-comedy night or all-horror. Find your "cousin" shows.

Typically, the shows you pick will have similar **formats**.

Format is a combination of two parts: **genre** and **running time**.

In TV there really are only two high-level genres: Drama and Comedy. *Game of Thrones* is Drama, as is *Lost*. *Modern Family*, *The Big Bang Theory*, *What We Do in the Shadows* are all Comedy. If you don't know if you're a drama or comedy, that might be an issue. It's better to know what you are and let your freak flag fly.

I'm gonna throw in one additional genre: Dramedy. Dramedy is drama with a lighter tone. Shows like *Fleabag*, *Shameless*, and *Succession* mix tears and angst with the yuk-yuks. These Drama/Comedy hybrids have been taking over TV in recent years, enough to get their own genre spot. Yay, dramedy!

For years TV show running times were pretty standard—comedies were half-hours, dramas were hour-longs. Things have gotten a little loose. Right now, there are several more choices:

1. **Hour-long drama** — *This Is Us*, *Game of Thrones*, *The Expanse*, *Better Call Saul*, *Ozark*, *Stranger Things*

2. **Hour-long dramedy** — *Orange Is the New Black*, *Jane the Virgin*, *Shameless*, *Crazy-Ex Girlfriend*

3. **Multi-cam comedy** (sitcoms shot on a stage, usually with an audience) — *The Big Bang Theory*, *The Ranch*, *The Conners*, *Friends*, *Seinfeld*, *Will & Grace*

4. **Half-hour comedy** (single-cam, shot like a movie) — *Barry*, *The Office*, *Silicon Valley*, *Veep*

5. **Half-hour drama or dramedy** — *Homecoming*, *Atlanta*, *Girls*

One caveat: hour-longs are rarely a whole hour and half-hours are usually 22 minutes or so. And a show like *The Mandalorian* might regularly clock in at 42 minutes, but it's labeled an "hour-long." Rule of thumb: if the show is around 40-minutes or more, it's an hour-long. Under 35, it's a half-hour.

SERIALIZED or EPISODIC?

In the days of yore (officially, the 1990s and before), we didn't have DVRs, On Demand, or binge-watching. If you missed an episode of *Moonlighting* on Tuesday night, you may have missed your chance. Forevs!

Maybe you could catch a rerun that summer or years later when the series went into syndication (another days-of-yore thing), or maybe you could buy a ginormous VHS collection of the entire run, but that was expensive and clunky.

Because of this old watch-it-or-lose-it world, everything was built so that you could just drop into a rando episode and totally get what was being put down. Franchise types were largely Blank of the Week procedurals or Trapped Together comedies. And while some shows thread barely noticeable serialized B Stories into the backgrounds of their seasons, their episodes were engineered to be standalone aka **episodics**.

In recent years, even the most episodic shows have a heavy helping of serialized storytelling. Except for some animation or an occasional cop show, almost every show mixes in some dose of serialized storytelling.

So the question is less if your show is purely serialized or episodic... and more is it *mostly* serialized or episodic?

A lot of this is determined by your franchise type. If you're a Blank of the Week, you're probably gonna be episodic. It's almost built-in. New blank shows up, new blank is resolved. Easy peasy. Likewise, if you're a Trapped Together and a comedy show, you might be episodic.

Almost every other franchise type leans serialized.

And even these episodic shows are gonna have light serialization running through them (*The Office*'s Pam & Jim, *Cheers*' Sam & Diane, *The X-Files*' deeper mythos). The key is their heroes and situations don't change from episode to episode and often don't even change from season to season. Remember, the audience can drop in at any time. So you don't want to drastically transform a character or a situation and confuse the heck out of everyone. An episode in an episodic series should end in the same general "situation" where it started.

Take a look at similar shows. Think about yours. And choose: serialized or episodic.

ARE YOU LIMITING YOURSELF?

Shows that are meant to be "one season and done" (and often have fewer episodes) are called **Limited Series**. If your show has a definitive conclusion that does not lend itself to a Season 2 or is a historical story that completes after a handful of episodes, you're in limited-series territory.

Most buyers would prefer an opportunity to have a Season 2 if the show is a massive hit. But even in the most extreme case, if a show does big business, they'll find a way to make a second season— even if they have to force it! Can't wait for *Chernobyl* Season 2!

Some shows are season-to-season anthologies. In a pinch, you can do what *American Horror Story, American Crime Story,* or *Fargo* do. They're brands that tell a limited story every season.

WHAT'S YOUR PLATFORM (NETWORK/CABLE/STREAMER)?

Platform is a fancy word for channel.

Again, break out those trusty comp shows. In addition to world, franchise, and format, platform comes down to **tone** and **audience**. Gritty and brutal shows may not work on CBS or ABC (though somehow the show *Hannibal* made it onto a major network). Multi-cam comedies and shows that cater to the entire family are not typically the stuff of Showtime or HBO. Got something that appeals to young viewers? Maybe the CW is your home.

If you want to have bad words, nudity, graphic violence, controversial themes or subject matter, you're a cable show. Or a streamer. Is your sitcom for kids? You're Disney XD or Nickelodeon or Disney+.

Do another comp list. This time drill down on characters, tones, realism, and, most importantly, audience. Find the channels your comps are playing on. That's where you belong. Most shows can play a range of networks, but it's good to know your target audience before you write, so you understand what you can and can't get away with.

Stranger Things or *The Walking Dead* would be different if they were on ABC or the CW or HBO or Shudder. *Friends* might have been quirkier and edgier on AMC or FX. Knowing your intended target audience and platform can help you tailor the delivery.

EXERCISES

1. Make a list of your 20 favorite shows. Determine their worlds and franchise types. Write out their genres, platforms, and running times while you're at it.

2. List all of your worlds. Go back and look at the brainstorming tips in this chapter. Dig deep. List the worlds you know, the worlds you've studied or want to study, or the type of worlds that only exist in your own imagination. Don't analyze... yet. Just write them. All your worlds. Do it!

3. For your list, pick some worlds that jump out as either ones you know inside-and-out or ones you'd love to become an expert in. Pair those worlds with various franchise types. Then go down the list of franchise types and brainstorm what that world + franchise type combo looks like as a TV show.

4. Once you find the perfect world + franchise type combo, find similar produced shows. Are they episodic? Or serialized? What are their formats (genre + running time)? What platforms are they on?

CHECK YOURSELF

1. Is your world fresh enough? Does it have a new spin?

2. Is it a world you know or want to spend time researching?

3. Does your world + franchise type compare to some obvious shows with similar tones?

4. Even now, in this raw form, can you think of 5-6 TV episodes for your world + franchise type? (This is the ultimate test; if you can't, you might have more work to do!)

🐾 WHO LIVES IN YOUR WORLD?

"TV is all about Character! Think about Character first! Character! Character! Character!"

That's all you'll hear when you start pitching TV.

Your world might be enough to get a viewer to watch a pilot, but if you want rabid bingers to commit to 10-30 hours of Season 1, you're going to have to go deeper. TV viewers are choose-ey. You gotta make a case for why your show is gonna be invited into their living rooms. Truth is, people spend more time with Walter White and Sheldon Cooper and Sheriff Rick Grimes than their extended families. These "guests" need depth, they need to not get on watchers' nerves, they need to be worthy of people's time.

In the words of Jerry Seinfeld: *who are these people?*

Let's figure it out.

WORLDS HAVE CHARACTERS

If you're doing a story about the CIA, you'll have analysts, field agents, tech experts, government officials, informants, enemy spies. You may even run this circle out to friends, family, and significant others. There may be others: reporters, lawyers, the person who runs the restaurant next store. Stories about the music world have record executives, singers, songwriters, producers, music engineers, PR people, marketing types, influencers, striving musicians working dive bars and open mics, spouses, and family members, etc., etc.

The more you're an expert in your world, the more specific you'll be able to get about who populates it. You'll start putting adjectives in front of these "first gasp" lists. You'll jot quick blurbs describing interesting traits or quirks or flaws. The idealistic lawyer. The pacifist tech expert. The nemesis spy who is mourning their dead spouse. Maybe you know these people, maybe you've worked with them. Maybe you are them. Or maybe you're mixing and matching, riffing and inventing, or at the very least embellishing.

These characters are a start. But right now they're just kind of paper dolls. We need to give them some life. Some soul.

WORLD THEMES

What's your show all about?

Not the meth trade. Not the CIA. Not stand-up comedy or women's wrestling.

What's it *really* about?

That's your show's **theme**.

People who can see theme in a vast garble of story ideas and trailer moments and cool characters are the ones who can see the Matrix. It's the key to making your story relevant to modern times, your viewers, and you.

Theme is the main ingredient on your plate.

When writing a feature film, many writers don't totally crack their theme until they write a draft or two (raises hand, shamefully). Then they go back in and rewrite, punching up the theme parts and making changes based on this new discovery.

But we're talking TV. You can't afford to do that here.

You can't wait until the end of Season 1 until you decide what your theme is.

You don't have a show until you figure out what it's really about.

The best place to start is your world. How does your world speak to humanity and life? How does it speak to you... spiritually?

WHY THIS WRITER, FOR THIS WORLD?

There's a reason you're attracted to your world. Something personal.

Dig in. Figure it out. Why are you the best person to write about this world? This story? These characters?

Write down your answers.

If you've actually lived in the world, had the job, endured the trauma, this shouldn't be hard. Your experience lends authority to the work.

But what if it's one of those other worlds. Ones we love but haven't lived in?

You need to find a personal connection.

Time for an example. If I was writing about my wrestling TV series, I might say: I'm fascinated by professional wrestlers. It's a brutal and dangerous career where people sacrifice not only their bodies but their personal lives, their relationships, and their bank accounts—all in pursuit of a dream. This personal drive is something I've wrestled with in my writing career. How far do I go and how much do I sacrifice in the name of a dream? For something with extremely long odds, is it worth the risk to put all my eggs into one basket and basically jump into a journey that might leave me penniless with little practical skills? Why do I continue? When do I throw in the towel? Like a wrestler who found his passion, would I be giving up on the thing that gives my life meaning?

Free write your own **personal connection statement**. Write from the heart. The more vulnerable you can be, the better. Your raw honesty will guide you to what the main theme of your show is and help you figure out your connection to the world's main characters. **The best themes are found at the intersection of you and the material**.

Let's say you're writing a story about the world of community theater—a Trapped Together with people from varying walks of life. Let's list a bunch of potential themes that come to mind:

- Seeking Acceptance — The show may be about people who are "misunderstood" in their ordinary lives but accepted here.
- Insecurity vs. Confidence — The show might feature people who are overly confident and misperceive their talents. Maybe they need humility or maybe they need to pump the brakes on their reckless pursuit of their dreams.

- Rebooting an Image — People are running to a place where no one knows the real them. Enjoying a place where they're not judged for their past or their baggage.
- Proving Others Wrong — Maybe the world has told your main character they're worthless... and now they're out to prove their value by any means necessary.
- Realizing One's Talents — Someone has a gift but for some reason can't recognize it, or is so self-sabotaging that they won't let it out of the box.

Your list will vary. It's your take on the world you handpicked. There must be something beyond "ain't it cool" that attracted you to it.

Ultimately, you'll have to choose a theme that can last for a season or two or seven. It takes some thought. Some soul-searching. This choice is almost as critical as your world or franchise type. It's what your story is all about.

WHY NOW?

The other big question that comes up during TV pitches is what's relevant about this show *right now*. In today's landscape. The answer is tied directly to theme.

Everything from *Game of Thrones* to *Hamilton* to *Parasite* has some timely relevance. Find the reason your world is relevant right now. It's likely tied to why it's relevant to you... right now.

YOUR SHOW NEEDS A STICKY HERO!

You need the types of main characters people want to invite back week after week or binge after binge. By the way, I'm going to call your main characters your **heroes**; they might be bad guys or jerks or literally kill people, but in their minds they're heroes. Even Hannibal Lector, he's not bad, he's just a misunderstood hero... in his mind.

For starters, your heroes need three elements:

1. A **flaw** — a personal problem that needs fixing.

2. A **want** — a trackable goal that they're pursuing.

3. A **need** — a life lesson that must be learned.

The want relates to the "tangible" aspects of the show (which may change over the course of a season or a series), while both the flaw and the need focus on the "internal" or "spiritual."

When we're talking spiritual, we're talking theme. **Character and theme go hand and hand**. Throughout a show's run, the hero's internal journey will reflect a larger theme. One way to tackle the big three is to approach it with a big theme hammer.

This hammer is named Mjölnir.

Not really.

Your theme is at the hub of a bunch of character tools that will help drive story and deliver a deeper meaning beyond the plot.

Theme can often be expressed as simple mission statements or summations of a lesson:

Selflessness is the key to happiness.

Being true to yourself is the path to success.

Honesty is the foundation of great relationships.

Once you identify a central theme, you can use it to inform all kinds of story choices.

The first and most obvious story choice: character flaws. If the theme is a lesson, what type of person needs to learn it? What type of character is best fixed by the lesson at hand? Flaws are critical. Flawless characters are cold, artificial, and dull. Characters with flaws have dimension and soul.

Once you decide on your character's flaws, you can figure out their **shard of glass**. The shard of glass is the origin story to your character's flaw. Maybe their flaw is that they distrust people because they were abandoned by their parents as a child. Maybe they feel a deep need to prove themselves because they were fired from the job just before the company went supernova.

The shard is buried deep within the character. To truly be fixed, it needs to be voluntarily pulled out.

The **want** is what a hero *thinks* will fix the problem. It should be specific. It can't just be that they "want to be happy." What do they think will make them happy? Getting a million dollars by any means necessary? Marrying their jerky lawyer boyfriend to finally win the sibling rivalry against their sister? To own their dream house?

The want is fool's gold. It won't make your hero happy and it won't fix your hero's life.

The **need** is the lesson that must be learned to fix the flaw and remove the shard of glass. You might recognize it. It's Mjölnir. That theme hammer we began with. The simple statement we used to derive our character's flaws in the first place.

Flaws, shards of glass, wants, needs—all should tie into your theme.

The TV show *Barry* is about how a distraught and emotionally numb ex-soldier and hitman is trying to find purpose and essentially save his soul. The show's hero, Barry, has the following big three:

- **Flaw** — believing life is meaningless and going through the motions of his sad and violent existence instead of reckoning with a traumatic past.
- **Want** — an acting career and lifestyle.
- **Need** — with support and help from those who care about him, to get in touch with his true feelings, honestly reconcile his violent past as a soldier, and deal with post-traumatic stress.

Heroes start the story unaware of their need. Awareness is something they sloooowly acquire throughout the series. Until then, they'll go in other directions—chasing wants dictated by their flawed views.

THE TRANSFORMATIONAL MAP

Your hero is going to start as a flawed person... and go on a journey of change. The perfect course is discovering the need, removing their shard of glass, and fixing the flaw forever.

In a TV show, that shard might just stay in place until the very last episode of the series or beyond. It's a long, long journey. You, the writer, are gonna need a map.

The first step is to figure out where your hero starts... and where they finish.

Will they go from Mr. Chips to Scarface? Or from devoted Russian spy to worried parent willing to sacrifice for the sake of their children? Will they start as a rogue pirate who refuses to stick their neck out for anybody and then transform into a person willing to give up their life for their new friends?

Character journeys (or **arcs**) are best expressed as "befores and afters."

Here's a handy template:

Transformation Map: (DESCRIPTION OF FLAWED CHARACTER) learns (NEED or LESSON LEARNED) through (HIGH-LEVEL OVERVIEW OF SHOW'S STORY) and transforms into a (LESS FLAWED CHARACTER).

Some examples:

Barry: An (insecure and aimless man) learns (confidence and humility) while (working with fellow theater people who sincerely care about him and want him to succeed) and transforms into an (empathetic team player).

The Good Place: A (self-centered, morally questionable young woman) learns (selflessness and self-confidence) while (trying to navigate how to keep her and her friends from spending eternity in a Hellish afterlife) and transforms into a (self-sacrificing good person).

Breaking Bad: A (stuck-in-a-rut chemistry teacher who is wasting his potential and going through the motions of life) learns (self-reliance and ambition and ego-driven selflessness) while (trying to work his way through the crystal meth biz) and transforms into a (drug kingpin).

Or you could just say Mr. Chips to Scarface.

It's important to know where your character starts and where they might end up. Later, when you figure out your seasonal or even episodic arcs, you can discover the waypoints on the journey or make transformation maps just for those story chunks.

THE BROKEN COMPASS

The **broken compass** is the wrong-way GPS that our hero obsessively follows along their spiritual journey. Screenwriting for any medium is character psychology in action. When it's time to write, the secret weapon for creating character-driven stories is to use your hero's broken compass to guide their reactions.

Walter White's broken compass is ego-driven. Long ago, he got a shard of glass stuck in him when he was screwed over by friends and ousted from a successful start-up he helped to create. Now, as he makes critical choices for his legacy and his family, that shard of glass is causing his broken compass to guide him to meth-making and crime instead of accepting charity or asking help from others. He's on a noble quest to help his family, but his compass points him to make the wrong moment-to-moment decisions. Good intentions... bad directions.

Ned Stark in *Game of Thrones* values duty over all else. Despite his misgivings, this personal trait compels him to serve as the hand of the king and follow a line of thinking that he'd be better off without. We know this code will lead to his downfall. But his compass is broken.

Personal codes and broken compasses go hand in hand. Dexter Morgan believes that if he can follow the code, he can be a serial killer and have a normal life. This broken compass gets him into one terrible predicament after another. Instead of learning the lessons that will fix his flaws, he blindly follows this compass.

One way to get a handle on your broken compass is to come up with **mission statements** or mantras for your characters based on their flaw. Use the words "always" or "never" in them.

Here are some examples:
I will never act like my father.
I will never let any sin slide.
I must always prove I'm the smartest person in the room.
I will never forgive.
I will never acknowledge my past.
I will always follow my code
I will never ask anyone for help.

These mission statements should be born directly from the shard of glass and reflect your hero's basic flaw. They embody the misguided philosophies that are causing havoc in your hero's life.

A perfect example is the pilot of *Better Call Saul*. Jimmy McGill (who will later become Saul) is trying to do whatever he can to make ends meet. In the first episode, he's driving a beat-up Suzuki Esteem, struggling to afford a strip-mall backroom office, and representing the lowest of the low clients. So when he gets a large check from his brother's law firm that will solve many of his problems, what does he do? He rips it up!

It's a great character moment setting up a broken compass through action. Jimmy will *never* take help from his old law firm! He'd rather go down all kinds of illegal ways to prove he can make it without their help. The series will later reveal the shard of glass: how he got screwed over by his brother and the firm.

Besides guiding you in the decisions your character makes, broken compasses help you make story decisions. Always lean into tension and choose situations that cause your hero to strain because of their mission statements. Show us how your hero won't bend no matter what the pain—that's character revelation, baby!

The broken compass is critical in television. It will help you make story choices and brainstorm episode ideas. Unlike in movies, your characters may never remove that nasty shard of glass and fix their flaws. They'll continue to bump up against it. Your hero will flirt with change. They'll experiment with it. The compass may move millimeters in the proper direction, only to cause them internal conflict and struggle along the way.

If you're writing something "more episodic," your character likely won't ever fix their compass. Archie Bunker, Lucy, Larry David, and George Costanza never change. Their broken compass is part of what makes them funny. These characters glimpse little lessons along the way but never enough to remove that pesky shard of glass. While we see snapshots of them "getting it," the lessons aren't enough to keep them from going down that wrong path the very next episode.

TV is about the struggle. It resembles real life in that way. Change is hard. Your job is to pick at the scab of the shard of glass, pour salt in the wound, bring the internal pain.

CREATING YOUR CHARACTERS

Theme helps you think up your characters.

Consider *Grey's Anatomy*. The first season centered on new interns trying to prove that they could make the grade as surgeons. Let's say the show's main theme was something like "What does it take to be a good surgeon?" Or a personal theme: "Am I good enough to be one of the greats?" Self-doubt is the key question. Learning to be confident. Learning to overcome baggage and shed the things that are holding you back from being the best you. But what are the deep-rooted flaws that are related to self-doubt?

The first step might be to make a list of some traits that make a great surgeon:

1. Focus
2. Humility
3. Professional Distance
4. Confidence
5. Aptitude

We can derive our lead interns' central flaws by using the above as what they need to aspire to:

1. **Focus.** Meredith Grey has the stuff to make the cut. But she has baggage. Her mom is a famous surgeon who now has dementia, and she's sleeping with a doctor from work and

therefore getting involved in workplace romance drama. Meredith is determined to "prove herself on her own merits"—almost to her detriment. Surviving the grueling path to become a surgeon is hard enough; she makes it harder by putting her own conditions on how she can do it. She spends time trying to live up to the image of her mom, thinking that means keeping secrets (about her mom and her relationship). That's a wrong-way goal. Being a good surgeon isn't about hiding things that make it seem like you're unfocused, it's about being honest with yourself and others to find your own way to tackle the difficult tasks at hand.

2. **Humility**. Cristina is another character who has the goods. But she knows it and is borderline arrogant. She has a tough time handling failure; her competitive nature fractures her relationships with coworkers, friends, and lovers. She needs to see that she lacks humility and empathy to be the best she can.

3. **Professional Distance**. On the opposite side of the humility spectrum is George. He's humble, introverted, not quick to speak up for himself, and almost cares too much about his patients, his fellow residents, and his mentors. He needs to be a little more "Cristina" to survive. He'll have to find his voice and self-advocate for himself if he wants to succeed.

4. **Confidence**. Izzie is blonde and attractive and often underestimated. She's filled with self-doubt, is almost the underdog in this war of intellects, and needs to fight extra-hard to prove she's worthy. She's a little out of her league at first—her journey will be one of learning, growing, and finding herself worthy.

Choose your central theme, then choose characters from your world and understand how they reflect the central questions

and dilemmas you've chosen to explore. Over the course of your series, characters and themes may change, but staring at the white page, it's best to dig into your theme for answers. It's the gift that keeps on giving.

WHO IS YOUR MAIN CHARACTER?

Unlike film, TV needs lots of characters. When you're in the middle of Episode 7 of Season 6, it's great to have options. More characters mean more story. Options!

While shows like *Ramy* and *The Marvelous Mrs. Maisel* and *The Mandalorian* have obvious main characters, other shows like *Lost*, *This Is Us*, *Stranger Things*, and *The Office* take a team approach to story and sometimes ruthlessly balance their character time within seasons or even episodes. Even in ensembles, shows often nudge a character slightly forward, like Steve Carrell's Michael in the first few seasons of *The Office*, Leonard in *The Big Bang Theory*, or everyman Mike in *Stranger Things*.

How do you know who your hero is? Here are some tips:
- They're the most like us.
- They often provide a window into the upside-down world of the show.
- They're the ones whose transformational map most embodies your show's theme.
- Their personal flaws put them in the most conflict with the world of your show.

WHY DOES ANYBODY CARE?

We're in the golden age of anti-heroes. Many of TV's most popular heroes are flat out "bad guys": Walter White, *Ozark*'s Marty Byrde, Elizabeth and Philip in *The Americans*, Saul Goodman, Dexter Morgan, the bloodsucking goofs of *What We Do in the Shadows*. Lucifer is even a hero of his own show.

Shows with so-called ordinary folk are filled with jerks and creeps and people that in real life might get on our last nerves. Think about *Mad Men*, *Curb Your Enthusiasm*, and *Veep*.

Flaws are indeed sexy.

This rise of the anti-hero highlights the difference between television and movies. In TV there's time to show the nuances. We have just as much time to spend with Tony Soprano at home with his wife and kids as we do with him beating people up and ordering others to be whacked.

In a movie, we might get about 10 minutes before the central plot takes over and takes us on a tension-filled ride. It's hard to make people care about psychopaths and jerks and crooks in that short of a time. Feature writers get just enough time to squeeze in one quick *Save the Cat!* scene and call it a day.

Quick note: **A *Save the Cat!* scene shows us the hero is worth fighting for.** 'Cause, yeah they may be a psychopathic killer... but at least they take the time to rescue a little kitty-cat, so there must be something redeeming buried inside their cold, calculating, villainous heart. And we're on board for their journey.

In TV, especially pilots, *Save the Cat!* scenes still work wonders. But you need even more.

YOUR CHARACTER'S ROOTING RESUME

Imagine we're going to create an online dating profile for your main character and the first question is "Why do you think (insert your character's name) deserves the viewer's emotional investment for a whopping 22 hours of television?" What is it you need in a character to get under your skin? To think about even when you turn off the show? To buy a T-shirt and wear it around proclaiming you're Team Walter White?

Here are some common traits you might list on the resume that give you something to root for:

1. **They're underdogs.**
    - We're all weirdos or freaks or nerds deep down and we empathize with people that don't fit in.
    - The world treats them unjustly.
    - They're Rodney Dangerfields — they get no respect.

- They're rookies trying to play in the big leagues — just because they're new to something doesn't mean they're failures, and we audience members know this. We know one day… they'll be contenders! And we're on their side when they're not yet cool. When they're just the new band at the club.
- They're economically challenged — they lack money or material things and live a difficult or maybe miserable existence.
- They're dealing with disease (physical or mental afflictions).

2. **They care about someone or something**.
   - A kid, a significant other, a grandma, a friend, a "Pam from the office," or a family.
   - A cat… which they save! Or any animal. But in this book, we'll say a cat. For marketing reasons.
   - An old neighborhood, a nostalgic item.
   - A cause!

3. **They try very hard to make their lives better**.
   - Dreamers — they have a dream, a way out, or a plan.
   - Failures — they often fall flat on their face. But they get up and try again.

4. **They're fun**.
   - Funny — whether it's a gift of gab like Buffy the Vampire Slayer or Chandler on *Friends*, or just next-level charming like *The Marvelous Mrs. Maisel* or *Lucifer* or *The New Girl*.
   - Sweetness
   - Charming personality
   - Va-va-voom sexy — we're primal animals after all. Some characters just bring the hotness in either looks or, more importantly, attitude.
   - Adorkable

5. **We know their struggle**.
   - They have secret pain.
   - They have a painful past.

- They confess their flaws.
- They're in mourning.

6. **We wish we were more like them.**
  - Self-sacrificing
  - Generous
  - Resourceful
  - Loyal
  - Smartest person in the room
  - Overcome their fears
  - Never-give-up
  - Cut through the BS
  - Live by an honorable code — Supergirl, Jack Bauer in *24*, *Homeland*'s Carrie Mathison, all have a drive or the personal ethics to do what's right.

7. **They're just like us.**
  - They share common mundane problems.
  - They live mundane lives.
  - They give us an honest vulnerable peek behind the curtain, revealing things we're embarrassed to admit about ourselves or things that remind us of those we love.

8. **They're the best at something**
  - Talents — Whether they're the best singer, the best butcher, the best driver, it's fun to "live" the lives of the best.

Check out two examples of rooting resumes that resonate:

Rooting resume for Walter White in *Breaking Bad*'s pilot:
  - In the opening teaser, he's in danger, desperate, and in big trouble.
  - He's in his tighty-whiteys, making him vulnerable and humiliated... all for our entertainment.
  - He makes a "If you find this message, I'm already dead" video for his family to find. It's sincere and from the heart, expressing love for his family and saying goodbye. Even in the end, he's a family man.

- He's got a future. At 50, a new baby is on the way. It's both a joy and a cause for anxiety.
- He's wicked smart. We even catch glimpses of his awards for "Proton Radiation" from his glory days. Others perceive him as smart too, even if they undervalue him in general.
- He's in a rut. His big 50th birthday is celebrated with a bacon breakfast spelling out the number "50" on his eggs. Even worse, it's veggie bacon (he's watching his cholesterol). Later his wife gives him the most unsexy birthday sex ever—all the while working on the computer and talking about their mundane schedule and all the chores poor Walt needs to do.
- His family is strapped for cash. They can't even afford a new water heater. He drives a crappy car (even the glove compartment is broken). And he has to work at a car wash to make ends meet.
- At the car wash, he's disrespected by his boss and the customers (his students who laugh at him). The job stinks but he suffers for the money his growing family needs.
- He's passionate about his job (chemistry teacher) even though the high-school students think he and chemistry are a waste of time.
- He has a great relationship with his special-needs son. They joke and have an easy way about them. A true friendship.
- He has lots of people who love him. His wife throws him a surprise party and it's filled with friends and family.
- His annoying brother in-law treats him like he's less than a man. Even when he's toasting Walt, the brother-in-law uses the moment to make some pointed digs.
- He's sick. In fact, he's dying.
- He's a massive underdog, in way over his head in the world of crime. He's not at all equipped to face the dangerous unhinged crooks and cartel members that occupy the volatile landscape of meth dealing.

Rooting resume for the titular character in *Fleabag*'s pilot:

- She confides in us. She stares right down the barrel at us and admits her deepest darkest secrets. We're her new BFF.
- She's funny and clever, constantly making jokes, often at her own expense.
- She's vulnerable and makes deep confessions of her vulnerability.
- She's kind and empathetic. She politely suffers all kinds of awkwardness.
- Her life is rough. She's recently been dumped. Her live-in boyfriend left her, which is apparently a frequent occurrence.
- She suffers an embarrassing moment right in front of us.
- She has money troubles and needs cash to keep her business (a small coffee shop) open.
- She's denied a small business loan she desperately needs.
- Her sister is "perfect"... everything Fleabag is not. And worst of all, Fleabag needs to borrow money from her.
- She loves her sister (and her sister loves her) even though they have a bit of a stony relationship.
- She does not seem to suffer fools and is usually the smartest person in the room (even if it's more street smarts).
- She helps a stranger on the street who seems high or drunk and rather helpless get a cab home safely.
- She shows up at her father's doorstep on the verge of tears, looking for comfort, and he rather rudely turns her away.
- Lastly, we find out that her best friend and business partner—who she loves more than anyone—recently died and our hero is lost in a world of grief.

YOUR SERIES ISN'T DONE UNTIL IT'S DONE

There are a lot of moving parts when it comes to designing your show. A great idea in the character-building phase may influence the types of stories you need to tell or even the theme.

It's okay.

Go back and adjust your franchise type or your world or your platform.

The goal isn't to follow some prescribed plan, it's to make the best TV show you can. Rarely will the process just flow in some one-two-three fashion. More often, you'll have to skip around, try things out, ask questions, and go back to the beginning. It's fine to start with a character then use it to figure out a world. Or jump from world to theme to character and then go back and see what kind of franchise type best suits those elements. As you break story on your show, you may need to adjust characters or themes or worlds.

So be it.

It's not done until it's all done.

So leave the door open.

EXERCISES

1. How does your world speak to you personally?

2. Why is now the right time for this show?

3. List the top 3-5 characters of your favorite shows. Who do you think is the main character? Can you describe their broken compasses?

4. What's your show's overall theme?

5. List the 3-5 main characters of your show. Describe how they relate to your show's theme. How do their flaws speak to the theme?

6. Choose your #1 main character.

7. What's their main flaw?

8. What's the shard of glass that caused the flaw?

9. What's their broken compass? Write their mission statements using the terms "always" and "never."

10. Come up with a rooting resume—what are some of the reasons audiences will want to invite these people into their living room?

CHECK YOURSELF

1. Is your overall theme a universal one?

2. Does your character's flaw relate to your theme?

3. Can you see how the flaw will influence the character's home, work, and play and create things that need fixing?

4. Imagine some possible scenarios your world suggests—does your character's broken compass indicate how they'll react when things get tough?

5. Does your hero have a clear rooting resume?

PART 2

BREAKING STORY

🐾 IT'S STORYTIME...

I've used the *Save the Cat!* method to write horror movies, biopics, kids' television shows, comic books, novels, commercials, documentaries, videogames, *D&D* campaigns, and wrestling psychology (that's Kayfabe for wrestling story structure, btw).

But TV is the wonkiest.

As we've discussed, shows aren't stories—they're springboards for stories. These spring-boarded stories take many forms: single well-crafted pilots, complete narratives made up of a single season's worth of serialized television, three-season arcs, self-contained bottle episodes, or even stories told across two weeks or two parts.

TV isn't doing anything avant-garde. It's just that the form is so wide-open and variable, any episode could be a chapter, a short story, or some kind of standalone side trip. There's an old proverb about blind men who learn about a new animal in town (an elephant) and want to check the little critter out for themselves. Each tries to describe the mysterious creature by examining a different part of its mammoth body. The interpretations are spectacularly wrong. They can't grasp the whole. So instead they try to frame each isolated fragment in some way without really having the big picture.

In TV, any individual episode can be a trunk, a tail, an ear, or a whole separate animal. To analyze any story you need the big picture, you need the frame. You can't just drill down on Season 4 Episode 2 in a vacuum and make assumptions. If you could see the whole elephant, you might be able to break it down in some sensible "3 or 4 act structure." But without such insight, it's hard to know exactly which part of the story elephant you're looking at.

For this reason, before diving into episodes, we need to lay down some *Save the Cat!* basics and temporarily separate them from any kind of format. We'll dig into how these basics relate specifically to TV later. For now, understand that *Save the Cat!* is really a method to create good stories of any type. For this chapter, it's easier to see the whole elephant as one two-hour movie than one episode of *Game of Thrones* or 130 episodes of *The Simpsons*. We'll circle back to TV in a bit.

WHAT'S YOUR STORY DNA?

I teach screenwriting to college students.

I read lots of scripts.

Lots.

All of them have problems. These are students. First-timers. Problems are good. Problems are learning.

Nine out of 10 times, I don't need to read an entire script to know something's wrong. I can figure out the biggest issues in less than two minutes.

> PROFESSOR NASH
> So... what's the pitch?

> COLLEGE STUDENT
> It's about a college student
> who wants to follow their dreams.

> PROFESSOR NASH
> Follow their dreams. Hmm.
> That could be a lot of
> different movies.

> COLLEGE STUDENT
> Um... well, this college student
> has a girlfriend and he needs to
> decide whether he wants to be
> with her or follow his own dreams
> of playing professional Twister.

                    PROFESSOR NASH
     Twister? That's new. Okay. But
     "deciding," that's a short movie.
     Only takes a minute to decide. A
     split-second.

                    COLLEGE STUDENT
     Well, it's also about them trying
     not to decide.

                    PROFESSOR NASH
     Not a lot of drama in trying
     not to do something. As someone
     famous once said — Do or do not...
     there is no try.

                    COLLEGE STUDENT
     Was that William Goldman?

                    PROFESSOR NASH

     ...uhhh...

This is when I get a long detailed explanation that sounds similar to someone recounting their bizarre dream about waking up in a cotton-candy factory with three people from their childhood and they're talking about putting on a play but none of them remember their lines. Sometimes these pitches sound like people babbling about their boring 9-to-5 or their aimless *Dungeons & Dragons* campaign.

It never fails though; most new writers can't describe their stories in a simple *trackable* way. Ninety percent of teaching screenwriting is just saying "What's the pitch?" again and again and listening to new writers stumble over themselves trying to figure it out.

I once watched a newbie screenwriter pal nearly break down

because he couldn't figure out what his logline was as he sat across from me at an Applebees. He kept stopping and starting and trying new angles and explaining different characters' backstories. It was like a bad stand-up comic on open mic night. I barely said anything. I just asked the question and listened as he fumbled his way again and again through disconnected characters and their disjointed internal needs.

That man was G.R.R. Martin.

No...it wasn't, but I still felt bad. And that moment gave me some insight into why most writers are terrified to pitch their stories.

Their stories are UNPITCHABLE!

They're unpitchable because they're not really stories. They're collections of disjointed scenes or a grab bag of characters loosely surrounded by setting or situation. They look like stories, they feel like stories, but they're *not* stories. They lack something from the start. They lack the genetic makeup of what storytelling is.

When I teach, I insist that my students have a bare minimum **Story DNA** mapped out before they move ahead to outlining. It's the baseline stuff my not-G.R.R. Martin friend couldn't figure out over margaritas. It's the stuff you need to have on lockdown before you ever try to pitch your story, let alone write 60 pages of it.

All good stories can be described in the following way:

1. A protagonist (**HERO**)...

2. ...who really wants something (**GOAL**),

3. but there's someone or something in the way (**OBSTACLE** or **VILLAIN**)...

4. ... and if they don't achieve their goal, something really bad will happen (**STAKES**).

Forcing yourself to figure this out before you write will level you up. You'll go from newbie to not-so-bad. It seems so rudimentary, but you'd be surprised how many people don't have these mission-critical elements in their scripts.

These four elements are also essential to crafting a good **log-line**. Let's look at *Wonder Woman*:

An Amazonian warrior (**HERO**) must embark on a harrowing journey through a dangerous and modern world she doesn't understand to hunt and slay the God of War Ares (**GOAL** and **OBSTACLE**) to stop the war that will end the world (**STAKES**).

Imagine *Wonder Woman* without any of these:

1. No hero — What is *Wonder Woman* without a Wonder Woman? Wonder Womanless!

2. No goal — Okay, I love Gal Gadot as much as the next person. But two straight hours of her doing nothing is not an international blockbuster. At best, it's a YouTube channel. I'd subscribe (it's Gal!), but it's not a movie.

3. No obstacle — Imagine if the way to stop the war was to simply step outside and scream, "Stop it, you idiots!" That's a short movie. Stories need obstacles. Big ones!

4. No stakes — If killing Ares doesn't spell the end of the war, Wonder Woman might have better things to do. Like practice magic lassoing or buff her battle-tiara. Even worse, without a life-or-death reason to continue, she might just quit the whole quest the first time she gets a knick in her bulletproof bling. Stories must have compelling reasons to keep characters on the move and taking action.

Every story you break needs each of these four elements. It's the DNA. You can't grow a full-blown story without it. Make it your prerequisite to moving forward on any story.

Now let's dig deeper into each element.

GOOOOOOAAAAALS

Here's another convo from one of my classes:

INT. CLASSROOM - DAY

> PROFESSOR NASH
> So who is your story's hero?

> STUDENT
> A college student. Like myself.

> PROFESSOR NASH
> Wow. How original and fresh.
> What's their goal in the story?

> STUDENT
> To be happy.

> PROFESSOR NASH
> Uhhhhhn.

> STUDENT
> Why are your eyes doing that?
> That eye-roll-ey thing.

> PROFESSOR NASH
> I have an eye issue. Allergies.
> Forgot my Zyrtec. Um... how
> is the audience going to track
> 'happy' in your story?

> STUDENT
> Duh. The actor will show happy
> in their performance.

> PROFESSOR NASH
> By actor, you mean your brother?
> The same actor in your last film?
> The one who can't remember his
> lines?

> STUDENT
> Well, maybe I'll write in some
> extra smileyfaces. And a music
> montage. Maybe my main character
> will dance in his kitchen a lot.
> Are you okay? Your eyes are
> going back in your head.

Please. Please. Please. Make your hero's goal **TANGIBLE**!

Choose a goal that audiences can track without having to mind-read the actor (or force you to write a kitchen dance scene that screams joy and happiness). Tangible goals are external goals. Slaying a dragon. Winning a trophy. Returning home.

> STUDENT
> But my story is about more than
> that! It's going to change the world.
> It's going to dig deep into the
> human psyche. I'm a character-writer.
> I scoff at plot. I paint with
> emotions and truth!

Okay, Terrence Malick, take a breath. All good movies are about characters and truth and emotions. *All of them.* If you just read the beautifully written character section that preceded this chapter, you know I think all of those intangible, spiritual things are ESSENTIAL. I even capitalized essential, so you know I'm serious.

But if you didn't skim the last few chapters (uh-huh, skimmer!), you'll remember that "what's it all about" is tied directly to the character's deeper **need**. The internals. It's at the heart of character arcs, transformation maps, character psychology, and broken compasses.

But this part is different.

We're talking goals now.

And when we're talking about goals, we're talking about what the character **wants**. Well-developed characters have both wants and needs. If your hero has an intangible goal, like "must cope with grief" or "must conquer their fears" or the ever-popular "must learn to be happy," you're in spiritual territory—not goal territory. You still have to figure out a want. *A tangible one.* An external one. A trackable one.

The need does relate to the want. If someone is desperate to deliver themselves from unhappiness, they check their broken compass and it points them in the direction of the want! They think the thing that will make them happy is winning the big job or buying the fancy house or winning the attention of the hunky new chief surgeon with the tight abs. The "need to be happy" is the *intangible* side. Dr. Abs is the want.

Indiana Jones might need to get his confidence back after failing to get the idol. He may think the answer to all his doubts is to defeat his competitor Belloq and capture the Lost Ark and solve the great mysteries of antiquity. The Ark becomes his external want—his goal. But Indy's need is to find acceptance or love or forgiveness from the person he left in favor of fortune and glory. Maybe he needs to care more about love and people than trinkets and history. And maybe, just maybe, when the Ark has finally opened, the reason he doesn't look at it like his "We're the same, you and I" rival is because he finally has what he needs and it's more important than what he wants.

Needs and wants go hand and hand.

BE MEANER: THE OBSTACLE (or VILLAIN)

Hey you.

Yeah, you.

Come closer.

I need to tell you something.

You listening?

Good.

You need to be a monster.

Seriously, the lowest of the low. Mean. Low-down. Cruel.

You have to rough your heroes up. Bang 'em around. Stress 'em out. Take 'em to their absolute limits. Then pour salt in the wounds.

In the words of Rocky's Russian opponent, Drago, "You must break them!"

It's your job. It's your main job. Make the obstacles in your poor hero's path excruciatingly hard. These torturous hurdles should have layers. A lasagna of agony! The obstacles will test your hero physically, intellectually, spiritually. Make your hero ugly-cry. Kick them in the soul. Break them.

Seeing your hero overcome the impossible shines a more glorious light on them. Weak-sauce obstacles make for weak-sauce stories. They lead to characters who have to shuffle their feet just to stretch out the narrative. Or stories that have to meander because there's just not enough story-meat on the bone in defeating the villain or overcoming the odds.

Be meaner.

WHAT'S YOUR 'OR ELSE'

Stakes make your hero take action.

Most of us are lazy. We deny the call of taking out the trash, doing the dishes, finishing our taxes, writing our next pilot. Imagine if we had a huge obstacle placed in our way. One created by the meanest of mean writers. Why would we ever do anything?

There's only one good reason: because if we didn't, we'd die. Or something would die. Our hope. Our wish. Our dream. Our sanity.

If CHAINSAW FACE bursts through the door right now... I'd have to act or get chainsawed. If an extinction-event meteor was streaking to earth and the only way to stop it was to do the dishes, dishes would get done.

Make your hero act right now, right this second!

You might not have a meteor or a CHAINSAW FACE in your story, but to your hero what is life-or-death? Is it the new job? Is it getting their kid into a fancy college? Is it finishing your screenplay before the midnight contest deadline?

Twist your hero's arm!

To the breaking point.

Make them act now. And don't allow them to quit.

It's get the goal *or else*.

The "or else" is your stakes.

WHAT HAPPENS NEXT

Do you know what the key is to make readers flip the pages? To make viewers binge the next episode?

The single most important tool a writer can have in their arsenal.

Do you know?

Okay, I'm gonna tell ya...

It's questions that need answering!

And the biggest question of all is: **What happens next?**

Questions are itches that need to be scratched.

Your Story DNA poses a question. This question creates the main tension in your story: "Will the hero overcome the obstacle and achieve the goal or will they suffer the horrible fate (aka stakes)?" This is often called **the dramatic question**—it boils down the Hero, Goal, Obstacle, and Stakes into a single statement:

Will Wonder Woman stop the God of War or will he be allowed to stoke the fires of World War I and destroy civilization?

At the root of all questions is tension. Storytelling is really about manipulating your audience's internal tension knobs.

First, you set up this dramatic question in the viewer's mind. They meet the character. They realize the problem. They feel the stakes. Then it's go-time!

You grab the tension dial and ride it like a madman, giving your watcher or reader lightning zaps of tension. *Will the hero succeed?* Doesn't seem like it. I'm worried. Oh, no! Are they gonna die? Is the world going to end?

Ups and downs.

A roller coaster of Good News/Worse News.

Hope and fear.

In the end, shut off the tension switch, release the safety bars, and let the audience go back to their normal lives.

How do you deliver the whens and the whys of tension? With great **structure**. Because if tension lets up too much or starts too late, there's a danger of being "too slow" or "not hooking" the audience. That's a structure issue. Having a solid *Save the Cat!* beat sheet ensures you have the tension goods.

What's a *Save the Cat!* beat sheet, you ask?

We'll get to that in the next chapter.

Ahh... an itch that needs to be scratched! Tension for the win!

LOGLINES ARE PRETTIED UP STORY DNA

```
INT. ELEVATOR - DAY
The doors close and the NEWBIE WRITER looks
up and Wowza, it's J.J. ABRAMS.

                J.J. ABRAMS
     Oh... no.

                NEWBIE WRITER
     Hey JJ. Big fan. Team Felicity. Star
Trek Kelvin era all the way.

                J.J. ABRAMS
     Why won't this elevator move?

Presses buttons frantically.
```

```
                    NEWBIE WRITER
        I'm a writer, you know.

                    J.J. ABRAMS
        Okay, look… we've got 10 floors
        to go. Probably 30 seconds. This
        is your big shot Tell me,
        what's your story about?
```

What's your story about?

It's that Applebee's moment I talked about earlier!

If you're taking a general meeting, or going to a film festival, or planning to be trapped in an elevator with an A-List producer or director, you GOTTA KNOW!

In the earliest days of your writing journey, loglines are the coin of the realm. When you communicate with agents and producers, they'll ask what you are working on. You'll answer with your logline.

A logline is a one-sentence summary of a story.

Warning: a logline is not a tagline.

Taglines are the things you see on posters like…

Size does matter. Nope.

In space, no one can hear you scream! Nope.

You'll believe a man can fly. Nope. Nope. Nope!

She did the laundry, washed the windows, and took out the trash—now she's going to clean up the streets. Um… *STC!* Easter Egg Alert!

None of those are loglines. A logline looks like this:

After a gigantic shark begins attacking people in a small beach town on the days leading up to the 4th of July, a police chief with a phobia of water must try to stop the hungry beast despite the greedy town officials who demand that the beaches stay open.

The basic form of a logline is this:

After (a CATALYST), (A HERO) must overcome (OBSTACLE) to achieve (GOAL) or else (STAKES).

The **Catalyst** is the moment that kicks your story off. It's Tony Soprano learning he has a mole in the gang or Sherlock learning about the latest mystery to be solved or when Walter White sees his former student and future partner Jesse flee a meth lab.

Check out these loglines:

After a night of drunken partying, three groomsmen lose their about-to-be-wed buddy, and now must go on a desperate hunt for the MIA groom-to-be, despite not having any memory of what happened the previous night... or he'll miss the big day!

After debris strikes her space station and strands her in orbit, an astronaut battles to survive and return safely to Earth.

After finding an old treasure map, a crew of misfit kids goes on a dangerous adventure in search of pirate treasure, trying to get the money before they lose their homes to foreclosure.

Once you have the basics down you can get jiggy with the template and experiment with the style and words—the key is to be sure all the Story DNA is clearly evident from the logline alone.

Here are some tips and warnings when formulating your logline:

1. **If your story is good, get out of the way** — A lot of new writers put a lot of effort into "fancying their loglines up." Don't bother. Great loglines are more about great stories, not great word choices. Yes, there is some work figuring out the best way to phrase your logline with clarity and economy... but if you find yourself dipping into cliché-speak and working over the logline like some lame Hallmark card, you might be overdoing it, or your Story DNA might be weak.

2. **Don't just pitch the Catalyst** — The biggest mistake new writers make is creating loglines that only pitch the Catalyst, leaving the real meat of the movie vague. "A boy is bit by a radioactive spider" isn't a logline. That could be 5,000 different stories. It could be a body-horror movie about radiation sickness or a movie where a team of experts chases the spider in attempts to save the boy or a movie about a boy who can suddenly talk to spiders. Why? Because Catalyst loglines do not tell us what the hero must do after the Catalyst occurs. The hero must have something they're trying to do. That's the engine for your story. And you can't have an obstacle or stakes without a hero and goal in place.

3. **Make sure there's a formidable obstacle** — If the goal doesn't feel like it's very hard to accomplish, there's probably no story there. Someone who "must decide" or "choose between X or Y" isn't a story, it's a story beat that's decided in one scene. Tangible goals with difficult obstacles are the key to making your logline pop.

4. **All your Story DNA must be evident to a reader after they read your logline** — A great way to test your logline is to let someone read it and then ask them to list the Hero, Goal, Obstacle, and Stakes. If they can't, your logline is either not clear or not complete.

Story DNA is the first step during the story-breaking process. It's important to have each of the elements on lockdown before you dive deeper. And we will be diving deeper, much much deeper, in the next few chapters.

ONE NOTE ABOUT TV AND LOGLINES

Loglines are descriptions of stories. But shows are not stories, they're story machines. And unless your show is a tightly serialized "extended movie" kind of show, it won't necessarily have a locked-down Story DNA.

However, your pilots are stories.

Your seasons are probably stories too.

Any given single episode of a show could be a complete stand-alone story, but it also might be one part of a continuing one.

Since we're going to focus on pilots, loglines are useful to pitch our story and to use the logline as a sort of a working thesis. Writing a pithy logline before you write your story is a splendid idea. And you'll be ready to pitch J.J. in the elevator.

EXERCISES

1. List a few of your favorite movies or books. Who is the hero? What's their goal? What's in the way? Why do they have to act *right now*, with no delay and no excuses?

2. Think of your favorite TV shows. For just their pilot episodes, think of the Hero, Goal, Obstacle, and Stakes.

3. For those story ideas you came up with for your own show in the previous chapter, write down the Hero, Goal, Obstacle, and Stakes for each of them.

4. For those same ideas, write a logline that clearly communicates the Hero, Goal, Obstacle, and Stakes.

CHECK YOURSELF

1. Is it clear who the story is about, who your hero is?

2. Is your hero's goal tangible, trackable, and external? If it's not, make sure you're not in "need territory." What does your flawed hero think will solve their need? That's your want and goal!

3. Is the obstacle a tough one? Are you being mean enough? Grrr.

4. What's making your hero take action *right now*? It better be something life-or-death. Don't let your hero have any wiggle room. Make them act!

5. Is your logline clearly stating the goal your hero will pursue in the story and not just the Catalyst?

🐾 THE SAME... BUT DIFFERENT

Pop Quiz Hotshot — What do all these movies and TV shows have in common?
- *A Bug's Life*
- *The Fast and the Furious*
- *Air Force One*
- *Warm Bodies*
- *Sons of Anarchy*
- *Cable Guy*
- *The Magnificent Seven*
- *Ten Things I Hate About You*
- *Disturbia*
- *Raiders of the Lost Ark*
- *House*
- *West Side Story*

Cue the *Jeopardy* music.

What could it be?

Hmmm.

Give up?

Turn the page...

They're the same… but different!
- *A Bug's Life* = *The Seven Samurai* with bugs
- *Air Force One* = *Die Hard* on Air Force One (with the POTUS)
- *The Fast and the Furious* = *Point Break* with race cars
- *Warm Bodies* = *Romeo & Juliet* with zombies
- *Sons of Anarchy* = *Hamlet* with bikers
- *Cable Guy* = *Fatal Attraction* as a comedy
- *The Magnificent Seven* = *The Seven Samurai* with cowboys
- *10 Things I Hate About You* = *The Taming of the Shrew* in high school
- *Disturbia* = *Rear Window* with a teenager
- *Raiders of the Lost Ark* = James Bond as an archaeologist
- *House* = Sherlock Holmes as a doctor
- *West Side Story* = *Romeo and Juliet* with street gangs

You see, there isn't anything completely new out there. And if there was, it's probably a tough watch. Too weird, too esoteric, too hard to comprehend, too new.

Most original ideas are two cool things merged for the first time. It's that peanut butter and chocolate mix that tastes great together.

You've probably seen that corny "This meets This" pitching shorthand:

It's *Jumanji* meets *The Notebook*!

It's *Elf* meets *Saving Private Ryan*!

On the surface, those are pretty eye roll-ey, but the shorthand can be useful to communicate certain "same but different" takes.

The *Rocky* "formula" has been done a gazillion times (even pre-dating *Rocky*). Look at all these *Rocky* rips (not really rip-offs, okay? Don't @me):

- *8 Mile* — Rocky raps.
- *Flashdance* — Rocky dumps a bucket of water on himself.
- *The Warrior* — Rocky makes people tap-out.
- *Cinderella Man* — Rocky boxes… in the 1930's.

- *Blades of Glory* — Rocky plays.
- *Dodgeball* — Rocky dodges wrenches.
- *Fame* — Rocky goes to the school for the arts.
- *Purple Rain* — Rocky tells us what it sounds like "When Doves Cry."
- *Drumline* — Rocky plays drums.
- *Rudy* — Rocky plays college football.
- *Pitch Perfect* — Rocky sings.

Rap meets *Rocky* might sound ridiculous, but it's communicating a story about an underdog (like Rocky!) overcoming the odds in the world of rap battles and hip hop.

If you watch enough movies, read enough books, binge enough TV, you'll recognize recurring patterns in storytelling. And these patterns are represented by the *Save the Cat!* **genres**.

The word "genres" is a bit confusing. It conjures images of 1990s Blockbuster Video stores with shelves separated by categories: sci-fi, horror, comedy, drama, fantasy, etc. These old-school genres were all about audiences and expectations—if you watched a horror movie, you'd want to be scared; if you checked out a comedy, you'd expect to laugh.

Save the Cat! genres are different. They speak to character goals, thematic tendencies, and common archetypes that repeat over and over in the stories we watch and read. What's really cool is an individual Blake Snyder genre isn't audience-specific. The same *STC!* genre can be found in an Oscar®-winning movie, a straight to video slasher, a lifetime drama, a gross-out comedy, or Shakespeare.

After you firm up your Story DNA (hero, goal, obstacle, and stakes), you'll start shaping the story you're trying to tell. Slotting it into a genre provides you further clarity. So let's take a look at how the *Save the Cat!* genres can help you.

The 10 *Save the Cat!* Genres

BUDDY LOVE – These are those "you complete me" stories. A spiritually incomplete hero finds a companion who somehow makes them more whole. Due to a complication, the two struggle to be together in the way they're meant to be. Buddy Love movies are your love stories, friendship stories, mother/daughter stories, boy-and-their-dog stories.

The three elements of a Buddy Love story are:
1) An **incomplete hero** who is missing something physical, ethical, or spiritual; (s)he needs another "someone" to be whole.
2) A **counterpart** who completes the hero or shines in the areas the hero lacks.
3) A **complication**, be it a misunderstanding, differing viewpoints, or the disapproval of society.

EXAMPLES: *Brokeback Mountain, Zootopia, When Harry Met Sally, Lethal Weapon, 48 Hours, Pretty Woman*

DUDE WITH A PROBLEM – An innocent hero is yanked into a life-or-death problem and, despite massive odds against them, must overcome it. Many stories are about dudes with problems. But the keys to this genre are innocent underdogs who are undeservingly pulled into a predicament and forced to react.

The three elements of a Dude with a Problem story are:
1) An **innocent hero** who is dragged into a messy situation without asking for it—or even aware of how they got involved.
2) A **sudden event** that yanks our poor dude into this world of hurt—without any warning.
3) A **life-or-death battle** putting the life of an individual, family, group, or society in question.

EXAMPLES: *Die Hard, The Martian, Hunger Games, Taken, North by Northwest*

FOOL TRIUMPHANT — An underestimated "fool" is pitted against an establishment but proves their hidden value to everyone, causing them to triumph! Fool Triumphant stories are about heroes who don't fit in but can teach us something about life.

The three elements of a Fool Triumphant story are:
1) A **fool** whose innocence is their strength and whose unassuming personality makes them likely to be ignored—by all but a jealous "Insider" who knows that something more lurks within.
2) An **establishment**, the people or group a fool butts up against, either within their midst or after being sent to a new place in which (s)he does not fit in... at first.
3) A **transmutation** in which the fool becomes someone or something new, often including a "name change" that's taken on either by accident or as a disguise.

EXAMPLES: *Elf, Boogie Nights, The King's Speech, Legally Blonde, Being There*

GOLDEN FLEECE — A hero and their team embark on a quest to win a prize or accomplish a mission. The mission/prize could be robbing a bank or dropping a magic ring into a volcano or winning the World Series. Sports movies, quests, and road trips all are the stuff of the Golden Fleece genre. The mission has a definable road whether it's a real road as in *The Wizard of Oz* or *Fury Road*... or a season as in *Major League* or *The Bad News Bears*. There should be a clear "prize" or "finish line" that the audience can track. Once the prize is captured, the story is over.

The three elements of a Golden Fleece story are:
1) A **road** spanning the globe, time, or even neighborhood blocks. With each length of the "road" traveled, the hero grows. The road often includes a "Road Apple" that stops the trip cold.
2) A **team** or a buddy that guides the hero along the way.

Usually, it's someone who represents something that the hero doesn't have: a skill, knowledge, or attitude.
3) A **prize** that's sought. Usually, it's something primal: going home, securing a treasure, or re-gaining a birthright.

EXAMPLES: *Raiders of the Lost Ark, Dodgeball, Little Miss Sunshine, 1917, Harold & Kumar Go to White Castle*

INSTITUTIONALIZED — A hero is entrenched inside a certain group, institution, or establishment. These stories are about how the hero fits into the system and their struggles therein. They must decide if being part of the group is worth it, and ultimately must choose to join, leave, or destroy it. Workplace stories and stories about institutions or establishments are the hallmark of institutionalized storytelling.

The three elements of an Institutionalized story are:
1.) A **group** (a family, an organization, or a business) that is unique and that the hero lives or works with, or must deal with.
2) A **choice**, the ongoing conflict pitting a "Brando" or "Naif" vs. the system's "Company Man."
3.) A **sacrifice** that must be made and results in one of three endings: join, burn it down... or commit "suicide."

EXAMPLES: *The Devil Wears Prada, Full Metal Jacket, Office Space, One Flew Over the Cuckoo's Nest*

MONSTER IN THE HOUSE — A hero is trapped in some location or situation (aka The House) and must survive a monster (human or otherwise). Monster in the House stories are commonly found in horror movies, urban thrillers, or comedies about people or things that just won't go away.

The three elements of a Monster in the House story are:
1.) A **monster** that is supernatural in its powers—even if its strength derives from insanity or determination.

2.) A **house** that traps the hero. It can include a family unit, an entire town, or even "the world."

3.) A **sin** that lets the monster in... a transgression that can include ignorance.

EXAMPLES: *Psycho, Jaws, The Conjuring, The Exorcist, A Quiet Place, IT, Get Out*

RITES OF PASSAGE – A hero suffering through a relatable life problem (divorce, growing up, death, mid-life crisis, etc.) tries to solve it by avoidance instead of tackling it head-on. Like most heroes, they choose the wrong path and ultimately need to learn the hard way.

The three elements of a Rites of Passage story are:

1.) A **life problem** that occurs anywhere from puberty to midlife to death—universal passages we all understand.

2.) A **wrong way** to attack the problem, usually a diversion from confronting the pain.

3.) **Acceptance** of a hard truth the hero has been fighting, and the knowledge it's the hero who must change to solve the problem, not the world around them.

EXAMPLES: *Ordinary People, Bridesmaids, Lost in Translation, Birdman*

OUT OF THE BOTTLE – An ordinary hero's life is changed by magic that either bestows a wish or a power or inflicts them with a curse. Whichever way, this magic changes the hero's life and makes things difficult. The magic is resolved in the end, but the lesson it teaches resonates with the hero forever.

The three elements of an Out of the Bottle story are:

1.) A **wish** asked for by the hero or another character, and a need to be delivered from the ordinary.

2.) A **spell** that bestows the magic and follows a set of clearly defined rules.

3.) A **lesson**: be careful what you wish for! A common theme for most OOTB stories is that life is good as it is.

EXAMPLES: *Groundhog Day, Freaky Friday, Click, Bruce Almighty, Big, Liar Liar, Field of Dreams*

SUPERHERO — A hero with a superpower (or compelling mission) faces a potent nemesis or catastrophic problem so large it challenges even their own mighty powers. These movies are about extraordinary people tested by the values of the world.

> The three elements of a Superhero story are:
> 1.) A special **power**, even if it's just a mission to be great or do good.
> 2.) A **nemesis** of equal or greater force, who is the "self-made" version of the hero.
> 3.) A **curse** for the hero that (s)he either surmounts or succumbs to as the price for who (s)he is.

EXAMPLES: *Superman, Spiderman, James Bond* movies, *Erin Brockovich*

WHYDUNIT — A hero/detective pursues a case where the real puzzle is "why" the case proves so compelling that (s)he is willing to dive into the darkness to find the answer.

> The three elements of a Whydunit story are:
> 1.) A **detective** who does not change. They can be any kind of gumshoe—from pro to amateur to imaginary.
> 2.) A **secret** within the case that is so strong it overwhelms the lures of money, sex, power, or fame. We must know! And the Whydunit hero must know too.
> 3.) A **dark turn** which shows that in pursuit of the secret, the detective will break the rules, even their own—often ones they have relied on for years to keep themselves safe. The pull of the secret is too great.

EXAMPLES: *Seven, Blade Runner, Body Heat, The Big Lebowski, Chinatown*

WHAT ARE GENRES GOOD FOR?

Genres help you with structure. Having clarity of the type of story you're telling helps early story decisions that bridge the gap from idea to outline.

Your process may vary. You might work the genre angle first to arrive at your Story DNA. If you have a general idea like "Ghost Exterminators for Hire" but aren't sure where to take the story, you can "try on" different genres and take 'em for a spin. A Monster in the House might pit those Ghostbusters in a single location with ghosts closing in. A Golden Fleece might be a story about competing to be the best Ghostbusters and winning the Ghostbusters Franchisee of the Year Award. Institutionalized might be about an everyman who gets hired into some weird cult-like job where he's indoctrinated into a "busting makes me feel good" lifestyle.

Genres are also my favorite way to research. Before I start a project, I like to watch shows and movies and read books that inspire me and give me ideas. The cool thing about genres is that you can find totally different stories (that appeal to different audiences) that you can stack on your research pile—so long as they share the same genre. Then, when you start to write, a comedy Monster In the House might provide insight into your urban thriller Monster In the House. Or a teenage Rite of Passage might help inform your Hallmark movie Rite of Passage.

In television, genres are directly applicable to season arcs and episodes but not so much the shows themselves. Shows can change genres from episode to episode. A series like *Buffy the Vampire Slayer* might jump from Monster in the House to Golden Fleece to Out of the Bottle to Rite of Passage—all within a single Dude With a Problem season!

We'll dig deeper into how you can use the *Save the Cat!* genres to write for TV when we get to breaking story on your first season and your series' pilot.

EXERCISES

1. Again, pick out some of your favorite movies and books—what *Save the Cat!* genres are they?

2. For the sample episodes you came up with for your own show earlier, what *Save the Cat!* genres best describe each one?

3. Now that you have a clearer understanding of the story you're telling, revise some of your sample episode loglines. Keep reworking those loglines at every step!

🐾 BEAT SHEETS... OR WHO NEEDS A WRITERS' ROOM?

The first few days in a new writers' room usually start with questions.

What's the first scene?

How do we introduce the main character?

What really kicks off the story?

What's the big twist?

How does it end?

Save the Cat! drags that story out of you in the same way a conference room full of expensive TV writers does. *Save the Cat!* won't stop nagging you until you have a complete story with good pacing, character transformation, and all the beats that are required for a story that sticks the landing. When you're done working through a story using the *Save the Cat!* method, you'll have the exact same thing writers' rooms produce: a detailed outline that's "script ready."

THE *SAVE THE CAT!* BEAT SHEET

"What's a beat?" you ask...

A **beat** is a storytelling moment. A beat describes what happens next from a high level. Think of the beats as instructions on how to put together IKEA furniture. They tell you to connect the legs of the chair to the seat but skip the little details that tell the whole story, like finding all the parts, keeping your dog away, and shouting obscenities when you put the legs on backward. The beats are the basic steps of how to put together your chair. Just enough to understand the big picture.

Since we're talking general story here and not a specific medium like novels, movies, or TV shows, we'll use percentage markers instead of page counts or minute designations in the parentheses that follow each beat name.

Here's a high-level description of the 15 *Save the Cat!* beats:

THE *SAVE THE CAT!* BEAT SHEET

ACT 1: The Ordinary World – Thesis

1. OPENING IMAGE (0-1%) – A thematic or grabbing visual image, scene, or short sequence which sets the tone of your movie. It often serves as the "before" picture of your hero (or world) that will transform throughout the story.

2. THEME STATED (5%) – A line of dialogue that organically states what your story is all about. The theme is typically voiced by another character to your hero, calling out the hero's deeper flaw or spiritual need for change.

3. SET-UP (1%-10%) – Reveals your main character's "ordinary life" or status quo. Takes time to demonstrate a character's flaws that negatively impact the hero's life. Describes the character's familiar world when it comes to home, work, and play, and introduces the main characters who inhabit the hero's life.

4. CATALYST (10%) – the life-changing moment that happens to the hero and sets the story in motion. Provides that initial shove onto the story roller coaster.

5. DEBATE (10%-20%) – The reaction to the Catalyst, usually presented in the form of a question ("Do I really have to go on this dangerous quest?"). Can be a sequence of doubt, denial, evasion, or even preparation. It lends weight to the life-changing bigger journey yet to come and foreshadows the new world as one that you do not enter lightly.

ACT 2: The Upside-Down World – Antithesis

6. BREAK INTO 2 (20%) – The hero decides to take action and locks in to accomplish a goal, venturing into a new world, or choosing a new way of thinking. This is a no-turning-back decision that separates the old, ordinary world from the new world.

7. B STORY (22%) — A thematic secondary story is kicked off. Often, this is a story about love or friendship or mentorship.

8. FUN & GAMES (20%-50%) — The hero is in the new world. This beat delivers on the *promise of the premise*. It's a large section of the story that essentially presents "the movie you came to see." Contains scenes and sequences that are shown in the trailer of movies or hinted at in the blurb on the back of the book or on that "Coming Next Week" teaser at the end of a TV show.

9. MIDPOINT (50%) — The middle of the story and culmination of the Fun & Games. Usually, this beat is a *false victory* or a *false defeat*. The Midpoint *raises the stakes* on the hero, forcing them to narrow their focus on winning the day or surviving. Often, a *ticking clock* is introduced here, ratcheting up tension and boosting the urgency.

10. BAD GUYS CLOSE IN (50%-75%) — Stakes have raised and tension is higher. External Bad Guys may be literally closing in or psychological, internal Bad Guys may be causing more problems.

11. ALL IS LOST (75%) — The moment the hero most feared actually happens. Now it looks like the hero will lose. Usually contains a *whiff of death* where someone has died or the threat of real death is in the air. This is the hero's rock-bottom moment.

12. DARK NIGHT OF THE SOUL (75%-80%) — A reaction to the All Is Lost where the hero wallows in sadness, mourning what was lost and lamenting that they are now worse off than before the story began. This is an opportunity to take stock, where meaningful learning happens on the way to transformation.

ACT 3: Merged World – Synthesis

13. BREAK INTO 3 (80%) — A new piece of information is discovered and the hero realizes what they must do to solve all the problems that have been created in Act 2.

14. FINALE (80%-99%) — The big showdown where the hero finally proves they've learned the lesson that was taught via their

struggles in Act 2. The quest is won, the dragon is slain, and when the smoke clears, the hero has changed. Their flaw is repaired and the world is indeed a better place.

15. FINAL IMAGE (99%-100%) — The "after photo" of the hero and the world. A mirror of the Opening Image. Shows how far the world and the hero have transformed.

So that's the beat sheet in a high-level nutshell. Now let's go more granular and dig deeper into each individual beat, highlight some key considerations, and show some examples.

I know we're using a lot of movie examples here. Trust me, it all applies to writing your TV shows and pilots, as you'll see in the TV pilot beat sheets "Coming Soon to a Chapter Near You!"

OPENING IMAGE (1%)
Single-Scene Beat

The Opening Image is your chance to hook the audience. It's everything you learned about the opening sentence in your 10th-grade composition class: grab 'em by the eyeballs at word one!

The Opening Image sets tone, establishes voice, and plants a thematic stake in the ground. Often, writers will use it to introduce us to their hero and visually illustrate their hero's flaws. This is the "before" picture: the vice that must be fixed to make life better.

If you're starting from scratch, I'd suggest brainstorming a scene that visually displays why your character must change. Show us how the hero's flaw is making a mess of things. *Die Hard* opens with John McClane alone and grumpily flying into Los Angeles, but he and his wife are in each other's arms by the end. *Rocky* opens with our favorite Italian Stallion fighting in a rinky-dink arena with little fanfare and ends with him winning over a crowd on the biggest stage, surrounded by people who love and care for him. These character goalposts can help stake out your hero's transformation. If you go with a more plot-driven teaser-based opening—like the first scene of *Jaws* where the shark feasts on his first victim or even a big CGI prelude scene like in *The Fellowship of the Ring*—you can kick your main character's introduction up to the first scene of the Set-Up.

When working on your Opening Image, brainstorm the Final Image, which is the mirror image to this beat. Use these two beats to show just how much things have changed from the open to the close of your story. Tackling these two beats at the start of your story-breaking gives a clear before-and-after picture of the journey your hero will endure, and can be instructive in generating everything in between.

THEME STATED (5%)
Single-Scene Beat

Somewhere in your well-crafted Set-Up, your hero demonstrates how their flaws manifest—and indicates someone is going to call them on it. This is your theme stated. It's an organic verbalization of "what it's all about." Usually, it's something said to your hero by another character.

In *Gravity*, it's George Clooney telling Sandra Bullock, "You've got to learn to let go. Learn how to let go..."

In *Pirates of the Caribbean*, it's Orlando Bloom being told "Pirate is in your blood, boy, and you'll have to square that someday"

In the *Shawshank Redemption*, it's Morgan Freeman saying, "Hope is a dangerous thing."

Heroes begin a story with something to learn. The story is an arm-wrestling match of change vs. the status quo. This beat is the opening salvo.

The Theme Stated is less its own beat and more a sub-beat that occurs within the Set-Up. The Theme Stated is a beat that floats. Sometimes it appears in the Debate or even later in the Fun & Games, but it usually lands at the 5% mark right in the middle of your Set-Up—the perfect place to call your imperfect hero on their imperfectness. Put it there and you can't go wrong.

SET-UP (1%-10%)
Multi-Scene Beat

Before the hero goes on the journey that will transform them forever, the pre-transformation hero needs to be established. Show their status quo. Paint a picture of the hero's ordinary world at home, work, and play. The viewer needs this "before" picture to fully appreciate how much things are about to change. You're establishing a baseline. There must be **things** here **that need fixing**. Living like this without any change means some kind of death. **Stasis = Death** is *CAT!*-speak for the hero's ordinary living situation that is so soul-crushing that to stay in it feels like death.

Stories are transformation machines. The hero's flaws are contaminating all aspects of the hero's life. Showing these things that need fixing are crucial to the Set-Up. The things that need fixing also serve as problems we can check off as the hero changes. *Does the hero still have issues with their ex? Are they still disrespected at work? Are they still hiding from their landlord?* These things slowly change as the hero internalizes facets of the lesson they need to learn.

In *Back to the Future*'s Set-Up, Marty is lacking confidence after an audition gone wrong, his dad lets Biff push him around, Marty's principal thinks he's a slacker, and overall his family is in a rut.

In *Joker*, the main character is leading a depressing life—he's disrespected at his job, made fun of and beaten up in public, has an invalid mother, and longs to be something more than he is.

Additionally, Set-Ups are places for *Save the Cat!* scenes and adding to your hero's **rooting resume**. Use this space to get us on their side, show us that they're underdogs, and give us a glimpse into what they do when no one is watching.

CATALYST (10%)
Single-Scene Beat

This action beat happens to the hero and kicks the story into gear. It's not a realization of the implications of some past event, it is THE EVENT!

It's typically the one "random coincidence" that happens to the hero (you only get one rando, so use it wisely).

The Catalyst is the debris hitting the space station in *Gravity* or the sudden arrival of government officers in *Raiders of the Lost Ark* or Harry meeting Sally. It's the moment Harry Potter hears the words, "You're a wizard, Harry."

If the ordinary world of the Set-Up is a pond, the Catalyst is a thrown rock that causes ripples underneath the very feet of the hero.

DEBATE (10%-20%)
Multi-Scene Beat

The Catalyst makes its ripples in the status-quo pond and now the hero must react. The Debate deals with whatever messiness the Catalyst is bringing into the hero's world. It creates questions, doubts, and concerns. This happening demands a response!

Typically, the hero tries to avoid the larger "call to adventure." Other times, it's less about trying to escape the call and more about preparing before they dive into the new upside-down world of the story.

When Luke Skywalker sees the hologram of Princess Leia, the hero in him is stirred, but he can't just walk out on his aunt and uncle who depend on him to milk the blue cow and farm moisture all the livelong day... but maybe he can pass the buck to old Obi-Wan Kenobi. In haunted house movies like *The Conjuring*, initial spooky doings lead to questions: Is it real? Is it dangerous? Can we move? Who we gonna call?

On the other hand, James Bond doesn't try to squirm out of a new mission. It's his job and he's good at it. Instead, he's briefed, drinks a martini, and gears up with the latest spy gadgets from Q.

The Debate is a good place to ask those nagging questions studio execs like to ask. Why don't they call the cops? Wouldn't they just move? How do they know it's not all a trick? Put these questions on the lips of your characters. They are questions real-life human people *should* ask when rando events sweep them into wacky predicaments.

BREAK INTO 2 (20%)
Single-Scene Beat

If the Catalyst is an invitation, this beat is the RSVP. It concludes the First Act and basically catapults us into the story we've been waiting to see. The First Act is the ordinary world, Act 2 is the opposite. The First Act is the thesis and Act 2 is the antithesis. It starts here—with a bold step taken by the hero. The protagonist makes a choice (or is forced into one) and enters this new **upside-down world**.

Remember that Story DNA (Hero, Goal, Obstacle, Stakes)? This is the spot where it all becomes crystal-clear in the viewer's mind. By this point, the viewer should be asking "what happens next?" Will the hero get the goal... or will the horrible thing happen?

The Break into 2 is a character moment. It's here where the hero must make a choice. They may be forced to make it after trying to shirk responsibility or effort since the Catalyst, but the choice is still theirs. They need to proactively take the big step into the upside-down world of Act 2.

In *Star Wars*, the stormtroopers track the two recently bought droids to Luke's farm and end up killing his aunt and uncle. Luke doesn't have much choice given the baddies are still hunting the droids and he has nothing to return to. He may be forced to, but Luke still makes the next move. He commits to escorting the droids to Alderan. He takes the first step into the upside-down world outside his safe home and into adventure.

Harry Potter boards a train. The upside-down world of Hogwarts awaits.

The Ghostbusters leave behind academia and go into business for themselves. An upside-down world of ghostbusting for hire ensues!

B STORY (20%)
Multi-Scene Beat

A thematic B Story kicks into gear. B Stories are theme Sherpas. It's their job to carry the theme and directly address the hero's need. B Stories are often relationship or love stories. This beat commonly introduces the hero's friend, lover, family member, or mentor, who will teach the hero something about the theme and what they need to learn to overcome their primary flaw. Sometimes these "helper characters" have already been introduced in the Set-Up, and this beat shines a light on them, a sort of "look at me" moment that says pay attention to this jabronie!

Often, mentors will step up for the first time, like *The Karate Kid*'s Mr. Miyagi. It's here he saves Daniel and puts himself in a position to be a mentor in both karate and life. Sometimes a nemesis that isn't the ultimate villain will emerge (I'm looking at you, Draco Malfoy). More often than not, a romantic interest like Peeta in *The Hunger Games* or the Irish cop in *Bridesmaids* will first make the acquaintance of our hero. In *Up*, as the house flies away and Carl escapes the world, he hears a knock on the door. It turns out he's got a stowaway in the form of annoying scout Russell, who is on his porch holding on for dear life! The relationship with Russell will be essential to Carl's growth and his learning how to move on from the grief of losing his wife.

The B Story is a multi-scene beat but with a caveat. The B Story scenes get sprinkled into the other multi-scene beats and sometimes even team-up with the A Story in the single-scene beats. This particular beat is meant for the scene that kicks the B Story off.

One other caveat: this beat can float a bit. Sometimes it's a little before the act break. But typically the B Story kicks off in the upside-down world, when the lesson starts to be taught. That can't happen till at least after the Catalyst and usually not until after the Break into 2.

FUN & GAMES (20%-50%)
Multi-Scene Beat

Welcome to all the cool parts! This beat delivers on the **promise of the premise** aka the movie that was pitched in the trailer. In a monster movie, the monster is eating people here! In a love story, the relationship is on! In a heist movie, the heisters are heisting!

From a Story DNA perspective, this is where the hero is trying to achieve the goal and slamming head-on into those obstacles that stand in the way!

It's the longest individual beat, spanning 25% of the story. It often taps into the home, work, and play of the Set-Up... now in an upside-down funhouse mirror way.

One way to tackle this inflated section is to approach it with its own mini-structure, a series of ups-and-downs or actions and reactions:

• The hero takes action — A hero with a goal brings the action (guided by their broken compass). Their plan fails or succeeds but leads to a new revelation that escalates matters! Ultimately, it's an uh-oh moment.

• The hero licks their wounds — the hero deals with the smackdown by retreating, falling into self-doubt, or immediately trying to put out fires. In doing so, they discover new information, get some new hope or inspiration, and use their broken compass to come up with their next move.

• Just rinse and repeat the "action/licks wounds" scenes and mix in some B & C Stories. Oftentimes the last "take action" scene ends in victory... the false victory of the Midpoint.

Beware of making your Fun & Games "too linear" or "too episodic." Too linear is the term for beats that read more like a checklist than a story. There's either no obstacle in the way of the hero achieving their goal or your beats lack those "blow up in the hero's face" moments that surprise us and force your hero to think on their feet (the ultimate way to express character). Without these mini-disasters, your story and your characters are predictable and, even worse, fast-forwardable. It's a bit like what we said about perfect characters being a snooze. If characters are always right and never fail, they're unrelatable... and boring.

On the flip side, being "too episodic" happens when scenes feel like they were plucked right off the white board and dropped into the script without any regard for why they need to happen *right now*. They have a checklist feel. Soulless. Inorganic. Like you had a bunch of scene ideas but didn't bother to figure out the cause/effect nature of how one moment inevitably leads to the next. Worst of all, they don't ever feel character-driven because the events aren't a result of your hero's choices, wins, and losses—they're just rando encounters.

The Fun & Games of *Die Hard* has Bruce Willis in a cat-and-mouse battle against the terrorists in the skyscraper. In *Bill & Ted's Excellent Adventure*, it's some most excellent time travel. In *Knives Out*, Daniel Craig is on the case interviewing suspects and following up on clues. In *The Hangover*, it's the guys trying to piece their night together to find the missing groom

NOTE: The Fun & Games is *not* necessarily fun for the hero. They might be getting chased by chainsaw killers or find themselves stranded on a desert island or being tortured by Jigsaw.

Not fun, for them... but *fun for us*.

MIDPOINT (50%)
Single-Scene Beat

The Midpoint is the place for rug-pull twists, public victories that go bad, and the sh#!-just-got-real moments.

Midpoints have three primary elements:

1. They **raise the stakes**.
2. They have **A and B Stories cross**.
3. They serve as **false victories** (when the hero gets a win... but then things go bad) or **false defeats** (the hero fails badly... but somehow it's not as bad as they think).

In the false victory, the hero is on an upward trajectory through the Fun & Games, which culminates at the Midpoint in a "big win." Sometimes there's even an epic party scene or public celebration to cap off their victory. Think about Superhero movies like *Spiderman* or *Iron Man* or *Ghostbusters*. They usually show supes flexing their muscles and then the Midpoint shows some public coming out or press conference. Then just when they start to get headlines, some big baddie wants to ruin the party or at least takes notice and decides to play spoiler to all their glory.

Conversely, movies that have downward trajectories in the Fun & Games tend to land on false defeats at the Midpoint. Imagine a horror movie where a poor soul is tortured by some mad killer or supernatural force for the start of Act 2. They often reach a point so low or so scary at the Midpoint that they must fight back! It's a harsh wake-up call—if they want to survive, they have to stop screaming and running around and do something.

The stakes raise in several ways. Villains become more focused. A new plot twist makes the hero realize the stakes are bigger or the obstacles are much harder. The A Story and B Story cross, making things personal. A sudden deadline is declared. A fuse is lit. A ransom is made. In love stories, a kiss, a confession, a night of passion can suddenly take things to the next level. There's more to lose, things are personal, the tension has been ratcheted up!

In Pixar's *Up*, during Carl and Russell's trek toward Paradise Falls, they're captured and brought to a large hidden cavern where Carl meets his hero, the great explorer Charles Muntz! This is the meeting Muntz-Fanboy Carl has always dreamed of. But it's a false victory, as we'll soon see that Muntz is no hero. His dark paranoia will make the rest of the story that much more dangerous and he'll ultimately prove to be the villain of the piece.

In *Avatar*, hero Jake Sully confesses his love for the native woman he's supposed to be spying on and she confesses her love for him. They join as one, and, in the tradition of the Na'vi people, become mated for life. Another false victory. Things just got personal and Jake is on a path to have a showdown with his superiors.

In *Get Out*, the hero encounters an old acquaintance who went mysteriously missing, and is not acting like himself. He uses the opportunity to call his sounding-board character back home (the B Story). It's an uptick in stakes (it's clear this isn't all just in his head) and the B Story mentor highlights it with simple advice: "Get out!"

It's pretty common to start **ticking clocks** here too. This is the spot in *Back to the Future* where Marty sees his family slowly fading from photos. He knows the clock is ticking. The longer he stays in the past, the closer he is to vanishing from existence.

The Midpoint also begins a shift in attitude for main characters. Somewhere around the Midpoint (it could be just before or after), circumstances become weird enough for the hero to realize they need to shake things up. Before the Midpoint, they're usually trying things the old failed way... now they start to dabble with new ideas and question past attitudes. They begin to slowly transform.

BAD GUYS CLOSE IN (50%-75%)
Multi-Scene Beat

Tension rises! Forces—both internal and external—align against our hero and begin to bring the pain. In fact, "Bring the Pain" could be another good title for this beat. In the Fun & Games, the hero was able to navigate the obstacles without feeling huge heat from the baddies. But here, the Bad Guys come back with John Wickian vengeance. It's time for you, the mean writer, to grab that tension dial and dime it, baby!

In movies like *Jurassic Park*, the monsters are loose and hungry. In *Titanic*, the heroes scramble to escape the sinking ship. Internal Bad Guys come to play in movies like *The Social Network* when Zuckerberg brings in new investors and is suddenly at odds with his old buddies. In *Whiplash* the hero feels the pain on all fronts — his psychotic bandleader is creating drama among the group. The hero takes it out on his father and breaks up with his girlfriend to focus on his goals that are growing increasingly more difficult to achieve.

Yikes! Pressure!

ALL IS LOST (75%)
Single-Scene Beat

Our hero's worst nightmare comes true. It's the rock-bottom moment. Remember that "Will the hero achieve the goal?" question that's been driving the story? Well, in All Is Lost all signs point to NO FRIGGIN WAY!

This is the spot where someone (or something) dies. It can be physical or emotional. This is the beat where mentors get killed, friends get kidnapped, and couples call it splitsies, ultimately forcing the hero to go it all alone. A **whiff of death** almost always accompanies the All Is Lost. This beat is also the place where the old way of thinking meets its demise and makes room for something new. Real change.

The All Is Lost is where Obi-Wan gets struck down, where Quint dies, and where Harry and Sally break up.

DARK NIGHT OF THE SOUL (75%-80%)
Multi-Scene Beat

Death needs to be mourned. The hero finds themselves distraught and broken. They wallow in intense sadness and whimper through woe-is-me monologues and usually have to break out the umbrellas because it often starts raining on their misery. It's also a spot where the hero reflects and realizes they are worse off now than when the story began. But we've endured enough stories to know that this is the dark before the dawn, the moment where the hero must be at their lowest to have an epiphany that will truly give birth to the new 2.0 version of themselves that can defeat the Bad Guys (both internal and external) and win the day! This epiphany is directly related to the lesson that needs to be learned and the **shard of glass** that must be removed.

This beat reflects back on the Theme Stated. It's a moment to wax philosophically, to openly challenge old ways, and to mourn the past.

In *The Hunger Games*, it's when Catniss buries Rue in flowers, hardening and becoming the hero who will go on to winning the Games. In *Star Wars*, it's sad Luke and friends mourning on the Millennium Falcon after Ben Kenobi's death—a moment to realize Luke is now on his own and must make Obi Wan's death matter.

BREAK INTO 3 (80%)
Single-scene beat

Thanks to a fresh idea, new inspiration, or last-minute thematic advice from a B Story character, the hero realizes a new path to victory! The hero chooses to try again, sometimes with a completely different goal than in Act 2. A and B Stories often connect and combine here as the hero steps forward for one last attempt to win it all.

Act 3 is the synthesis of the two other worlds. Remember, Act 1 was the thesis and Act 2 was the antithesis. Act 3 combines who the hero was when they started with the lesson they've learned. It's this new person—a product of both worlds—who can win the day.

In *Star Wars*, the team gets away with the Death Star plans. Now an attack is possible! A new goal arises: take out the Death Star! In *The Silence of the Lambs*, Clarice figures out another clue—"He knew her!"—and takes the step to investigate one more lead, one that will ultimately bring her face to face with the serial killer Buffalo Bill.

FINALE (80%-99%)
Multi-Scene Beat

The Finale is where the Bad Guys are defeated, B Stories are resolved, and victory is won. It's also the time when that life-wrecking shard of glass is finally removed.

The main character incorporates what they've learned into their fight for the goal because they have experience from the A Story and context from the B Story. The Finale is about synthesis! Combining the old world and the new. Bringing it all together. And winning! The hero wins because they've changed and in the Finale, they prove their new way of living is better by doing something the character could not have done at any other point in the story.

Think of the Finale as a mini-movie. You should be able to define it with new Story DNA. Who is the hero, what's their goal? What's the big obstacle? What are the life-or-death stakes? The answers to these questions may be the same as they were in the Fun & Games section. But not always. Sometimes it's a more locked-in version of them or even a spinoff from succeeding or failing to obtain the original goal.

Think of *Star Wars*. The movie starts as a journey to deliver the droid with the secret plans to the rebels, but it ends with an attack on the Death Star. The goal has changed to "destroy the Death Star," a spinoff from the success of the original "deliver the Death Star plans to the Rebels." *The Silence of the Lambs* is a movie where Clarice's original goal is to find a serial killer and a kidnapped girl. In the Finale, her goal is to survive a serial killer and rescue the girl from his lair.

The Finale is another mega-beat, built from several scenes. To help guide you, we have a handy-dandy thing we Cats like to call the Five-Point Finale. It breaks the Finale into five steps, a good roadmap to creating your mini-movie:

1. *Gather the Team* — Whether it's a team of many or one, this is the time to gather 'em up. This is where plans are laid out, people suit up (lots of snapping utility belts on or sliding swords into belts!), and the heroes give last-minute "good lucks." Sometimes this is just your hero gathering their courage or resolve to tackle the big moment. Your hero has a goal and a plan to win—this is the preparation.

2. *Storm the Castle* — It's time to execute that plan! Storm the castle! Race to the airport to stop the love of their life from boarding the plane. Bring down the villain once and for all.

3. *The High Tower Surprise* — Plot twist! We're writers, which means we must be mean to our heroes, so surprise... the plan does not work! Either the villains were way ahead of the hero or something about the hero's plan just isn't right. Regardless, hope and enthusiasm are pulled out from under them. In our mini-movie Finale, this is a Midpoint and All Is Lost jumbled into one.

4. *Dig Down Deep* — Now it's time to dig down deep. Show that our hero is different than when they started. This point

reflects back on the theme and the Dark Night of the Soul. Our hero has changed and can only win the day because they're a new person.

5. *Execution of the New Plan* — The hero executes the new plan (the one they can only do because of what they've learned) and wins the day.

FINAL IMAGE (100%)
Single-Scene Beat

This is the bookend of the Opening Image. This visual moment shows how far we've come in the story, how much the hero has changed, and how the hero's ordinary world will never be the same.

· · ·

Before we punt these movies examples to the curb, let's take a look at the beats in action, with a movie that hits 'em all.

E.T. the Extra-Terrestrial Beat Sheet

Written by: Melissa Mathison

Genre: Buddy Love (boy and his alien)

OPENING IMAGE: A starry sky. Far below, in the dense woods, is the large mothership. Lit up like a Christmas tree. The aliens have landed. As they wander around the dark forest gathering samples, headlights cut through the trees, trucks rush to the scene. The aliens race back to the ship. One is left behind. This is E.T.

SET-UP: A bunch of teenagers play *Dungeons & Dragons*. We meet Elliot, the younger brother of one of the teens (Michael). Elliot gets no respect. The others ignore his pleas to play. It's like he's invisible. They send him out to meet the pizza wagon.

CATALYST: Outside, pizza in hand, he encounters something in the shed. He tosses a ball in, and it's thrown back. He escapes inside, dropping the pizza. Splat! The other boys and Elliot's mother race out to investigate. They find some tracks inside the shed: "Coyotes are back."

THEME STATED: The theme comes during the Debate (see, told ya, wiggle-room). After a heated (post-Catalyst) conversation where Elliot tries to convince everyone what he saw wasn't just "alligators in the sewers," Elliot gets angry and spills the beans about his dad's new girlfriend, upsetting his mom. Michael says, "Why don't you grow up and think about how other people feel for a change?" There is a lot of talk about "feelings" as the movie goes on. At one point Michael says Elliot "feels what E.T. feels." That's the theme in a nutshell: selfish thinking leads to loneliness and longing, but empathy—especially with a stranger from another planet!—leads to acceptance and true friendship. Ignored by his family, Elliott starts out trying to convince people to think his ideas and feelings are important—it's all about him. But by the end, he puts others (E.T.'s) feelings and needs in front of his own, and becomes a kid-of-action to save his bestbud and win the respect of all those around him.

DEBATE: The Debate often revolves around a question triggered by the Catalyst. In this case, it's "What in the name of Marvin the Martian is hiding in our garage?" Everybody doubts Elliot—they always do; it makes for good *rooting resume* material. We know he's right but everybody thinks he's a dorky kid with a big imagination. His *broken compass* points firmly in the "I will prove everyone wrong whether I die trying!" direction. In bed, Elliot hears noises outside the window. There's no way it was a coyote! So he does what every unsupervised latchkey '80s kid would do, he goes out in the backyard and sleeps with a flashlight hoping to catch a glimpse of the monster. There he spots E.T. in the corn. They both scream in terror and run away from each other.

BREAK INTO 2: The next day Elliot takes action! He lays his Reese's Pieces trail to lure the thing back to him. E.T. shows up in the backyard munching Elliot's candy bait. Elliot leads him into the house and up to his bedroom. E.T. likes the candy and, taking his own step into the upside-down world, puts his trust in Elliot.

B STORY: The B Story beat is usually a spot where a key "B Story character" shows up or becomes more important. Here we get our first real look at E.T. This is a friendship (Buddy Love) story and the warm relationship is the heart of our theme. Learning to be a great friend is what Elliot needs to grow. Another key sub-thread kicks off here: The unnerving hunt for E.T. by the authorities is constantly present as Keys, the lead scientist, finds Reese's Pieces in the woods. The film comes back to Keys every couple of beats, and every time he's a little closer! It's a *ticking clock*, allowing us a slower pace to dig into the relationship while maintaining the tension as these "hunters" keep the heat on at every turn.

FUN & GAMES: Elliot fakes sickness. Hangs at home with E.T. Shows him toys and starts their friendship. He introduces his brother Michael and sister, Gertie, to E.T. as well. The kids learn about E.T. and witness his telekinetic abilities. All the while, Keys closes in, taking pictures of Elliot's neighborhood, ultimately roaming around the woods in Elliot's backyard. Elliot goes to school and we see the telepathic empathy E.T. and Elliot share as E.T. drinks beer from the fridge and magically gets Elliot drunk. Elliot frees the dissected frogs, evidence that he's starting to feel what others feel (even frogs). Somehow feeling what E.T. feels directly opens Elliot up to this new way of thinking. The *transformation machine* is working its magic and changing Elliot. Meanwhile, during this drunken interlude, E.T. learns to speak via a Speak-N-Spell toy.

MIDPOINT: E.T. phone home! E.T. wants to phone home and gets an idea from a Flash Gordon comic strip: he'll build a communicator out of toys and household items. It's a *false victory* since as Michael and Elliot are gathering equipment, surveillance crews are listening to them. They know exactly where E.T. is at this point. A *ticking clock* is engaged when Michael says, "He's not looking good." Elliot tells Michael E.T. will be fine once he's back on his home planet.

BAD GUYS CLOSE IN: The next day is Halloween. The kids sneak E.T. out dressed up as a trick-or-treating ghost and head off to the woods to set up the "phone." E.T. takes Elliot's bike on a "flying trip." Once everyone is out of Elliot's house, the Bad Guys/scientists swoop in and scan with instruments. The next morning, Elliot is missing; the cops are taking a report. When Elliot shows up, he's looking very ill. He tells Michael to go get E.T. Michael finds a sick looking E.T. by the river near the make-shift communicator as helicopters circle the woods. The Bad Guys are closing in! Michael takes E.T. back home and Mom freaks out as she sees E.T. for the first time (in an embarrassing coffee spilling cliché that I would cut in the next Special Edition). Just then guys in astronaut suits crash the party! Take everyone hostage! And cover the house in Saran Wrap. E.T. and Elliot are side by side on medical beds. Keys interviews the family.

ALL IS LOST: E.T. dies on the medical table. The telepathic link to Elliot is broken.

DARK NIGHT OF THE SOUL: Gertie cries. Keys consoles Elliot. E.T.'s packed in ice and a Ziploc bag. Elliot gets some alone time with E.T.'s body. He reflects back on the Theme Stated, speaking to his empathetic connection with the alien:"I'm so sorry. You must be dead 'cause I don't know how to feel."He begins to cry. His connection to E.T. goes beyond the supernatural.

BREAK INTO 3: As Elliot says a tearful goodbye,E.T.'s heart light shines! He's alive! But the heart light means his mothership has returned. Elliot must save E.T.!

FINALE: Elliot and Michael hatch a plan to get E.T. back to the ship. They enlist the help of Michael's friends. The crew hijacks the van E.T. is to be transported in (along with E.T.). They all end up on bikes with the government types in hot pursuit. They finally escape doing the bike-flying trick and end up in the woods where the space-ship awaits. They say their goodbyes. E.T. says, "I'll be right here," suggesting that friends remain in our hearts and feelings forever.

FINAL IMAGE: As the ship flies off into the same sky we opened with, we hang on Elliot's face. And we can tell he's a changed man...err...kid, happy for his friend's triumphant return home.

Okay, now that we understand the basic beats, we'll jump back to TV World to see how they help break story for seasons and, most importantly, TV pilots.

🐾 BREAKING SEASON 1

You've found a unique world. You've determined the best franchise type that will pop out compelling reasons for viewers to come back week after week or binge night after night. You even have great characters.

Now we have yet another chicken and egg situation: do you dive right into your pilot or think up Season 1 first?

If you're working on one of those rare 100% episodic shows—a Blank of the Week cop show or an animated Trapped Together or a kid sitcom—you don't have to do too much season planning before you leap into the pilot.

But even those shows usually have a season-long runner story. The Jim & Pam of it all. The Sam & Diane (if you're old school or just like *Cheers*).

It's best to have a handle on those season-spanning stories before you jump.

Do you really have to plot the whole season out? Is that what this crazy CAT!-man is saying?

Emphatic *NO*.

But you need enough info that if someone asks, "What's Season 1?" you'll have an exciting answer full of twists and turns and OMG moments. You'll have enough story that they'll lean forward and go, "Mmmm-hmmm, that is good. I think you've got something."

Before going deep into your pilot, sketch out the high-level beats of Season 1. Emphasis on HIGH-LEVEL.

Let.

Me.

Repeat.

HIGH-LEVEL!

You only need about 1-2 pages of a season arc that spell out the big turning points and where your characters land when the credits roll in the final episode. Sure, you can go deeper. But your time and effort are better spent elsewhere (ahem, writing more pilots). That's where the money is. Don't get distracted. Stick to the big beats. Write out a 1-2 page beat sheet and move on to your pilot. Got it? Good!

SEASONS AS TRANSFORMATION MACHINES

Stories are transformations. You take a character that needs to change and put them through a story-grinder so they come out different.

In *A Christmas Carol*, Ebenezer Scrooge is a miser and a curmudgeon and he's got a bad case of the Bah Humbugs! He won't change. Ever. Even little Tiny Tim can't crack Scrooge's snowball-cold heart. So we drop a story bomb on the grumpy miser. We hit him with three time-traveling ghosts and a night of Yuletide history-hopping that ultimately forces the old coot to become Mr. Christmas.

In TV, any given episode may serve a specific purpose: setting up a character, playing out a particular conflict (a standalone or bottle episode may even serve a side character). Typically, there's not a major character change within an episode. TV characters have to maintain their flaws and hang-ups for episodes and seasons that may span years or decades. If you change your hero each episode, there won't be much to do in Season 7.

A lot of shows run out of steam using up all their character transformation potential or just streeeeetch out the transformation so long that the show is in a bit of a rut and risks wearing out audiences with the same-old-same-old.

The trick is to identify some change across a season but still leave plenty of flaws and internal demons to wrestle with. Sometimes the season transformation can just be an awakening to a new life or way of thinking. The new life might even be fraught with danger and present different flaws for Season 2. It may put the hero at odds with the upside-down world they now inhabit. If after a season of bloodshed and therapy, Tony Soprano starts thinking he needs to "be a better person," it makes his world that much more dangerous. He's playing the mobster game with an arm tied behind his back. He'll be severely tested in the next season.

Seasons also end with heroes struggling and realizing something's got to give, but refusing to transform. That elevates the tension and leaves them in even bigger jeopardy and conflict in the unfolding story to come... next season!

If you've already worked out your main character's transformation map, you have an idea where they're going. If they're gonna be Mr. Chips and turn to Scarface throughout the entire run of the show, where do they land at the end of Season 1?

If Mr. Chips was level 1 and Scarface was level 10, what's level 2? In *Breaking Bad*, it's Walt being in deep enough that it's easier to keep working the meth biz, but not so deep he's looking to take on the cartel or become the Voldemort of crystal meth. He still thinks drug dealing is something he's doing for his family, so that when he makes enough money he'll find a soft place to land.

That's where he has to end up at the end of Season 1.

That's the trajectory.

Your first and most important step in breaking your Season 1 is planting those goalposts.

How does the hero start?

Where do they finish?

Write it down.

Fill in the blank:

My Hero starts Season 1 _____ and ends Season 1 _____.

Once you have those posts planted firmly at the opposite ends of your Season 1 playing field, you're ready to build the bridge that takes you from start to finish.

BEAT OUT YOUR SEASON

The *Save the Cat!* beat sheet is an efficient way to create the twists and turns to construct the transformational story inside your show and season. Yet we know television is wonky. Any given show may be juggling several distinct stories in a season. Even an individual B or C or D Story may stretch out to almost a feature's length worth of time. Television networks sometimes require more episodes than a show's main story really dictates. A series might be filled out with standalone stories, flashback episodes, or other devices that don't entirely move the season arc forward but add layers to the over-all story.

For less serialized shows, the primary hook is that week's story. Season arcs are sprinkled wherever they're needed. Storylines might be lightly seeded in early episodes but save the bulk of their narrative for later.

Because television isn't meant to be watched in one marathon sitting (unless you're me watching a new season of *Ozark*), the pacing demands aren't as stringent season-wide as they are "within an episode." For example, a TV arc's "Midpoint twist" may come in Episode 6 of 10, but if Episodes 4 and 5 are delivering their own breakneck story-within-a-story pacing, nobody will notice or care that the Midpoint was a little late.

But beware: the quickest way to lose your series' audience is to slow-burn the season-long story, not providing the necessary stake-raisers, plot twists, and emotional turning points that viewers crave.

Fear not! *Save the Cat!* is here to make sure you don't make those mistakes. Because **even though we use the beat sheet as a story analysis tool, it's primarily a story-breaking tool**.

By way of example, let's map out a season of *The Good Place*, a highly serialized and highly regarded Dude with a Season-Long Problem comedy. Serialized comedy shows on network TV are a new thing. *The Good Place* and *Last Man on Earth* manage to tell all the twists and turns of a must-binge serialized show, while also delivering a light, fun tone and lots of laughs.

There are so many twists and turns in an entire season of *The Good Place*, I could slice this story about 5 different ways. For a moment, let's pretend no one has ever seen *The Good Place*... like it was all our idea… like that movie *Yesterday*, where no one could remember the Beatles… but instead of John Lennon and *Hey Jude!*, nobody's heard of Ted Danson and "Forkin!"

THE GOOD PLACE "SEASON 1"
World: The afterlife
Franchise Type: Dudette with a Season-Long Problem
Platform: NBC
TV Genre: Half-Hour Comedy — Serialized

OPENING IMAGE: Eleanor blinks awake and sees: "WELCOME! EVERYTHING IS FINE!" She's called into Michael's office and he introduces her to the afterlife (yep, she's dead). But good news! She's in The Good Place!

SET-UP: Michael gives Eleanor the guided tour. It's Utopia with Frogurt. Nice homes, a quaint town, and all the karma-worthy people. Everyone is living their best afterlife. We're introduced to the rules, rewards, and also to Janet, the sort of robot/Siri that runs the place and can make things appear and disappear in a blink.

CATALYST: Eleanor explores her new home (a modest, small place with icky clown paintings) and meets her soul mate, Chidi, a professor of ethics. But there's a big forkin' problem (and not just that every time she curses, her words turn into goofy airplane-entertainment-version obscenities). When Eleanor is shown a video screen in which she can review the entire history of her life, she realizes they've got the wrong girl. They think she's this amazing saint. But that's not her.

DEBATE: Eleanor reveals to Chidi that she's not supposed to be here. She's a party girl, with an aimless life and a not-so-great moral compass. Ethics-obsessed Chidi begins to stress over having to keep Eleanor's real identity under wraps, but they realize The Bad Place is just as horrible as we could imagine. Torturing! Screaming! Bad stuff! He can't just damn her to The Bad Place… can he? At a big party, we meet the silent Jason (though everybody calls him Jianyu now, we won't find out his real name until later), a Buddhist monk who took a vow of silence, and the host Tehani, a rich British socialite. They'll round out our ensemble. A frustrated Eleanor's true colors begin to show; she starts stealing shrimp and making fun of people.

THEME STATED: At Tehani's party, Eleanor questions whether any of these people are really better than her. It's a Theme Stated for the entire series: what is good and what makes a good person? That is the heart of the show.

BREAK INTO 2: Eleanor's behavior seemingly causes an apocalyptic incident that is instigated by her "non-Good" actions the night before. Realizing she's responsible, Eleanor takes action. She asks Chidi to make her a better person, someone worthy of The Good Place. Together they set out to change her before anyone finds out she's not supposed to be there.

B STORY: Eleanor's relationship with Chidi takes a turn for the better as he becomes her Yoda of ethics. Their rapport is directly related to the theme of "am I a good person?" They'll ultimately find love, but right now he's her guide to becoming a better Eleanor. And she'll help him lighten up.

There are other stories here concerning the other characters and even flashbacks to Eleanor's past life. All of the threads supplement the greater theme of "who is really good?"

FUN & GAMES: Eleanor sets out to fit in, but her slip-ups continue to cause disasters. Lucky for her, Chidi seems to be on Team Eleanor. She also begins to notice the other residents aren't so great either. Buddhist monk Jason finally speaks aloud when he reveals to Eleanor that he also doesn't belong in The Good Place. Hmmm. The boss of The Good Place, Michael worries that things aren't looking so great, and as the mayor/architect/project manager, he ends up blaming himself and announces his own retirement. That means going to The Bad Place and living an eternity of pure torture. Eleanor, now struggling to be her good self, can't let Michael go. The entire group realizes that robotic Janet, who is sort of The Good Place's enforcer, will be the one required to retire Michael (aka sending him to The Bad Place), and they set out to stop her. Chidi ends up hitting the reboot button on Janet (basically killing her). Michael begins an investigation into the murder of Janet.

MIDPOINT: *B Story crosses A Story* when Eleanor admits she loves Chidi, but also confesses to everyone she doesn't belong in The Good Place and is in fact "the problem." It's a moral win for Eleanor; she's truly becoming a better person, but it also means she's likely just damned herself to The Bad Place.

BAD GUYS CLOSE IN: A train arrives from The Bad Place with a sleazeball named Trevor. He's come to trade Eleanor for the "real" Eleanor (who has been in The Bad Place the entire time). Chidi admits to killing Janet and pleads to Trevor and Michael to leave Eleanor alone. She's trying to be a good person after all.

Demons from The Bad Place show up to negotiate. Internal Bad Guys close in too: Chidi and the "real" Eleanor bond, giving our Eleanor doubts about her relationship with Chidi. Now a judge gets involved. The judge will decide Eleanor's fate as she is put on trial. A test of sorts is proposed: if Eleanor can achieve 1,200,000 points via doing good deeds in The Good Place, she'll be able to stay. We see Eleanor on the right track but—like most well-told stories—the road to success usually leads to the biggest roadblock of all.

ALL IS LOST: Eleanor is denied points for her good deeds because they were intended for self-preservation. She's screwed! Michael learns that Jason doesn't belong in the Good Place either. Double rock bottom!

DARK NIGHT OF THE SOUL: Eleanor pleads with Chidi to accept the "real Eleanor" as his soul mate before she gives up and escapes with Jason and Janet on the train to The Medium Place, where they hope to live a better life and learn to become better people. In The Medium Place, they meet Mindy St. Claire, an attorney who bears some similarities to Eleanor. Eleanor sees herself and her fate in the lawyer. Back at The Good Place, an antagonistic judge must decide the fate of Eleanor and Jason in their absence. Michael, Chidi, and Tehani argue in their defense, but the judge isn't swayed.

BREAK INTO 3: The judge makes a ruling: if Eleanor and Jason don't come back, he'll send Chidi and Tehani to The Bad Place as substitutes. Eleanor pleads with Janet and Jason to go back to The Good Place to save the day. They agree to return.

FINALE: Once there, the judge gives the entire group the responsibility to decide their own fate and pick which two people will go to The Bad Place. True to the show's philosophical underpinnings, the group argues the various pairings like a college ethics course. Just when things are reaching their most tense, Eleanor realizes the big truth: this isn't The Good Place at all. It's The Bad Place! This whole thing has been set up as a way to torture the four of them for eternity. Michael is revealed as the sinister architect of this whole twisted scheme... and now it's ruined. He begs the judge for a do-over to erase their minds and start from the very beginning. The judge grants his wish to try the experiment again, but right before Eleanor loses her memory and everything gets rebooted, she writes a note to herself that says "Find Chidi" and hides it inside Janet's mouth.

FINAL IMAGE: Eleanor wakes up in the exact same place as she started at the beginning of the story. Only this time we know what's up and so will she—once she finds the clue she made for herself.

· · ·

The beat sheet is an awesome tool for getting a handle on your Season 1 without having to write every episode. Okay, okay, I know what you're thinking. I can read your mind right now, it's shouting to me in all caps and in bold ...

DO I REALLY NEED TO DO ALL THAT WORK TO WRITE A PILOT?

That's an un-emphatic *yes*.

It's a yes-*ish*.

While you can write a 20-page treatment on Season 1 if you feel inspired, to write your pilot you only need a high-level Season 1 beat sheet. We're talking a 1- or 2-pager. 3-5 if you can't help yourself.

One-sentence beats let you focus on high-level storytelling. A beat sheet of single-sentence beats will give you enough story to figure out what you need for your pilot, which is really the goal of this whole exercise! Brevity for the win!

Let's take a look at what *The Good Place* looks like as a one-sentence-per-beat beat sheet.

OPENING IMAGE: Eleanor awakes in an office and Michael tells her she's dead but there's "Good news": she's in The Good Place.

SET-UP: Michael gives Eleanor a tour of the small town that is populated by people who earned their way in through good deeds and meets her new friends, Tehani and Jason.

THEME STATED: Eleanor questions whether or not any of these people are really better than her: what makes them so good?

CATALYST: Eleanor explores her new home and meets her soul mate, Chidi, but realizes her new neighbors think she's someone else and doesn't deserve to be here!

DEBATE: Eleanor admits to Chidi that she doesn't belong and together they try to figure out what to do next.

BREAK INTO 2: Eleanor's behavior seemingly causes apocalyptic damage to The Good Place, so Eleanor asks Chidi to help teach her how to be a better person, someone worthy of The Good Place.

B STORY: Chidi is both a mentor and a romantic interest—they'll learn from each other what it means to be a good person.

FUN & GAMES: Eleanor tries to be a better person while working with and growing closer to Chidi (and covering up the ever-worsening problems her presence is causing), but she begins to suspect something is up with The Good Place when Jason admits he doesn't belong either.

MIDPOINT: The stress is getting to her; Eleanor finally admits to everyone that she doesn't belong in The Good Place and she's in fact "the problem."

BAD GUYS CLOSE IN: Michael tries to figure out what to do and an investigation and trial of sorts take place as Eleanor's fate hangs in the balance.

ALL IS LOST: Eleanor is to be sent to The Bad Place (along with Jason)!

DARK NIGHT OF THE SOUL: Eleanor and Jason escape to a limbo area, leaving their friends to deal with the mess.

BREAK INTO 3: A judge orders that if Eleanor and Jason aren't available to go to The Bad Place, their friends will have to take their place, so our heroes return to save the day.

FINALE: Eleanor realizes this isn't The Good Place at all and Michael is the sinister architect of this whole twisted scheme, which now is ruined.

FINAL IMAGE: Michael gets a do-over and Eleanor wakes up in the exact same place as she started... only this time we know what's up and so will she, once she finds the clue she made for herself.

See! Quick, pithy, and all you need to have in your back pocket for writing your pilot.

. . .

Both of these beat sheets leave out many of the twists and turns and runner stories and tangents that fill out the actual first season of *The Good Place*.

And that's the point.

Season beat sheets should lay out the skeleton of a season. They show the path, but they leave lots of room for exploration. They allow you to identify payoffs that need to be set up in the pilot.

After your show is greenlit, you'll have a team of writers working on the big Midpoint twist in Episode 3 or Episode 7's B Story. For now, yadda yadda that stuff, save it for the writer's room. You only need the bare minimum to get you writing your pilot. Focus on that.

ENSEMBLES & RUNNER STORIES

If you have a show with an ensemble cast of almost equal weight, it's often easier to break character beat sheets out separately. Shows like *Stranger Things* or *This Is Us* are obvious candidates. TV writers' rooms often break separate story threads in isolation and then bring them together when they write their scripts (a step called "The Blend").

Similarly, if you are writing an episodic show and have a runner story that gets spread out every so often, you can use the single-sentence beat sheet to make sure the story has all the twists and turns and momentum it needs. In theory, these beats would be sprinkled over episodes throughout a season where they are warranted.

Again, for your season beat sheet keep your eyes on the prize. The goal is to break enough story so that you can write your pilot and perhaps pitch the high-level show to potential buyers. The goal is not to write your entire show or know exactly what happens in Season 1 Episode 10.

Tread lightly.

Eyes on the prize.

The prize is the pilot!

DO I *REALLY* NEED TO BREAK AN ENTIRE SEASON TO WRITE A PILOT?

Ish.

The more you understand your show before you write your pilot, the better your pilot will be. And there's a bonus: if you're called to pitch your series, you'll need to be ready to walk execs through the big moments of Season 1.

But if you're itching to get started on your pilot, and don't feel like tangling with the Dark Night of the Soul in Season 1, I have a high-level brainstorming technique that can cut your work in half. It's also a great way to break new ground on your standard beat sheets!

THE PILLAR BEATS

Tackling the 15 beats may be a bit daunting.

Sometimes it's hard to know where to start.

Do you just jump in at the Opening Image and keep going? Do you start at the Closing Image because you already envision that? Skip to the Catalyst? Which beat do you start with?

Whatever works for you, works for you.

In our screenwriting workshops, we have a battle-tested plan: the pillar beats! The pillar beats are a collection of single-scene beats that anchor your overall story. In our workshops, we often speak of *six* pillar beats, but I like to add the All Is Lost as a pillar. I find that beat gives context to the Break into 3, so that you realize what the "All" is to your hero.

Here are the seven pillar beats:

1. Opening Image
2. Catalyst
3. Break into 2
4. Midpoint
5. All Is Lost
6. Break into 3
7. Final Image

Using the pillar beats is a quick way to whip up a high-level story framework before you dig deeper. In the case of your high-level season, it might be enough just to come up with the pillar beats, then go write your pilot. Regardless of your strategy, the pillar beats are a great first step toward creating your beat sheet.

EXERCISES

1. Dig up one of your favorite shows on Netflix or Amazon Prime. Choose a serialized show (not episodic!) that you binged. Come up with a logline for its first season.

2. For this same show, do a one-sentence-per-beat beat sheet for Season 1. Keep it short. One-page of Season 1 story goodness.

3. Now, it's time to do one for your own show's Season 1.
   a. Write your Story DNA and logline first. Be sure you have a tough obstacle and life-or-death stakes.
   b. Figure out what *Save the Cat!* genre your season logline falls under.
   c. Next, do your pillar beats. Remember to keep them at one-sentence per beat. You don't need to write your whole season!
   d. Okay, it's time: fill in the rest of the beats so that you complete a one-sentence beat sheet for your entire season

CHECK YOURSELF

1. Does your Season 1 Set-Up clearly express characters' flaws and the things that need fixing? Does it introduce all your main characters?

2. Does the Catalyst happen to your hero and disrupt their ordinary world?

3. Does the Break into 2 show a hero taking definitive action to enter the upside-down world?

4. Does the B Story clearly reflect and enforce your show's theme?

5. Does the season Midpoint raise the stakes? Do things somehow get more personal?

6. Does the Break into 3 represent a shift in the character, taking action their old selves may not have ever imagined?

7. Does the season's Final Image reflect a character transformation, while clearly leaving more room for growth in the seasons to come?

8. Does the season leave questions to be answered or story threads to be explored in future seasons?

🐾 THE WONKY LAWS OF PILOT PHYSICS

You've come up with a show that can sustain multiple seasons, identified compelling relationship-worthy characters, and sketched out a high-level Season 1 story that hits all the beats.

A pilot is nothing compared to that, right?

You've done the real work.

This next part will be a cakewalk.

Bwahahahahahaha.

Pilots are impossible. You have to take all that hard show-building work and cram it into an exciting attention-grabbing 30- or 50-page script that will not only launch your show but also your TV writing career.

Easy-peasy.

Your pilot is a proof-of-concept, a sales pitch, an audition, a set-up, an Act 1, a character study, and a cathartic story all at once. It wears a lot of hats... and needs to wear them with flair.

Here are some of the key duties of your pilot script:

1. **A pilot is a promise** — It demonstrates what a typical future episode might be in terms of tone, execution, and story potential—all within the context of the format and platform of your show.

2. **A pilot is a first date** — It presents compelling characters with rooting resumes that hook the viewer into a long-term (perhaps several years) relationship.

3. **A pilot is a set-up** — It positions the character at the start of a transformation that will range from stasis = death to at least some movement. Their world has been shaken and they can't help but notice and take some action. The character makes the first step into a new life. A whiff of change is in the air and the character's transformational theme is evident.

4. **A pilot is a launchpad** — It needs to make people watch the next episode and begin a story with enough energy and potential that it lasts one, two, or 10 seasons.

5. **A pilot is awesome** — The #1 goal is to tell a complete story with a cathartic ending and that's what the *Save the Cat!* beat sheet can help you achieve.

6. **A pilot is you-on-a-plate** — A unique you-on-a-plate story that demonstrates your voice and represents who you are as a writer and a person.

PREMISE PILOT VS. NON-PREMISE PILOT

Premise pilots are origin stories for your show. They kick off some new event that melds together the world + franchise type + characters for essentially the first time.

If it's a Blank of the Week, the hero accepts a duty or a job or moves to a new location or makes a discovery that will now force them to deal with a myriad of new blanks on a weekly basis. If you have a (Wo)Man with a Plan, your pilot will probably be all about the thing that kicks off the plan. Dude with a Season-Long Problem stories sweep the innocent hero into the problem. Trapped Togethers introduce the new job or situation or living condition or at least introduce some new person or element to the mix.

Counter to that, **non-premise pilots** are first episodes that feel like Episode 4. We join these stories with their world + franchise type + characters already rolling along. They demonstrate what week-to-week episodes feel like by dumping us right into the mix without wasting time with any origin story hijinks. They're typically the pilots for old-school episodic shows (procedurals, sitcoms, animated comedies, kid shows, etc.).

While non-premise pilots skip the origins, they still need to serve as introductions. In fact, **both premise and non-premise pilots have to thoroughly introduce all the key elements**: your hero and why we care, their life at home and work and play, the franchise type, the tone, etc. But in non-premise pilots, the writer must make all of these introductions while telling a story that "feels" like it's a rando episode even though they're carefully engineered to organically introduce the show without feeling like that's what they're doing.

WHAT'S THE NEW SITUATION?

Premise pilots establish a new situation for the main character(s). Sometimes this is your hero landing in the world of the show—a character might move into a new neighborhood, get stranded on a mysterious island, land a new job, or die and wake up in The Good Place.

Sometimes the world is a "situational world"—a new relationship, a special mystery to solve, a monster to hunt. Shows that feel like extended movies—like *Homeland*, *The Walking Dead*, and *Stranger Things*—introduce dangerous situations that threaten our main characters and drag them into these new worlds. In pilots for shows like *Broadchurch*, *The Killing*, or *Homeland*, the main character already lives inside the world of the show (a profession: police work, CIA, medicine, law, chef, etc.), but the new disruptor comes along that shakes things up.

In other shows, the new situation might be a mindset or a philosophy—almost always tied to the theme of the show or at least the central question or dilemma the hero will deal with through the first season or the overall series.

Shows like *The Mandalorian* or *Justified* or even *The Marvelous Mrs. Maisel* feature characters that begin to question their old lives or ways. The new attitude or notion is almost as important to the ongoing story engine as the external conflict.

Non-premise pilots begin in the world + franchise type + character situation but something new enters the mix. Choosing stories that introduce the audience to this world are key. Focus on stories that center around the very nature of the situation. Often these pilots will feature a disruption to the status quo: someone new entering the world, a promotion, a new idea that throws things into question, a chance to leave, or some other minor ripple to the already established situation.

GET PERSONAL

We're meeting your main character for the first time. We need to be introduced to all their dimensions. Show us how their flaws are messing up everything. Establish the hero's broken compass. Illustrate how this broken compass leads them to make surprising decisions, often ones that make their lives harder. Construct your story around something that tests and stresses their secret mantras, demonstrating how their personal makeup leads to conflict. Not every episode of a series will be intensely personal to the hero. But the pilot must be. You need to show your hero's flaws, their rooting resumes, their things that need fixing—and the best way to do this is to come up with a story that specifically pushes against their internal buttons.

THROAT PUNCH 'EM IN THE FEELS

Anybody can write a joke or give a thrill or hit a plot twist, but the shows we love go straight for the heart. If you can move the audience, make them feel something, give them a cry... you'll have the stuff of great pilots.

Character & Empathy is the special sauce. First you get people to empathize with your character, using your rooting resume. Then you run the hero through an emotional ringer.

You'll see it in almost all the pilots we breakdown later. *The Marvelous Mrs. Maisel* will have her life ripped out from under her. *Grey's Anatomy* side character George O'Malley will have to break the news of a patient who died in surgery to the family he's promised "everything will be fine." Hitman Barry (from *Barry*) will be forced to admit everything he hates about himself. *Stranger Things'* Hopper will be reminded of his own dead child when a local kid goes missing on his watch.

From an emotional standpoint, your pilot needs to lean on your character's shard of glass, twist it around, make it hurt. That's the best way to hit the audience in the feels.

YOUR SERIES THEME IS YOUR PILOT THEME

Individual episode themes often vary, sometimes diverging from series' themes.

But the theme of your pilot's story is born from your series' overall theme.

Properly introducing your series' theme ensures that your pilot tells a story that directly relates to your hero's theme-based flaws.

THE WHIFF OF CHANGE

We've said that stories are about transformation and that movies and books have strong character arcs. Yet in TV there will be many episodes or seasons where your hero does not change even a little bit.

TV is about keeping the same thing running... foreves!

So what gives?

Your standalone episodes or season arcs are stories, pure and simple, which means they require at least a spoonful of spiritual change. Your main character (or sometimes others in non-pilot standalone episodes) should dip a toe into their transformative journey.

This is the **whiff of change**!

The hero will see or sense the bigger world out there. Maybe they're just open to a new idea, something related to the theme of the show. It's enough to let them think, maybe for the first time, that "Stasis might just equal Death." It's not an all-encompassing movie-style, most-important-moment-of-my-life change... it's the *whiff* of change.

The whiff of change is critical in pilot episodes. It's the special sauce that makes your pilot feel cathartic while a typical Episode 4 might intentionally leave you wanting.

In the pilot episode of *The Marvelous Mrs. Maisel*, our hero, Midge, starts as the epitome of a picture-perfect Jewish housewife. She ends up with no husband, off on a bender, and starting to think... maybe I should try comedy?

Similarly, in *Barry*, Barry goes from being a soulless hit man to... a soulless hitman with a new idea: "I'm going to be an actor."

In both, the whiff of change is in the air! These are the first steps on the road to bigger transformations. On their overall transformation map, they're millimeters from the starting line with long, long roads ahead. But in your pilot, they take that first baby step.

In other standalones or episodics, the whiff might be a small hint that our hero may one day change, often sort of forgotten in the next episode.

But it's there if you sniff.

Other changes will occur in your pilot. Situational ones. Material ones. For example, your hero might win a prize or get a new job.

But the whiff of change is different. The whiff of change is a deeper, psychological, person-transforming path.

And it must be in your pilot.

🐾 LET'S GET WONKIER

Before jumping into writing a *Save the Cat!* beat sheet for your pilot, there's some weird stuff we need to talk about. The wonky stuff. The stuff you'll see if you watch tons of pilots back-to-back-to-back-to-back: patterns and recurring devices the pros use to clearly pitch their shows while delivering awesome-sauce TV that makes us set our DVRs or binge the weekend away.

THE OPENING PITCH

Back in the day, shows like *The Fresh Prince of Bel-Air*, *The Nanny*, *The Beverly Hillbillies*, *The Brady Bunch*, and *Gilligan's Island* packed everything you needed to know about the world and franchise type into their opening theme song.

Here's the story...

Of a lovely lady...

Who is bringing up three very lovely girls...

Everybody! Sing along!

If only *Breaking Bad* had gone that route. Sing it with me...

He had a tumor...

He met a dealer...

And they knew it was much more than a hunch...

Ah! The good old days. Just from the catchy opening jingle, you'd know that the Fresh Prince was "West Philadelphia born and raised" and the castaways of Gilligan's Island went on a "3-hour tour." Credits, a montage, a little earworm, and in 30 seconds you had all the backstory you needed to enjoy the show.

The **opening pitch** is like that without the sweet tune-age. Many pilots pitch the entire show's essence in a quick 2-3 minute opening teaser. These opening pitches feel like writer pitch documents rolling off the lips of your lead characters. They lay out situations, worlds, themes, character wants and flaws.

Everything but the music!

The *Goldbergs* pilot uses a voice-over montage that introduces the sibling lead characters, the grumpy dad in his underwear, and the Smother Mother. It also introduces our moviemaking hero, his pop-culture-obsessed attitude, and the nostalgia-shellacked veneer of the show. The first episode of *Black-ish* does the same. The main character, Dre, introduces the family, the theme, and dishes a healthy dose of his smooth POV which flavors every episode to come. In both pilots, the opening pitch does the heavy-lifting of the Set-Up, clearing the way for a non-premise pilot that truly reflects a regular episode without all the expositional baggage.

Just like the Fresh Prince!

Other times, opening pitches come in the form of speeches given by characters that confess the "before picture" internals of a character in a revealing monologue as in *Insecure* or *The Marvelous Mrs. Maisel* (which also mixes in some montage-ey stuff). These opening pitches take care of some serious groundwork right upfront, letting our characters speak their truths, giving us flaws, *Save the Cat!* moments, and rooting resumes—all in the first couple minutes of a new show.

Another type of opening pitch is the **mini-episode**. It's more of a show-don't-tell version, where the first couple minutes deliver a sort of warp-speed version of the show. The pilots for *The Mandalorian*, *Rick & Morty,* and *Justified* drop us right into a little 3-minute short story that encapsulates everything about the new series.

Some pilots, like *Breaking Bad*, flash-forward deep into the world and the conflict, previewing an intense and attention-grabbing moment we'll see later. In *Breaking Bad*'s opening seconds we get New Mexico! Cow pastures! Dead bodies! A mobile drug lab! A guy in a gasmask... in his underwear. And a desperate *Blair Witch*-style last goodbye spoken into a video camera. It's *Breaking Bad* on a plate!

These techniques don't work for every story (but you'll find some version of them in more pilots than not) and may even seem a bit heavy-handed at first blush, but when handled elegantly, organically, and eye-poppingly, they can take care of a lot of heavy lifting in a super-economical way for your pilot. And economy in pilot-world is everything.

MOVING TRAINS & STORY-BEFORE-THE-STORY

Most of the pilots I break down in this book drop us on a **moving train**, and force the viewer to catch up. These stories-in-motion are not typically the pilot's main story; they could be a **story-before-the-story** that gets interrupted or even one that's about to wrap up.

In *Grey's Anatomy*, we meet Meredith as she wakes from a one-night stand and she's late for work on the most important day of her life. *The Good Place* opens with the hero finding out she's dead! *Rick & Morty* starts with... *Rick & Morty* stuff.

Begin with someone getting arrested, or hustling to get to that life-or-death job interview, or introduce them on the day they're moving to a scary new town. Give us a situation. Give us questions. Give us conflict. Conflict is the best way to show us who your hero really is and to bring out that mission-critical flaw.

AND IN THIS CORNER...

As we've said before, TV is about three things: Character, Character, Character! You need to sell your characters from the moment they appear on screen. Give your main characters strong and memorable introductions. When we first meet them, it should be clear that they're important. Take the time to show us why they're wicked cool or awful or funny or lonely. Make their unique traits pop. Give them a star moment that shows them at their best or their worst.

You know I like my pro wrestling. In wrestling, the stars are introduced via some eye-popping intro. Fog machines, pyro, a rocking entrance theme. Whether it's your cold open or the very first scene after the title credits, this is your character's chance to win people over. Bring the fireworks!

In the opening sequence of *Justified*, Raylan Givens apprehends a fugitive with all the quiet cool of a spaghetti-western gunslinger and then manages to outgun two men in a brutal but quick shoot out.

Liz Lemon of *30 Rock* is introduced in line at a hot dog cart, where she gets into an argument with a rude bunch of customers over which line to wait in. It's a chance to see how she acts under pressure and how she deserves our rooting interest when she buys up all the hot dogs in the stand... and gifts them to everyone but those unruly other customers! Talk about a *Save the Cat!* moment!

The most celebrated moment of the HBO series *The Newsroom* was the introduction of news anchor Will McAvoy, who goes on a lengthy rant about how America is no longer the greatest country in the world. This character intro is so well written that it almost outshines the entire show, living on in YouTube clips and almost single-handedly responsible for landing Jeff Daniels an Emmy®.

So throw away your boring waking up and eating breakfast introductions. Skip those "ordinary day on the job" get-to-know-you scenes. Give your heroes big, unforgettable, character-revealing intros. Earn that second date. Hook the audience. And win some Emmys.

OPEN A WINDOW (CHARACTER)

A **window character** (aka a fish-out-of-water) is one who doesn't know the show's world and can be introduced to it along with the audience. In pilots, it's often the main character, like in *Grey's Anatomy* where Meredith Grey is going into her first day of work as a surgical intern. Other times, like in Shonda Rhimes's other huge hit, *Scandal*, it can be a side character like Quinn who is being brought into the main character's world for the very first time, providing a way to introduce the world and the main character's awesomeness all at once. These characters can ask the dumb questions. *Who is that guy? Why is this important? What's going on in this wacky place?* It gives you a great excuse to break out another pilot staple: the guided tour.

THE GUIDED TOUR

Many pilots give the viewer a **guided tour** of the world and its people. Usually, the window character is shown around the office by another character who lives or is an expert in the show's world already and knows all of its ins and outs. The guided tour is a great way to introduce a large cast quickly: *That's the office. That's the bar. That's Norm, he sits on a chair all day and drinks beer. That's Carla, don't mess with her.* She'll punch you in the throat... yadda, yadda.

SKIP BREAKFAST

Beware of starting with the dreaded "Breakfast Scene." A lot of pilots drop a breakfast scene around the 2-4 minute mark (even shows I'll breakdown later, like *Black-ish* and *Rick & Morty*, give us some coffee & bacon goodness right at the 2-minute mark, and *Breaking Bad*'s pilot drops into one after the flash-forward). While stellar execution can even make a cliché fun, breakfast scenes almost always start at 0 mph. It's a quick-and-easy way to set up character relationships and jump right into opportunities to show things that need fixing, but breakfast scenes are often the opposite of the moving train... so tread cautiously.

THINGS THAT NEED FIXING... WON'T GET FIXED!

Film is a closed loop. You set some bowling pins up, you knock 'em down.

In TV, those same bowling pins might still be standing until Episode 10 or Season 4 or the reunion episode on HBO Max.

Those things that need fixing in your Set-Up, well, you won't fix them all in the pilot. Instead, you'll offer some glimmer of hope that maybe one day they'll get fixed. Your savvy audience will see the potential in your hero and want and hope for change as the series progresses.

SET-UP... AND MUCH MUCH MUCH LATER... PAYOFF

Your pilot should have a cathartic standalone vibe.

But it's just a vibe.

You pose mysteries that don't get solved, you throw out tantalizing ideas, you even save heaps of character backstory and development for later.

Things can play out throughout a season and or even a series' run. Tell your pilot story to completion (or cliff-hanger), but don't try to answer every question. Pilots serve a great meal and tantalize the audience with a long menu they'll be sampling in weeks to come.

SET-UPS AREN'T JUST IN THE SET-UP BEAT

The entire pilot serves as a set-up for your show. So while your show has a Set-Up beat that relates things relevant to the pilot—the ordinary world's home, work, and play; the things that need fixing; and the theme—think of the entire pilot as your set-up for your show. If a character or thread is important to your show and needs to be set up in your pilot, it can appear in a place outside of your Set-Up beat.

The Mandalorian saves the biggest *Save the Cat!* moment for the end of the pilot episode. *Barry* sets up its main ensemble in the B Story (not the Set-Up).

Speaking of B Stories, a pilot often sets up season-long B Stories. Sometimes the B Story gets a quick scene that introduces a runner story and that's it. Often this scene introduces a villain or other conflict that's lingering out there, and will collide head-on with our hero in future episodes.

Take caution in your pilot that these season-long B Story introductions don't feel too random. The key is that the audience "sees where this is going." While dropping a pair of FBI agents investigating the cartel in a show like *Ozark* is obvious "future conflict" stuff, showing an incidental scene of a kid working at an ice cream shop isn't. Use this as your test: does setting up your B Story hint at the potential for future conflict or in some ways raise the stakes? If not, you might want to save the rando B Story for a later episode or find a way to connect it more organically to your pilot.

PILOTS ARE THE ACT 1 TO YOUR SHOW

Pilots take a hero and pull them out of their ordinary world into some dilemma.

This dilemma is similar to the Debate section of the *Save the Cat!* beat sheet. Often a question is asked: Is meth dealing viable? Is there something more in life than being a hitman? What will I do with my life now that my husband's left me? Do I have what it takes to be a surgeon?

The pilot provides a blow-by-blow debate to this question that often resolves in a commitment by the hero—and that commitment is the **Break into the Series**!! It brings the hero together with the franchise type so that future episodes can deliver on the promise of the premise of the overall show.

In some ways, that makes pilots Act Ones for your entire show, with the Debate beat being spread across all the other beats. From a high-level, you can view your pilot like the following structure:

SERIES BEATS	PILOT BEATS
SERIES SET-UP (ORDINARY WORLD)	OPENING IMAGE THEME STATED SET-UP CATALYST
SERIES DEBATE (LIFE IN FLUX)	DEBATE BREAK INTO 2 B STORY FUN & GAMES MIDPOINT BAD GUYS CLOSE IN ALL IS LOST DARK NIGHT OF THE SOUL
BREAK INTO SERIES (COMMITMENT TO THE FRANCHISE TYPE/WORLD/SITUATION)	BREAK INTO 3 FINALE FINAL IMAGE

SOMETIMES BREAK INTO 3... IS BREAK INTO SERIES

Ready to get really wonky? Some TV episodes skip the Finale or zoom through it without giving it a lot of meat. Remember, your pilot's last three beats are all about getting your hero to commit to the series' situation. In a sense, it's getting your hero to commit to the "new world" of franchise type/world/situation. Pilots are engineered to get the hero into a position where there's no turning back. This can be a choice to enter the new world, to try a new philosophy, or commit to a course of action. A choice that must be made!

Sometimes the hero commits to this new way at the end of the Break into 3 beat, which essentially brings about an end to the central conflict or at least the urgency of the final episode. They might be committing to a series-wide adventure or quest—something that simply cannot resolve in 10 minutes... by design!

It's not that the conflict of the episode is always resolved, but the urgency of it might be, and once the new choice is made, we realize it's much bigger than a single 10-minute Finale can contain. The implications of the decision are game-changing or at least deserve a whole episode or season.

In these pilots, the Finale feels more like a stretched out Break into 3. It wraps up loose ends. It might show how the hero's life is immediately affected by the decision. These endings often get montage-ey and become more about gearing up for next week, hyping what's about to happen or the bigger world the hero is stepping into. Other times, they'll just end on the big decision, creating a cliffhanger for the next week's episode.

We'll see this in a couple of the shows we analyze. Keep in mind it's an option, not a requirement.

THE WHIFF OF CHANGE... *STATED*

Remember the whiff of change? The whiff of change is so dang important that it's often highlighted with a big yellow metaphoric marker at the end of your episode. In the closing moments of a show, heroes often make grand statements, sometimes declaring something they're struggling with, or a new personal revelation that'll set up a season, or a character mission statement.

At the end of the pilot of *Justified*—a show about Raylon, a US Marshall who's beginning to have doubts about his shoot-first-ask-questions-later ways—Raylon asks about a shooting that happens at the very beginning of the show and has been weighing on his conscience ever since: "Was I justified?" That's the whiff of change... stated!

In the breakdowns you'll read later in the book, you'll see a bunch of whiffs of change stated.

In *Grey's Anatomy*, Grey confidently says "I am a doctor" after her first day. In *Barry*, Barry says "I am an actor." At the end of the pilot of *The Marvelous Mrs. Maisel*, Midge doesn't outright say it, but she asks her stand-up comedy mentor Lenny Bruce whether he "loves it"—signaling her intention to put herself out there and give it a go.

These moments typically land right at the Final Image beat of your story.

Sketch your whiff of change... stated into your Final Image when you start breaking your beat sheet. Then go earn it.

IF IT'S IN THE SHOW, IT'S IN THE PILOT

Pilots are often shot as tests to see if the shows will work before decisions are made to greenlight the entire series. If you have an element that's going to play a major part in the show—be it a character, a location, a tone, etc.—it belongs in the pilot. The pilot needs to serve as both a launchpad and a microcosm of your show and first season, so be sure you're introducing the primary components, including side characters and B Stories that might not pay off until later.

One last note: Don't save anything super-cool for Episode 2 because the only way the second episode will see the light of day is if the pilot rocks.

🐾 YOUR PILOT STORY DNA

The first step in writing your pilot is the same as writing any story: you need to nail down the high-level basics.

If you're working on a non-premise pilot, decide on a story that truly represents what your show will feel like episode to episode, allowing the opportunity to properly introduce your characters, situation, and settings. Choose stories that highlight your show's unique situation. Pick stuff that challenges the norm in some way or introduces the world via a new window character, getting very personal and landing us with a whiff of change.

If you're writing a premise pilot (and you probably are), it's time to look back into your Season 1 beat sheet. The question is how much of a story chunk do you want to bite off? The answer likely lies in between your Opening Image and your Break into 2. If you take that chunk, you should see an episode-worthy small journey for your main character. It takes a hero from their ordinary world to a point where they must make a decision to fully embrace the world of the show; they don't change, but they make a decision to change (yep, whiff of change for the win!). There's a good chance that's your pilot. It might feel like a big chunk, but remember when you go to actually make the series, your show will have a beginning, middle, middle, middle, middle, middle, middle, and end. So you'll be adding a lot of middle.

Your pilot story is everything now.

Make the most amazing pilot you can and take no prisoners!

Your season beat sheet might be a springboard. If making an awesome pilot means stealing the Midpoint or the All Is Lost from your season beat sheet, so be it. If it means taking your Season 1's Opening Image and expanding it to a full-on standalone story, then that's what you need to do.

You can always change things up after your pilot blows the doors off the world and you're getting invited to pitch meetings and interviews for jobs in writers' rooms. But right now, the goal is to get into those rooms. To blow the doors off. And that's why you need to write an attention-grabbing pilot that ticks all the boxes.

LET YOUR FRANCHISE TYPE GUIDE YOU

The franchise types are literally story engines. They're meant to take worlds in and spit stories out the other side. They are Story DNA prompts. Let's see what they might suggest for your pilot.

1. **TRAPPED TOGETHER** — Your pilot will be about the origin of the trap or the introduction of a new person (be it a new character who brings lots of tension or very often the main character)—people getting new jobs, moving into a new place, finding themselves trapped in a place or situation. Trapped Togethers derive conflict from both the traps and the trapped. The first episode should draw tension from both. Sometimes the hero will be struggling to escape or adjust or survive the new situation (or old one in the case of the premise pilot), only to realize they are indeed stuck and need to adjust (in a way other than escape—escape is Dude with a Season-Long Problem or (Wo)Man with a Plan territory). The whiff of change is often: Wow, I'm trapped! Oh well, I better try to deal with it.

2. **BLANK OF THE WEEK** — In a premise pilot, a hero accepts a new duty or job or situation that will bring them into conflict with their very first blank which must be solved. Remember this must be an "of the week" blank, as opposed to season-long ones that fit into the other franchise types like WhyDunIts and Dude with a Season-Long Problem. The deck should be clear for a new blank the next week. The whiff of change is usually: I can handle this, bring me the next blank.

3. **(WO)MAN WITH A PLAN** — The hero gets the idea or motivation to enact the plan or chase the season/series-long goal. The pilot is often a catalyst episode: the hero's world

must be shaken, and their specific skills or competence will be on display setting up the type of plan to come. The primary conflict derived in ongoing episodes will be the formidable obstacles in the way of executing the plan. The whiff of change is usually: I need to put all my effort into winning the prize or getting revenge or whatever that series/season-long goal is!

4. **DUDE WITH A SEASON-LONG PROBLEM** — The innocent hero's life is interrupted by the problem. It's their first taste of the life-or-death issue that will engage them in a season-long battle for survival. The conflict in the first episode and throughout the season will be surviving and trying to solve the problem. The whiff of change is often: this problem isn't going away, I'm in a fight for survival!

5. **WHYDUNIT** — The "detective" will be introduced to the season-long mystery and will likely realize it's worthy of their talents and time by the end of the first episode. The season conflict will be the mystery, and the pilot presents the initial clues and evidence. The whiff of change usually is: this case is deeper than I thought... and I gotta commit (for a season/series of investigation)!

6. **FOOL TRIUMPHANT** — The fool will be introduced to the new world. Their unique personality and POV will immediately be at odds with that world. They don't fit in. The whiff of change is usually similar to a trapped together, where the world and the fool realize they must try to deal with each other.

7. **BUDDY LOVE** — The buddies meet. The complication that will be the fly in the ointment of the relationship rears its ugly head and will be the main source of tension in both the pilot and the season to come. The whiff of change is usually a "I can't quit you" revelation; either by circumstance or spiritual connection, there's an awareness that the other buddy must be tolerated, pursued, or gotten rid of.

8. **MAD, MAD WORLD** — These are tricky—which might be why you don't see many from new writers—because they encompass elements of many franchise types and act almost as a catchall. They sometimes narrow in on particular stories that can provide introductions to the world. World-building is the key. Setting that up early is everything. Cast a wide net on the world and demonstrate conflicts lurking in the many corners that the show will explore.

MAP OUT YOUR PILOT'S STORY DNA

Whether you've broken the show's Season 1 or just jumped from story world to pilot script, the first step to finding a cathartic story is to identify your pilot's Story DNA. Then you know you have the goods.

1. **Who is your hero?**
2. **What's their goal in the pilot episode?**
3. **What's the obstacle stopping them in the pilot episode?**
4. **What's at stake if they don't get it? Why must they take action now?**

In *Breaking Bad*, Walt learns he has a tumor and takes action to secure his family's finances by diving into his first meth deal. It's a microcosm of what we'll see going forward, but his goal in Episode 1 is really just that one job. In later episodes, Walt's actions lead to bigger complications that will have to be dealt with, namely, cleaning up the mess he's made in the pilot, covering up his shady dealings from his family, and continually securing his family's finances before his disease claims his life.

When deciding your hero's goal in the pilot episode, make sure there is a formidable obstacle in their path. This is your one shot to make an impression. Hit the conflict hard. Don't waffle on it. I see a lot of new writers who crank out pilots that are so focused on setting up the ordinary world, the scripts are mired in the expositional blahs. The best way to show us a character or a world is to collide with conflict head-on. Give us something to doubt the outcome, to stress over and give our hero something to overcome, so we know how they roll when the going gets tough.

YOUR PILOT'S *SAVE THE CAT!* GENRE

Shows aren't stories but pilots are. After pinning down the Story DNA for your pilot, it's time to determine the kind of story you're telling, aka what's the *STC!* Genre? Use your Story DNA and your hero's transformation map to ask the questions below. Remember, while there is overlap between franchise type and *Save the Cat!* story genre, they are not the same. (While I'm No Fool, Dude with a Season-Long Problem, and WhyDunIts have direct genre cousins, Trapped Together or Blank of the Week do not.)

1. Is your hero trapped with a monster in a battle for survival? Hello, you're a **Monster In the House**.

2. Is your hero on a quest to win a trophy or slay a dragon or get to a location? Go get that **Golden Fleece**.

3. Does your hero need to be taught a lesson and they get the lesson in the form of some magic spell or curse? Alakazam! You're **Out of the Bottle**!

4. Do you have an innocent hero going about their day, who lands in a situation that has nothing to do with them yet they must rise to the occasion—yep, **Dude with a Problem**.

5. Is your hero dealing with some identifiable life problem (divorce, birth, parenthood, teenage years) and must discover their actual problem lies within? You're about to learn a life lesson or undergo a **Rite of Passage**.

6. Do you have an inadequate hero who needs someone else to accomplish their goal and become whole? **Buddy Love**!

7. Is your hero a determined detective (be it professional or amateur) seeking to solve a mystery at all costs... even if it costs them everything? **WhyDunIt**!

8. Do you have an innocent hero who is underestimated because of their eccentric or atypical POV or personality, and must win the day without being able to change who they are? That's a **Fool Triumphant**.

9. Is your hero an outsider in a group or world that's trying to force them to integrate into the fold? You're about to be **Institutionalized**!

10. Does your main character have a special power? Must they face an even more powerful nemesis? It's a bird, it's a plane, it's... a **Superhero**!

The genre will help guide you. You can go back and review the common traits of the genre to help with your overall storyline. And once you get the DNA right, it's time to write a logline.

WRITE YOUR PILOT'S LOGLINE

Write a logline for your pilot. Make sure it's more than just your pilot's Catalyst! Because your pilot will lay out a cathartic end-to-end story in its own right, the logline must clearly communicate each key element of Story DNA (Hero, Goal, Obstacle, Stakes). Let's take another look at our basic logline template:

After (a CATALYST), (A HERO) must overcome (OBSTACLE) to achieve (GOAL) or else (STAKES).

Remember this logline is for your pilot! Pitch it like it's a standalone movie. Don't pitch extraneous stuff from your show unless it directly plays a part in the pilot episode.

EXERCISES

1. Using your Season 1 beat sheet, determine the story chunk you'll use for your pilot.

2. Write out your pilot's Story DNA.

3. Choose a *Save the Cat!* genre for your pilot.

4. Write a logline for your pilot.

CHECK YOURSELF

1. Does your pilot have strong Story DNA? Is your main character the hero? Do they have a compelling goal, an obstacle (remember to be mean), and stakes that compels them to take action *right now*?

2. From what you have, is your pilot story character-forward?

3. Does your pilot story imply ways to introduce other stories and situations? Does it imply window characters to your new world or opportunities for opening pitches or opening mini-episode teasers?

🐾 YOUR PILOT BEAT SHEET

Got your world and franchise type? Check.

Got your characters derived from theme and a clear understanding of their broken compasses? Check. Check.

Have you done the work to suss out Story DNA for your pilot? Chose your pilot's genre and written up a logline? Check. Check. Check.

Okay, you're cleared for take-off!

Let's write a pilot beat sheet.

This chapter is meant to be your co-pilot (pun intended!). It'll walk you through each beat, giving you some pilot specific things to think about.

SAVE THE CAT! BEAT SHEETS FOR TV

TV is the same... but different.

Unlike feature films which have relatively rigid running times, telling end-to-end stories in TV gets wonky. It's that elephant thing again. You might be telling an eight episode story or a 100 episode one. There are serialized shows and week-to-week episodic shows or a mix of both. Episodic shows will have serialized runners as B Stories in the middle of otherwise standalone episodes, while serialized shows will drop standalone episodes about side characters to deepen characters and shake things up. Then there are the running times: there are hour longs, half-hours, and British shows with four 90-minute episodes per season.

See? Totally wonky.

In movie-land, the Fun & Games beat is a strict 25-35 minutes of trailer-moment, promise-of-the-premise glory. In a 22-minute TV comedy, the Fun & Games might only get one quick scene that you almost heavy thumb over with the DVR's skip chapter button. Some Set-Ups are 19 minutes of a 48-minute show; other times they're done in a super-quick teaser that ends with the Catalyst before you even hit the title sequence. Finales get compressed, Midpoints can happen well after the middle at 40 minutes into a 60-minute show. That's hardly the Midpoint. It's more the Midpoint-ish!

How do we handle this complete chaos?

"Story finds a way," says the foremost expert of Chaos theory, Jeff Goldblum.

Even if showrunners don't map out their shows using some tried-and-true method (some do), they've internalized what makes a story great and use their experience and craft to break well-structured episodes.

They're *Save the Cat!*ing. They might not call it that. They might not even have ever heard of it (for shame!), but their story-telling instincts originate from the same cues and sources as Blake Snyder's original principles.

The beats are found in every TV story and happen in the order we've already laid out.

But wonkiness is afoot.

How long you choose to spend in each beat depends on the story and which beats you intend to emphasize.

TV IS AN ITINERARY, NOT A CALENDAR OF APPOINTMENTS

By the nature of its format and audience expectations, a movie has a certain rigidity to its beat sheet. If it were a trip to New York, a movie beat sheet would have a specific schedule, like so:

8am — Stand outside of the *Today* show and wave like an idiot.

10am — Check out the Statue of Liberty.

Noon — Ice skating. Break leg.

1pm — Hansom cab ride through a dangerous neighborhood.

2pm — Check out 30 Rock. Sneak onto the set of *SNL*.

That's the feature film version or maybe even the novel.

TV is looser in the minute-by-minute aspects and often stricter in the overall time restraints. Think of your *Save the Cat!* beat sheet for TV as an ordered itinerary, not a rock-solid schedule. If you want to hang at the Statue of Liberty for an extra 20 minutes, fine.

If you want to skip out on the ice skating after one lap, cool beans. Maybe the part you really want to hit is an extra-long Hansom cab around Times Square. Do it! It's TV. It's all good. Just make sure you hit all the hot spots (err... beats) and know you have to be home by 2pm. So spending extra time in one place will cost you in another. In TV, that's okay. Because Set-Ups may have happened in previous episodes or, just the opposite, a new character or situation Set-Up might hog 10-12 minutes, stealing runtime from the Fun & Games and Bad Guys Close In beats.

WHERE TO START?

Do you just jump in at the Opening Image and keep going? Do you move to the end? Skip to the Catalyst? There are a lot of beats. Where, oh where, do you start?

I start with the pillar beats! You might remember these from the Season Breaking chapter—the pillar beats are a collection of single-scene beats that anchor your overall story.

As a reminder, here are the pillars:

1. Opening Image
2. Catalyst
3. Break Into 2
4. Midpoint
5. All Is Lost
6. Break into 3
7. Final Image

Here's how I use the pillars to tackle my pilot beat sheet:

1. **Stake your bookends first: the Opening and Final Images** — Decide where you want your hero to start and where you want them to end. What's that whiff of change that you want to hit in your Final Image? Figuring out where you want to land is paramount.

2. **The Catalyst and the Break into 2 are usually found right in the Logline/Story DNA** — Let's first check

some high-level loglines of movies. *After being bit by a radio-active spider, a teenager develops spider-powers and uses them to fight crime.* Do you see the **Catalyst**? It pops out at you like a bad 3D movie: "After being bit." Being bit is the thing that kicks off the story. It takes Peter Parker from status quo to story world. Here's another: *After finding a shark-attacked body of a swimmer, a beach-town sheriff must hunt down the shark before it kills again on the crowded 4th of July weekend.* See the Catalyst? Yep, that's right, finding that shark-munched body on the beach. It's what sets the hero in motion.

But what about the **Break Into 2**? Well, that's the extra beat where the hero takes action. While the Catalyst introduces the ripple in the pond, the Break into 2 is the hero saying,"Yes, I need to deal with this and here's how I'm gonna do it!" In its purest sense, the Break into 2 is simply the moment your hero chooses to pursue the Story DNA's stated goal. Figure out the final push that makes them commit and you've got it. The beat really can be boiled down to: "After a hero realizes stakes will happen, they decide to pursue the goal."

3. **The Midpoint is an inevitable conclusion of pursuing the goal... with a twist** — After you figure out the Break into 2, the Midpoint is often an inevitable victory or an inevitable defeat on the way to achieving the goal. It's not *the* victory or *the* defeat but a major step or bump along the way. In *Star Wars*, the heroes have a goal of "getting the Death Star plans to the rebels." The Midpoint hits when they jump out of hyperspace and there it is—Alderaan! The planet with the good guys. In *Jaws*, a shark is captured! The beach can open. But in both cases there's a twist! In *Star Wars*, just when they reach their destination—KA-BOOM—the planet explodes into a gazillion pieces courtesy of the Death Star. In *Jaws*, they've caught the wrong shark and now the town has let its guard down.

Take your Break into 2 and figure out some logical false victories or false defeats that might be reached in the hero's pursuit of the goal... and then give them a twist. That's your Midpoint.

4. **The All Is Lost is the worst thing that could happen to your hero.** All hope of ever achieving their goal is lost and their spirits sink to an all-time low.

5. **Break into 3: What's gonna finally turn the tide?** — After the All Is Lost, there's some wallowing and soul searching. The Break into 3 is a moment where we get that glimmer of hope... a new plan even! What will your hero's final plan be to win the day and earn that Final Image? Figure that out at this point. Remember, the Break into 3 can be a completely different goal for the hero than what we set up in the Break into 2. For example, in *Star Wars* Luke & Company deliver the Death Star Plans at the end of Act 2. It's good news... but now the Death Star is closing in with aims to blow up the rebel base. A new goal comes into play—survival!—and the group decides to launch an attack against the Empire's weapon. That's the Break into 3! Sometimes this new goal is the goal of the hero for the series. Sometimes it's one last hurdle to clear and the big decision is saved for a whiff of change, to be stated in the Final Image.

Wow! Most of your beats are done! Now, it's time to figure out the rest. How do we do that? We ask our hero!

LET YOUR HERO BE YOUR CO-WRITER

Most of the single-scene beats are actually beats that happen *to* the hero (Catalyst, Midpoint, All Is Lost). The key to creating character-driven stories is to show us how your three-dimensional hero with needs and flaws and a handy-dandy broken compass takes action in response to those life-rattling events. If you've chosen a pilot story that uniquely targets the hero's flaws, then the hero's broken compass will guide you in a direction that reveals character through action and generates maximum internal tension (to go along with the plot-driven external stuff).

FOR EVERY ACTION BEAT, THERE'S A GREATER REACTION BEAT

Each of the single-scene beats has a reaction beat.

1. The **Debate** shows how your hero deals with the life-disrupting Catalyst. Break out your hero's broken compass. What action would your uniquely flawed hero take? If the hero is offered a job, are they questioning it? Do they have to prepare? If a threat is leveled against them, are they trying to escape it? Or calling in the authorities? Or maybe logicing their way out of it. The Debate section is a great place to show your character in action. How do they react to problems and opportunities?

2. The Break into 2 is a beat of action and reaction. The **Fun & Games** embodies both the repercussions of your hero's choice to enter the new world and an opportunity for the hero to try to achieve their goals their way, i.e., they let their broken compass guide the way.

3. The **Bad Guys Close In** is the spot where your hero reacts to the events of the Midpoint and its stake-raising implications.

4. The **Dark Night of the Soul** is how your hero reacts to the worst thing that could possibly happen.

5. The Break into 3 and the **Finale** have a similar symbiotic relationship to the Break into 2 and The Fun & Games. The Break Into 3 presents new information. The hero takes it and comes up with a way to win the day, using all the knowledge and life lessons they've learned throughout the story.

When you're not sure where to go, ask your hero to lead the way. They'll *always* have the best answers.

FINALES ARE SOMETIMES WRAP-UPS

In some rare cases, the Break into 3 is a Break into Series, because the decision made in the Break into 3 sets the hero into a larger conflict that's bigger than the 10-minute Finale allows—often a philosophical change that might affect the entire season or series to come.

In these cases, the Finales act as wrap-ups, handling loose ends, showing how the new choice affects the hero's immediate life (the one shown in the pilot), and sometimes dropping in hints of conflicts or runner stories to come. These Finales are less about the fireworks of the hero tackling new obstacles and more about showing the resonance of the decision made in the Break into 3.

In the first-episode breakdowns in the next chapter, you'll see *Ozark* has a Break into 3 where the hero commits to a difficult mission that will play out through the season. The Finale becomes one of preparation and moving to the world where this mission will take place. In *Grey's Anatomy*, the pilot provides a test of whether or not the hero can survive this cutthroat world. In the Break into 3, Meredith Grey decides she can and chooses to sit in on the surgery she earned. It's an acceptance of her place in the new world. Here, instead of dealing with conflict, the Finale is more of an epilogue, tying story threads in a bow and showing the hero actively pursuing success, embracing both their position and competitiveness—something that will bring a series' worth of conflict to come.

B STORIES, C STORIES, D STORIES, ETC., ETC.

Pilots use the *Save the Cat!* B Story beat in the same way all good stories do: to introduce a new character or highlight a previously seen character. Many shows have large ensembles they need to service and will often juggle several stories, just so we don't forget about one of their major characters. In true ensemble shows, where equal weight is given to several characters, it's not unheard of that an hour-long pilot might have 4 or 5 concurrent storylines. Sometimes these shows break story for each individual character.

Typically, one character gets more of a nudge than the others. Aside from the A Story, there might not be enough real estate to give all the characters every *Save the Cat!* beat. The *Stranger Things* pilot (examined later) is like this. Hopper and Joyce get the most beats. The other characters' storylines get thorough Set-Ups but either combine beats or skip a couple in the name of run time.

TV writers break each story separately, giving each their own high-level beat sheet, then do a step called **The Blend**, where they mix and match the several threads into a coherent episode beat sheet. Multi-scene beats are the place to do the Blend. Sometimes various stories will crossover with single-scene beats (especially the Midpoint).

If you're making a show that has several equally weighted ensemble characters, you might try a process like this:

1. Write out the Story DNA and story loglines for each subplot.

2. Break your A Story into a *Save the Cat!* beat sheet.

3. Break Your B Stories — For each individual story thread, break out descriptions for the Beginning, Middle, End. The Beginning should introduce the B Story characters and their Story DNA. The Middle should show the hero fighting obstacles in an attempt to accomplish their goal. The End should resolve the tension and wrap up any loose ends.

4. Do the Blend — slot those B Story beats into all the non-single-scene sections: Set-Up, Fun & Games, Bad Guys Close In, Dark Night of the Soul, Finale.

The other unique thing pilots may do is introduce season-long B Stories (aka runners). TV writers often break these season-long runners separately, and then divvy up the runner beats among episodes wherever they best fit. This happens a lot with procedural shows that might have some larger threat looming that will come to a head at the end of the season. Let's say you have a *Hawaii Five-0* episode and it has a season-long runner about a serial killer who is playing some twisted game with the cops. These season-long runners often kickoff in the pilot B Story beat to hint at potential fireworks later in the season.

HOLD UP!!! WHAT ABOUT TV ACT OUTS?

You've googled about TV writing, watched a YouTube video, you've even zipped through Shonda Rhimes' Masterclass at 1.5x speed. And now one big thought is going through your head:

TV is 4 or 5 acts plus a teaser! This is all bunk!! Why is this *Save the Cat!* nerd talking all this 3-act nonsense!! Bunk I say! Bunk!

Feel better? Good. Here's the skinny: we're talking about two different things. In television, act breaks aren't about Aristotle, they're about Coca-Cola and dog vitamins and heart meds. They're about the dollar bills, y'all.

"Acts" in TV refer to commercial breaks.

In fact, it would make all of our lives easier if they just started calling them "Commercial Breaks" or "Breaks" or "Timeouts" or anything to avoid the confusion altogether. But they never listen to me! So, we're stuck with "acts." It's just the way it is.

For years, hour-longs had 4 acts (err, commercial breaks!) and a teaser, and sitcoms had 2 acts and maybe a cold open. Things have changed. Networks started sneaking in extra commercials to squeeze out every ounce of juicy commerce. Hour-longs can be 5 acts and sitcoms might be 3. Or two with teaser and tag. Or whatever crazy scheme works for selling Wendy's and Mountain Dew and Viagra.

Different networks mandate different rules for how their commercials are parceled out into shows. AMC might ask *The Walking Dead* to have 5 acts. A 30-minute Nickelodeon sitcom might have 3 acts and a tag (a quick denouement or "button" scene). Other shows on the same network even have different "Act Out" requirements.

What does this mean to us?

The mere mortal?

The newbie pilot writer?

First off, HBO, Showtime, Netflix, Amazon Prime, and many others don't do commercials at all. Shows like *Game of Thrones* and *Billions* never even think about McDonald's or Pepsi. Neither do *The Mandalorian, Stranger Things*, or *The Handmaid's Tale.*

So for the most part, you can 100% punt the commercials if you're writing a pilot. TV folks are used to pilots that don't have commercial breaks. Honestly, if it gives you a headache to even think about... don't. Skip it.

If you know the show you're writing is targeted specifically for network TV—maybe you're outlining a multi-cam sitcom for ABC, for example, and maybe that's the destination your brand of writing best fits—you might want to write in the act breaks, even if it's just to prove that you get it.

TV act breaks commonly (but not always) land right after the single-scene beats of our *Save the Cat!* beat sheet.

Just for reference, here are the single-scene beats:
1. OPENING IMAGE
2. CATALYST
3. BREAK INTO 2
4. MIDPOINT
5. ALL IS LOST
6. BREAK INTO 3
7. FINAL IMAGE

The Opening Image is usually your teaser. The Final Image is usually your tag. So that leaves the following:
1. CATALYST
2. BREAK INTO 2
3. MIDPOINT
4. ALL IS LOST
5. BREAK INTO 3

Basically, your Act Outs will drop immediately after any of the 5 beats above. You get to choose where you want the commercials. Pick the moments you think provide the biggest cliffhangers, plot twists, or new mysteries that present questions that need to be answered. The goal is to plant a seed in your viewer that will carry them through a series of boring ads about the *The Masked Singer*, the latest diet plan discount, and full-body shampoo for tangled hair. Pick the beats that create a need to be scratched. Sentences that need to be completed. Then boom: ACT OUT!

Big character moments sometimes get Act Outs too—moments of intense emotion that resonate through commercial breaks. The type of character body blows that take our breath away. They're not cliffhangers, but they're powerful and they sit with us, leaving us with the question: how will our new favorite people deal with this emotional gut punch?

Here's a quick test. If you can say either *Duhn, Duhn, DUHHHH* after your Act Out or hum the *Twilight Zone* theme or yell out, "THE PLOT THICKENS!", you have a satisfying act break. If not... keep trying.

While original pilots don't require act breaks, a lot of professional writers still outline with a TV act-out mentality. They hit these spots with big twists and turns that give momentum into the next story chunk and make people ask: *what happens next*?

The single-scene beats of *Save the Cat!* are story boosters. If you hit them with the serious push and escalation they warrant, it ensures good pacing throughout your story. It forces you to tweak your story to make sure it has that What Happens Next vibe running end-to-end.

So regardless of whether you're using Act Outs, hit those single-scene beats hard. Make your scripts page-turners. Make those viewers stick through the commercial! Sell those Guacritos! And earn your *Duhn, Duhn, DUHHH!*

ONE LAST BEAT SHEET TRICK FOR PILOTS

This is like that fortune cookie thing where you add "...in bed" to the end of each fortune. At the end of your Final Image beat, where "THE END" might logically go, write:

> *"Let the games begin!"*

Do it. This isn't a joke. It's important. I'd pre-print it for you but the editors already think I'm a madman.

Go.

Do it.

Now.

Done?

Good.

Now, you have to earn it.

Whether it's Mrs. Maisel deciding she's going to pursue a career in stand-up. Or Barry Birkman deciding he's going to make a go of acting. Or the Mandalorian choosing to spare the life of Baby Yoda. The reader or viewer must be thinking or even saying aloud...

Let the games begin!!

EXERCISES

1. Before you jump into your own beat sheet, read the next chapter, which contains lots of sample beat sheets.

2. Start your own beat sheet by cracking the Opening and Final Images for your pilot. Depending on your story, consider opening with an opening pitch, mini-episode, or moving train to grab the viewers' attention and give your characters great introductions that show how they work under pressure.

3. Make sure your Final Image shows the whiff of change (write a whiff of change... stated just to give yourself a goal to work toward).

4. Write out your pillar beats. Some will be easy (Catalyst and Break into 2); others will require some deep thinking.

5. Finish your entire beat sheet. Try doing the one-sentence per beat version first. Then once it's feeling right, go in and add depth and description. Beat sheets can be 1-2 pages or 15. It's your call. My recommendation is you probably should build it to at least 4-7 pages to make sure you're accurately describing those multi-scene beats (including your Five-Point Finale!).

CHECK YOURSELF

1. Do your Opening and Final Images demonstrate the shake-up in your hero's world? Does the contrast between those 2 beats hint at a whiff of change in the pilot?

2. Is your Story DNA obvious to the viewer by the time you reach your Fun & Games?

3. Is the hero's flaw and things that need fixing clearly set up in the pilot?

4. Does the pilot's theme reflect the overall theme of the show?

5. Are all the major characters introduced in your pilot?

6. Is your Fun & Games section too linear or episodic?

7. Does the Midpoint effectively increase tension?

8. Do your hero's choices communicate a unique broken compass that will be part of the ongoing tension of the show?

9. Does the pilot clearly introduce the world and franchise type of the show to the reader or viewer?

10. Does your pilot earn its "Let the games begin!"?

🐾 PILOT BEAT SHEETS

This chapter breaks down several pilots to see the beat sheet and other pilot techniques in action. We're going to be spoiling everything, so I'd advise you to watch them first. While platforms change all the time, the pilot episodes presented here were all found on one of the major streaming services. I'll be spoiling the shows with reckless abandon—so don't say I didn't warn ya.

PREMISE PILOTS

Barry: "Chapter 1: Make Your Mark"
Written by: Alec Berg & Bill Hader
Franchise Type: Trapped Together (with hints of Dude With a Season-Long Problem and Blank of the Week)
The World: Hitmen and Aspiring Actors
Episode Genre: Golden Fleece
Platform: HBO
TV Genre: Half-Hour Comedy
Story DNA:

- **Hero**: Barry — a soul-searching hitman
- **Goal**: To do his job and kill his target
- **Obstacle**: He's searching for meaning, questioning if he wants to continue his hitman ways. The man he has to kill is nice and also helpful to Barry in what might just be Barry's new path in life. The mixed feelings prevent him from finishing the gig the normal way, which leads to external obstacles he'll have to overcome to complete his job.
- **Stakes**: If he doesn't kill the man, he'll be in serious danger with the people that hired him.

Certain day jobs make great story engines, especially 9-to-5's that are dangerous or illegal and have new cases and people and problems every week. While *Barry* isn't a Blank of the Week franchise, the first episode is framed like one. Its framework eases us into Barry's ordinary world with a familiar story-telling pattern and then diverges into a new world… one more mundane but alien to both the hero and to us.

Barry is a window character into this new world of aspiring actors. In the series, Barry's life becomes a balancing act between his hitman job and his acting aspirations. The pilot balances both evenly. We get a full dose of home, work, and play, but not just in the Set-Up. The whole pilot serves as a Set-Up.

- **Home** — Barry lives a lonely existence, going through the motions and feeling depressed. It's all motels and rental cars. His only "family and friend" is his Uncle Fukes, who actually acts as Barry's shady boss and seems to be in it just for the money.
- **Work** — Barry kills people. It's a soulless and boring job. He deals with wacky clients, horrible air travel, bad rental cars, and a very unglamorous life.
- **Play** — Barry's acting class, his new buddies, and the people who will be catalysts in his life.

OPENING IMAGE (0-1): We open on a dead man lying in bed with a bullet hole in his noggin. A victim of a hit. Our killer for hire, Barry has just done the deed. He has a gun with a silencer in hand. This is his job and as violent as it looks, the tone is about as mundane as a Best Buy Geek Squad worker resetting an iPhone password. Barry's punching a clock, doing the same-old-same-old and sleepwalking through life. Character introductions are critical in pilots. This is an attention-grabbing one that sets up Barry's *stasis = death* existence from the very first shot.

SET-UP (1-3): The hitman lifestyle is just as lame as any other traveling businessman's career. It even has a crappy, clueless boss (or… ahem… agent), Fukes. Fukes is always cutting corners. Barry's life is filled with discount motels, cheap car rentals, getting stuck in traffic. James Bond this is not. Fukes claims that Barry was aimless before he started to kill for a living. Aimlessness and searching for purpose is a central issue for Barry. Barry's *broken compass* tells him that he can find happiness without fixing the deeper psychological issues within himself. He thinks if he can just find something that feels like a purpose, he'll be good.

CATALYST (3-4): At the three-minute market, Fukes announces Barry's next job. It's in Los Angeles, a hit for the Chechen mob. If they can get in with the Chechens, Fukes and Barry might be able to retire. Like it or not, Barry has a new gig. We know this is going to go sideways.

DEBATE (4-9): Debates go two ways: challenging the invitation or readying for the task ahead. The question at the heart of a planning debate is "Am I ready?" There is some doubt as to whether Barry can land this job in his current depressed state, so Fukes coaches him up, pitching ideas of how to make a good impression with the new client. Barry meets with the goofy mobsters (while they're mostly sidelined in this episode, this scene sets up their comedic value for future episodes), and they lay out the basics of the mission. Barry tries to offer some weird, extra-violent suggestions on how he can kill his target, which freaks out his new clients. They just want him to kill the target the normal way. Barry gets the gun via Fed Ex (no silencer, thanks to cheap Fukes).

BREAK INTO ACT 2 (9-10): Barry's ready and on the hunt. He follows the target into a mysterious building. Bored and waiting, Barry heads inside and finds an acting class.

B STORY(11): In some ways, the entire acting class serves as the B Story character, and his classmates are all introduced here. First up, Barry meets Sally. Sally will be a key helper/love story throughout the series. She'll also serve as a mentor in both acting and Barry's emotional journey. While feature films *always* pay off this B Story character completely and wholeheartedly during their 2-hourish run times, pilots can play the long game. They drop mentor characters in this spot that pay off in later episodes. Sally plays a small role in the first episode, but she'll play a much bigger one in the season to come. The entire acting crew serve as a chorus of mentors. They get Barry thinking differently. Is this his tribe? Is this what will give him purpose? The B Story immediately lays out a dramatic question: will Barry join the class?

B Stories reflect theme. The acting class gives Barry new ideas about life and allows characters to actively voice thematic dialogue. Also in this beat, Gene Cousineau hits the stage. He's the mentor figure in this episode. When we meet him, he's teaching Sally. He makes her cry. Then he does some Mr. Miyagi acting magic and Sally delivers a performance breakthrough. This is Barry's surrogate father figure that Fukes isn't. He'll also get the big moment at the episode's Finale.

THEME STATED (12): 92.7% of the time when a teacher talks or writes on a blackboard, that's the theme! Here, Gene tells the class, "That's what this is about — LIFE — I want you to create a life right on this stage."

FUN & GAMES (12-14): Welcome to the *upside-down world* of "acting." Barry marvels over the class. He stares wide-eyed and a bit confused at everything. Then he meets Ryan, the man he's supposed to kill. Before he knows it, Ryan drags him up on the stage to be his scene partner. This is crossing a professional line hitman-wise but Barry goes with it. *A & B Stories intersect* dangerously as Barry performs a scene with his target. And Barry kills... in the actor sense... not in his typical hitman style. Barry gets the applause and for a moment he forgets he's on a mission. It's a short but important Fun & Games, showing the *promise of the premise* of the episode. The pilot is only 24 minutes long and spends extra time in the Set-Up, so we skimp a bit here. This is a good example of how a TV script hits the beats but chooses where to skimp or invest extra time. Remember: TV beats are an itinerary, not a strict schedule!

MIDPOINT (14): Barry's touched. A change has stirred in him. But change is dangerous. Sally apologizes to him about treating him rudely earlier. She now realizes Barry's a fellow actor, so she affords him respect. Hmm, interesting. Sally invites him to go to the bar afterward with his new friends, again *crossing A and B Stories.*

BAD GUYS CLOSE IN (15-19): Being this close to his target is hella risky. Barry's blown any chance of not getting involved. This makes his job waaaay harder. There's even a sort of "Sex @ 60" when Barry spots Sally dancing with abandon in lovely slow motion. He likes these people. But empathy only makes his mission harder. If this is his tribe, should he be killing one of them? Might that ruin his chances of being a part of this new community? In later episodes, we'll see how this mission affects his new path. But for now, internal bad guys are making his life rough! It's almost as if his *broken compass* doesn't allow him to see how fraught with danger his hitman ways are. He starts chatting up the guy he's supposed to kill. The guy is really friendly. Barry ends up driving the guy home. He can't seem to kill him. His internal change is disrupting his job needs. The guy gifts him with a book by Gene (our mentor) and compliments Barry on his acting.

ALL IS LOST (19): Instead of killing him, Barry gives his target a big old hug. This is bad. The Chechen mobsters are spying and they've seen it all. The *B Story crosses with the A Story* again. In the worst possible way.

DARK NIGHT OF THE SOUL (20-23): Fukes has heard from the Chechens about the hug and questions Barry. Hugging your target is not a good look on a hitman. But Barry's "feeling really good about himself." He thinks acting could be his purpose. Fukes provides the voice of the internal bad guys. He's the devil on the shoulder to Gene's angel (two surrogate fathers who will battle for Barry's soul throughout the season). Fukes explains all the reasons why this acting nonsense is a bad idea. He even says "Stop thinking, kill Ryan." Any other path is certain death.

BREAK INTO 3 (23-24): Barry sucks it up and goes back to class the next night, tracking down his prey, ready to finish the job. He waits in the parking lot to make his move.

FINALE (24-25):

Five Point Finale:

1. **Gathering the Team:** The class breaks and heads to their cars. A gun and Gene's acting book at his side, Barry gathers his resolve. It's go time!

2. **Execution of the Plan:** Instead of killing the actor dude, Barry marches over to Gene, who is in his car, and asks if he was good enough to be in the class. We see where his priorities are.

3. **The High-Tower Surprise:** Gene calls him a bad actor. Ouch!

4. **Dig Down Deep:** Barry must dig down deep and act honestly. He decides to confess his heart.

5. **The Execution of the New Plan:** Very un-Barry-like, he admits that he's good at killing people. For the first time, he speaks his truth. From the bottom of his dark hitman heart. Every chilling detail. What he does, how he feels. He ends it with, "I know there's more to me than that. Or maybe there's not."—the central question of the entire show. Gene thinks Barry's confession is all an act and he's impressed with the truth of Barry's "performance." He invites Barry to join the class. Buzzing with confidence, Barry knows there's still unfinished business. The hit job almost has its own 5-step Finale. Barry goes to kill the guy and finds out he's already dead! Shot through the windshield by the Chechens, who then turn their weapons on Barry. A gunfight ensues. Barry is forced to kill them.

FINAL IMAGE (29): As police converge on the scene, Barry hides out in a diner. A waitress tells him that she's an actress and has an audition tomorrow. Barry replies, "So am I." His *whiff of change… stated*. He's taken the first step into a new way of life.

Let the games begin…

Grey's Anatomy: "A Hard Day's Night"
Written by: Shonda Rhimes
Franchise Type: Trapped Together (with lots of Blank of the Week action)
The World: Surgical Interns
Episode Genre: Institutionalized
Platform: ABC
TV Genre: Hour-Long Drama
Story DNA:

- **Hero**: Meredith Grey — surgical intern
- **Goal**: To survive her first marathon day of surgical rounds and prove she belongs
- **Obstacle**: The teachers, the medicine, the competition, the patience, the long hours
- **Stakes**: Her time and identity are so invested in making this work. If she fails, it will be the end of life as she knows it.

Shonda Rhimes spins lots of plates... and by plates, I mean hit network series. She's also a great writer. Her pilots pop and there are tons to be learned from them and her. Shonda really gets the whole "it's the characters, doofus." I'm not much for getting choked up over movies or TV, but this pilot has a character beat so well executed it still gives me the feels a decade and a half after I first saw it.

THEME STATED (1): Grey's kicks off with an *opening pitch* voice-over that drops a theme bomb on us from its very first line. Voiceovers often get eye rolls in screenwriting circles, but pilots are all about economy and in this pilot the VO does the job of getting some needed data to the viewer quickly. There's no time to fuss over the virtue of using any tool at your disposal. Do what works. Our main character, Meredith Grey, lays out a thesis statement in the opening line: "The Game. They say a person either has what it takes or they don't. My mom was one of the greats. Me on the other hand, I'm kinda screwed." That's the focus of the first season. In the pilot, Meredith and the soon-to-be-introduced fellow interns will experience the hardest day of their lives. Do they have what it takes? Meredith's mom was "one of the greats." Her mom's legacy is an internal hurdle Meredith will deal with in the episodes to come.

OPENING IMAGE (1-3): We start with a *moving train*. It's the morning after a one-night stand. Meredith wakes up with some dude still in her place. A dreamy dude, in fact. But Meredith's in a big hurry. She's going to be late for her first day at her important new job. The guy makes a remark about her house and she mentions it's her mom's. Then she lets him off the hook saying they don't have to "do the thing where they pretend to care." She can't even remember his name. (Derek, by the way.) It's good to start in a hurry! This opening scene grabs attention, yet leaves us guessing about Meredith and the mom and the new job and how Derek fits in. Meredith arrives late as Dr. Webber is giving a speech laying out the whole franchise type: they are first-year students, most of them will flake out, it's an arena, and this is their competition. Meredith ends the teaser with "I'm screwed." This *opening pitch* could be a teaser trailer. The stage is set for some first day of surgical intern hijinks! **(TEASER OUT - 3 min)**

SET-UP (3-6): Meredith begins her first day. Making Meredith a newbie *window character* allows us to be introduced to the show's world as she is. It also sets up the *guided tour* where we meet all the characters as Meredith does. She's introduced to her drill-sergeant-esque boss, Dr. Bailey, the other interns who will be part of the main cast, and even some of the senior surgeons. The interns are on the move seeing the locations for the first time, getting a lay of the land. It might as well be a network pitch for the entire franchise as Bailey gives them their "training day" speech and tells them the rules and the norms, all in a tense don't-screw-up sort of way.

CATALYST (7): A new patient arrives, a pageant girl named Katie. It's an emergency situation and Meredith ends up with the assignment. Grey's first day and first patient. The new world is ramping up quickly. Is she ready?

DEBATE (7-10): Grey gets to know her new patient. Katie, a typically annoyed teenager, is not happy about being here and already realizes Meredith, who can't even find her way around the hospital, is clueless. Meanwhile, the other interns get tested in similar ways. Izzy is doing rectal exams. Cristina is jockeying to be the one to get invited to scrub in, a traditional surgery she's heard only one intern gets on the first day. George has a heart patient and is screwing up the blood draw. Cocky Alex is struggling with stitches. They all get to know each other. They all know about Grey's mom too, who was a legendary surgeon. George is picked to scrub in on the surgery. It sets up a rivalry among the others.

BREAK INTO 2 (10-11): Meredith gets grilled by her patient's worried parents. Seeking answers, Meredith discovers that the new doctor in charge is—plot twist!—Derek (the one-night-stand from the opening)!! (**ACT OUT #1 – 11 min**) Juicy tension ensues. We'll have to wait till after the commercial to see how Meredith reacts!

B STORY (11): Meredith protests that their one-night stand backstory is not the look she wants on her first day. She's all business and feels like continuing their extracurricular relationship would be highly inappropriate.

FUN & GAMES (11-20): George scrubs in for the big surgery. The other interns bet on his failure, treating all of this like it's a sporting event. They make snarky comments as poor George fumbles through, and Meredith scolds them: "That's one of us down there. The first one of us. Where's your loyalty?" The struggle between her own empathy vs. the cutthroat nature of being a surgeon is what's at stake in this first episode. Can she be as ruthless and cold as everyone else? Or will her good nature limit her? George's surgery is going well... until it's not. He screws up royally and now gets the nickname "007"—license to kill. This is a tough gig. No mercy.

The Fun & Games deliver on the story's *promise of the premise*: surgical interns on their first day. Grey deals with her Beauty Queen patient. Cristina jockeys to impress her superiors, showing how competitive she is. Izzie battles to stay on Bailey's good side. Poor George struggles with his confidence after his public failure. We even get a taste of Alex, who doesn't have a huge role in this episode, but if a character is in the show, they must be in the pilot! He's a bit of a jerk, treating nurses with disrespect and not realizing Meredith is also a surgical intern.

MIDPOINT (20-23): Meredith's patient, Katie, goes into seizure. This just got real! Grey freezes in fear. (**ACT OUT #2 – 20 min**) She recovers and jumps into action. She grabs the defibrillator paddles and shocks her patient back to life. She's got the chops. She hesitated under pressure but recovered and acted like a real doctor. It's a bit of a *false victory*. She's saved a life but will catch all kinds of flack about it.

BAD GUYS CLOSE IN (23-29): A title card comes up—we're 24 hours in. It's a *ticking clock*, a reminder of just how long these interns have been at it. As time ticks away, they're getting less sharp, more snippy, and we know things will be getting more tense by the minute. The pageant girl is getting worse and none of her doctors have diagnosed her problem. The parents of the girl want Derek fired from the case. They demand answers. Derek turns to the interns for help. (**ACT OUT #3 – 25 min**) He asks them to play detective. He dangles an incentive: whoever finds the answers gets to scrub in with him on the big surgery!

It's a huge reward and sets them all scrambling. Cristina offers Meredith an alliance. They'll work together, giving both a better chance to win the opportunity. Meredith is willing to team-up but doesn't want to work with Derek at all, which is music to Cristina's ears: one less person to compete with. Off they go as a team to find a solution. As Cristina & Meredith research, they bond and Meredith admits to Cristina that she's had a one-night stand with Derek. But none of that matters right now. Meredith is focused on saving her teenage pageant queen's life. If the girl dies, she'll never have a chance to grow into a better person. That's the stakes for Meredith: saving a life and a future, not some mere learning opportunity. A random comment gives her a clue: the girl says she fell on a ball. It gives her an idea that leads to the the answer! Cristina and Meredith win the prize!

ALL IS LOST (29): Derek picks Meredith as the one to scrub in. Cristina feels betrayed (and thinks Meredith's only won because of her relationship with Derek). The new friendship is now splitsville! George's story gets its own All Is Lost here when his patient dies on the table. Dr. Burke shrugs it off, but George is stunned. George promised the family that the man would make it through. George gets dressed down by Burke about ever promising anything to families. It's a *whiff of death* and an emotional career punch all at once.

DARK NIGHT OF THE SOUL (29-37): Cristina accuses Meredith of being cutthroat and even questions whether Meredith's famous mother is buying her preferential treatment, which hits a nerve. Meanwhile, George has to break the news of the patient's death to the family. And this is the scene that made me choke up even on rewatch. Maybe I identify the most with George's self-doubting empath guy. And this moment would probably be the end of my surgery career. **(ACT OUT #4 – 37)**

BREAK INTO 3 (37): It's HOUR 40. They shave Katie's head in preparation for surgery. Meredith asks Derek to let Cristina scrub in. Derek advises her not to let petty personal issues interfere with her career. This is Meredith's big moment. Can she step up and enter the game? Or does she not have what it takes? She makes the choice to scrub in. This is a Break into Series, and the moment pretty much is a tension ender. The question on the first day of "does she belong" is answered. The rest of the episode is an epilogue of sorts, the bigger conflict from her decision lies in the episodes and seasons to come.

FINALE (37-41): In a wrap-up style Finale, Meredith is welcomed into the game. She sums up in voiceover: "I could quit... but I love the playing field." She performs the surgery, saving Katie— it's a huge high. Cristina watches her from behind the observation window. There's respect there. They're war buddies. As her first shift comes to an end, Meredith heads off with her new comrades in arms. They've all survived the first day. The game requires a certain level of shrewdness. She'll be different tomorrow. But she can still maintain her humanity, her empathy, and even her newfound relationships...

right? These internal struggles will fuel the conflict in the episodes to come.

FINAL IMAGE (41-42): The pilot is bookended by the only two "away from the hospital" scenes. First the Opening Image with Derek, and now a gentle moment with Meredith's mom at a nursing home. The opening scene was about joy and optimism and a young woman with her whole life ahead of her. Now, Meredith Grey interacts with her dementia-afflicted mother, who doesn't recognize her. Her mom asks if Meredith is her doctor. "I'm not your doctor, but I am a doctor," Meredith says, having earned the title. It's a *whiff of change... stated.* The show will be about a woman finding her identity in her mother's long shadow, and earning her own way in a world that doesn't allow for sentimentality or short cuts.

Let the games begin!

The Mandalorian: "Chapter 1 The Mandalorian"
Written by: Jon Favreau, created by Jon Favreau, based on characters created by George Lucas
Franchise Type: Dude With a Season-Long Problem (with hints of Blank of the Week)
The World: Make-Believe World — The Star Wars Universe
Episode Genre: Golden Fleece
Platform: Disney+
TV Genre: Hour-Long Drama
Story DNA:
- **Hero**: Mandalorian — intergalactic bounty-hunter badass
- **Goal**: To capture an unknown bounty
- **Obstacle**: Fortifications/guards /the dangers of the hunt
- **Stakes**: Money is short. The Mandalorian needs money for himself and his order.

The Mandalorian is a western-style tale of an anti-hero bounty hunter with no name. Its first episode is "almost" a non-premise pilot. It follows another dangerous job in the life of a bounty hunter. The procedural storyline has a Blank of the Week feel, and the series has some Blank of the Week tendencies balancing its serialized storyline and standalone episodes. But in the Final Image of this episode, it's revealed the whole pilot is built to kick off a more serialized Dude with a Season-Long Problem. May the Force Be With You.

OPENING IMAGE/TEASER (1-3): The Mandalorian (Mando to his friends) stares down at a small cluster of buildings (almost a wild west town). Our titular armor-clad bounty hunter is at the tail end of one of his missions. It's a James Bond-style cold open, a sequence that gives us a taste of how bounty hunting works in this universe and how Mando takes care of business (introducing the bounty pucks, the grappling hook, the special steel of his uniform). He steps into a shady bar and goes to work. He takes out six guys—a good way of "showing, not telling" that this guy has skills—and gets his man. He can bring him in "warm or cold." Right now, the choice is warm.

SET-UP (3-11): Mando drags his prisoner away, hailing an Uber (err...landspeeder). More examples of Mando's tools, methods, and world abound. He avoids a monstrous threat lurking in the ice. We see his cool ship, watch him pilot it, and when his bounty tries to escape, we get a demonstration of how he carbon-freezes his captives. In yet another seedy bar that has similarities to the Cantina scene from the first *Star Wars* movie, Mando delivers his guy and receives his payment. This universe is running on fumes and money is hard to come by. There are lots of *things that need fixing*: It feels like Mando is a Mercedes in a Ford Fiesta world. He's hurting for cash and there's a vibe that this new normal is squeezing Mando out. Mando is part of a "cult of warriors" and has a rigid code that will be tested to the extreme.

Who will bend first... him or the world? Money is an issue and so is maintaining his precious armor, which is more than just a piece of metal—it's part of The Way. The types of jobs he's willing to take are dwindling. As are the types of people he can trust. The universe is dirty and lawless.

CATALYST (12): After getting his meager wages from his middleman, Greef Carga, he's given the best job Carga can offer: an under-the-table gig that seems plenty shady. This beat feels very Blank of the Week procedural... but this mission is different somehow. Lots of secrecy and dread surround it.

DEBATE (12-16): The Debate poses the question: "What is this mysterious case?" The Underworld? No names? Extra money? It's suspicious. Verrry suspicious. Mando creeps through some back alleys and knocks on a door where he's greeted by Stormtroopers. Even though the Empire's been turned to ashes in a spectacular ball of fire (thank you, Ewoks!), we know these disenfranchised troopers are up to no good. Mando meets "The Client," who gives him a nebulous mission: no bounty puck, just a last-known location of the target. Shadiness abounds.

THEME STATED (16): The show's long teaser and Set-Up bring us a late Theme Stated beat. The Client gives Mando a parting comment in their meeting during the Debate, "It is good to restore the natural order of things... after a period of such disarray." In the face of disarray and disorder, is it good to restore things to the old way, if the old way wasn't so good? Or is it better to move on? Much like in a typical western, Mando is a man trapped at the cusp of a changing time. The old ways are dying... it's time to evolve. The story will find Mando ultimately breaking his personal code and putting himself at odds with the world he lives in. At odds with the old order of things.

BREAK INTO 2 (17): Hard up for money, Mando accepts the mission and goes off to hunt his bounty. It's a pretty common procedural Break into 2: the hero accepts the job and we're off. At the 17-minute mark, it's late for a Break into 2 for the short running time (this hour-long only goes 36 minutes). But this pilot is choosing to linger in the world-building and character Set-Up parts. We've already had the teaser fight, the monster attack, the little scene in the ship. Action! Action! And more *Star Wars*-ey action! Now we're getting almost a movie-length introduction of the episode's mission, emphasizing the weight this one has—somehow it's special. But spending so much time here means compression elsewhere. It will lead to a condensed Fun & Games with a quick Finale and a big-twist ending.

B STORY (18): We meet a B Story character, the Beskar Armorer. Mando offers the special metal brick he got for the bounty and the Armorer creates a new plate for him. The armor and blacksmithing are almost spiritual. In a flashback, we get glimpses of Mando's past (parents giving him away during "the purge"). These scenes are mysteries planted in the pilot which highlight a key piece of pilot weirdness: it's perfectly okay to plant unanswered questions or threads in a pilot. Having loose threads to get the reader or viewer thinking about potential future stories is not only a good idea, it's a promise of more to come and an itch that needs to be scratched.

FUN & GAMES (17-26): As often happens in the Fun & Games beat, we travel to a new world. Mando tracks his prey to a desert planet and the hunt is on! *The Mandalorian* is all about *Star Wars* action and bounty hunting and it delivers. Mando is attacked by a massive beast and meets a new friend, an Ugnaught (a cool alien species whose action figure we all owned back in *The Empire Strikes Back* days) named Kuiil. Mando has to learn to ride a Blurg.

MIDPOINT (27): Through a rugged test of wills, Mando tames the beast and it seems like a win. Mando is on his way and the Ugnaught agrees to help. It's a *false victory* as Kuiil warns Mando about what he's in store for: gunmen and a fortress. This ain't no dark cantina. It's a *stake raiser*! He's getting closer and a formidable showdown lays in wait. We're also curious to find out... who is this fortress-worthy bounty?

BAD GUYS CLOSE IN (28-30): Mando gets to the fortress. There's already a guy... errr... droid... on the scene: IG-11. A shootout ensues, the most *Star-Wars*-ey action in the episode. Mando and the droid are ambushed and have to fight through dozens of blaster-wielding baddies. The target is even closer. Tension is increasing.

ALL IS LOST (31): Uh-oh! Mando and IG-11 find themselves trapped and outgunned. They shelter behind some pillars and walls as laser blasts explode around them. Not only will they not complete their mission, they won't make it out alive. IG-11 initiates self-destruct mode. Smell that! It's the *whiff of death*! Their own death!

DARK NIGHT OF THE SOUL (32): Mando is not a guy for much wallowing. There is no crying in bounty hunting. He and IG-11 try to escape, but they're pinned down and the baddies have aimed a big cannon their way. Still, Mando insists: "Do not self destruct!" This isn't time for some big character arc and *shard of glass* therapy. He stays true to his warrior code. There's no self-destruction in his psyche.

BREAK INTO 3 (33): Mando has to convince IG-11 that they can shoot their way out of this death trap. He gives the droid a quick pep talk and they spring into action.

FINALE (34-36): They pull a wild gun-fight maneuver and Mando takes out everyone. IG is battered but still alive. He deactivates his self-destruct mode. They use the big laser cannon to blast their way inside the door, enter the fortress, and discover that their 50-year-old target is... BABY YODA. A dilemma. He's so cute! IG goes to kill the baby... and Mando blasts the droid. This is a mission like no other. The hunter is now the protector. He's crossed a line and he can't go back. A *whiff of change* is in the air.

FINAL IMAGE (36): The Mandalorian reaches out to touch the baby. This whole story has built up to this glorious *Save the Yoda!* moment for our hero.

Let the games begin!

The Marvelous Mrs. Maisel: Pilot

Written by: Amy Sherman-Palladino

Franchise Type: I'm No Fool/Woman with a Plan

The World: The 1950s comedy scene and 1950s NYC

Episode Genre: Fool Triumphant — not that she's anybody's fool, but in this world, she's underestimated. Even though we know she's massively talented and *marvelous*... the world overlooks her. So she's going to have to prove them wrong. Just the stuff of Fool Triumphant stories!

Platform: Amazon

TV Genre: Hour-Long Drama

Story DNA:

- **Hero**: Mrs. Maisel — a marvelous mom with a hidden, underutilized talent for comedy
- **Goal**: To make her husband's comedy set the best it can be
- **Obstacle**: The tough world of comedy, her husband, and the world in general
- **Stakes**: Her perfect life

The Marvelous Mrs. Maisel is my favorite show. Each new season is heralded like an event in my humble abode. I do my best to pace myself marveling over every set, every costume, every crackle of dialogue, every nostalgic morsel of the comedy scene. And then after 48 hours, I've watched every episode of the season... and post-*Maisel* depression takes hold.

Let's dive in...

OPENING IMAGE (1): "Who gives a toast at their own wedding?" Mrs. Maisel (aka Midge) says into a mic with the same showperson's pizzaz we'll see later in her stand-up act. "I do." Boom! We dive right into the *opening pitch*. And you can hear a million Twitter screenwriting gurus shouting out into the universe: "Never do flashbacks! Never do voice-overs! Never do preludes!" Welcome to flashback-voice-over-prelude-land, as Mrs. Maisel narrates a lightning-quick tour of how she got here. She's lived a somewhat privileged lifestyle. We see her private-school days, meeting her groom, Joel, and their perfect love affair. She and Joel bond over comedy, especially that dangerous rascal Lenny Bruce (who will play a big part in the series). Midge wraps up her wedding speech by saying there's shrimp in the eggrolls. She's so scandalous! It's a great character intro. We put her on a stage, give her a spotlight, and highlight the banter and storytelling that sets her apart from everyone else in this world. Sheer talent is her superpower. So is spunk. We know everything we need to know... and we're madly in love with her. She's getting invited back to our TVs anytime she wants. She's funny, smart, caring, and magical. The whole speech could have been lifted right out of a *Mrs. Maisel* show bible and dropped onto page one of the script. Of course, there's great craft required to condense all of that pitch stuff into a crackling fast teaser—all in the uber-charming style that sets up her skills at the mic and natural talent entertaining a crowd.

SET-UP (5- 11): A few years and babies later and Midge is thrilled. She's got the rabbi for Yom Kippur! Everything is coming up roses for Midge. She's living the perfect Upper Westside New Yorker's life, the one she was meant for. But this is the 1950s. There's a polite undercurrent of chauvinism and misogyny running through everything. Midge must keep herself beautiful and play the perfect mom and wife (never more evident than in the sequence where she secretly takes off her makeup at night, then puts it back on in the morning before her husband wakes up). Even the backstory she gives at the opening "romanticizes" the reality. This is an idealized world in denial. And she's going right along with the script. But after seeing her wedding speech, we know there's a big *thing that needs fixing*. She's got too much to give than this conservative cookie-cutter existence allows. She's mastered this world and runs circles around everyone.

She's destined for something, something special. Her eyes aren't really open to it yet (they will be soon enough) and she's not at all unhappy. She's optimistic and go-getting. But we know *stasis = death* when we see it. This world is gaslighting her (the name of the club that figures prominently into the show is The Gaslight) into thinking this is as good as it gets. Then there's her husband. Something is off with the guy. He seems bored at work and is more interested in slipping out to the comedy club and telling bad jokes than dealing with his clients. Midge is all-in with him, but he's not appreciating her quite as much as we know he should.

THEME STATED (12-13): "Anyone who knows me, knows I plan. Perfection..." Midge even measures herself daily. She's a bit of a control freak and can see all the twists and turns coming a mile away. What will happen when that plan unravels? Or is that plan actually keeping her from true happiness?

CATALYST (12-13): At the local night club, Joel takes his amateur-comedy talents up on stage. Midge is making it all work. Coaching. Cheering him on. Tracking the number of laughs he gets. Winning him the best time slot by bribing the club manager with pot roast. Joel hits the stage and has everyone in stitches. Everyone except that woman behind the bar, Susie Myerson! Susie is rolling her eyes at Joel's jokes. This is a glitch in the Matrix to Midge's world. Everyone else is laughing... why would Susie be throwing shade at Midge's man?

DEBATE (13-21): Is something off with Joel's act? Midge seems more into Joel's show than he does. She takes notes on his jokes and makes suggestions on how to punch up the act. He discounts her opinion at every turn. He's the comedy expert after all, right? It doesn't seem like he's putting the work in. Midge's mom questions the whole comedy act too. What's the point? They're adults. Why are they wasting time with this? Do they need money? Then Midge catches Bob Newhart doing Joel's exact same act on the TV, and she realizes Joel stole the whole bit. Midge is disappointed. Her "perfect husband" has some dents in his armor. Maybe Susie was on to something.

BREAK INTO 2 (22-24): The next day, Midge gets a call from Joel. He's in a panic. He didn't get a stage time at the club and their good friends are coming to see him do his stand-up. Midge responds, "This whole comedy thing is supposed to be fun... that's why we do it, right?" The words are prophetic. Maybe it's not just for fun. This is a bit of a *broken compass* goal in the pilot. Midge thinks making her husband happy and sticking to the pre-ordained plan is what will make her happy. She's investing so much in this pre-planned version of her life, she'll eventually realize that taking the reins and making her own way will take her in directions that she deserves. Eventually. Many pilots, especially character-driven ones like this, spend extra minutes in their opening acts. This one almost uses up half the pilot's runtime. But the pace will quicken as twists and turns and tension abound in the second half.

B STORY (26): Midge again faces off with Susie. While the B Story often introduces a new character, it sometimes shines a spotlight on someone we've already seen. The usual bartender is out and Susie is filling in, also serving as the gatekeeper to the club. The old pot-roast trick is not going to work! Susie questions why Joel isn't over there asking for a spot. She does what every good mentor/helper character does and points out the cold hard truth: Midge is doing Joel's work. Who wants this more, Joel or Midge? Susie will become Midge's talent manager and comedy mentor in the episodes to come. Their relationship is the B Story of both the pilot and the first season.

FUN & GAMES (24-29): Welcome to the *upside-down world*. The comedy game isn't the carefree "everything goes right" party it was before. It's this world that a comedian has to endure and survive to make it, and Joel has comedy dreams. But things ain't looking rosy. Midge and Joel are going to be late. His sweater has a hole in it. Ever the problem-solver, Midge is trying to calm him down and fix things. But Joel's unraveling. As they hurry into the club, she's coaching him up on jokes, suggesting he use some of this real-life stuff in his act (subtextually still worried about his joke-stealing). Midge and Joel sit in the crowd, the tension growing, unsure if he'll even get a spot as *time ticks* away. This is a disaster. It's also a relatively quick Fun & Games.

MIDPOINT (29-31): At the last minute, Joel gets the call to go on stage. He opens with the jokes about tonight's troubles, the ones that Midge suggested. No one laughs. Then he goes back to his old rip-off act. And bombs horribly. We can smell the flop sweat as his entire set goes down in flames.

BAD GUYS CLOSE IN (31-35): During a tense cab ride home, Joel blames Midge for everything. This is followed by an even rougher bedroom scene. "I have to leave," he says out of nowhere. Midge's perfect life is crumbling in the blink of an eye. Joel admits what he's been hiding. He always thought he was supposed to be something different. Like Midge, he had a plan, but this wasn't it. Joel is ahead of Midge in some ways. He already knows this life isn't what he dreamed of and he's impulsively hitting the eject button. He laments, "I'll never be a professional comedian." "No, of course not," Midge snaps back in a bit of unfiltered honesty. She never thought he was serious about his comedy. Her plan was this life and she made the best of what they had. A fight that's been a long time coming explodes as this one-big-scene Bad Guys beat spills over into the next beat.

ALL IS LOST (35-37): Midge is completely blindsided as Joel confesses he's been sleeping with his secretary. He doesn't want this life anymore. On the eve of Yom Kippur, Joel leaves Midge.

DARK NIGHT OF THE SOUL (37-41): Midge watches Joel go in stunned sadness. Now comes the hard part; she's left to tell her parents. Their reaction is to blame her. They act like they're the ones who have the issue. Dad's advice is to win Joel back. Btw, it's raining! Classic Dark Night stuff! Midge grabs a wine bottle and heads out, drinking on the subway, and staggering into The Gaslight in her drenched nightgown to retrieve her pot-roast dish.

BREAK INTO 3 (41-42): Midge drunkenly wanders onto the stage, ready to give everyone a piece of her mind.

FINALE (42-54):

Five Point Finale:

1. **Gathering the Team** — Midge grabs the mic and takes the stage.
2. **Storm the Castle** — Midge gives a raw and hilarious stand-up comedy performance, baring her soul in the process.

3. **The High Tower Surprise** — The routine goes a bit off-color and when the cops try to shut it down, she hurls some insults and flashes them. She gets arrested and ends up in the backseat of a police car with good ole Lenny Bruce.

4. **Dig Down Deep** — Susie bails Midge out. Susie's impressed— Midge has got something! Back at the club, Midge turns down her offer to be her manager at first, but then after seeing some boring comics bomb on stage, she reconsiders. She's better than those hacks!

5. **The Execution of the New Plan** — She tells Susie she's in! And it's time to get to work.

FINAL IMAGE (54): After a long night, Midge heads back to the jail and bails out Lenny Bruce. She asks him a question,"Do you love it?" He will only give her a shrug. She nods and says "Yes, he loves it." A *whiff of change* is in the air! Midge has transformed from the picture-perfect Jewish New York woman to someone about to dive into the raucous Lenny Bruce world of stand-up comedy.

Let the games begin!

Ozark: "Sugarwood"
Written by: Bill Dubuque
Story by/Created by: Bill Dubuque & Mark Williams
Franchise Type: Dude with a Season-Long Problem (Man with a Plan)
The World: Money Laundering and the Ozarks
Episode Genre: Dude with a Problem
Platform: Netflix
TV Genre: Hour-Long Drama
Story DNA:
  • **Hero**: Marty Byrde
  • **Goal**: Survive the cartel and keep his family alive
  • **Obstacle**: The cartel and their main contact, Del
  • **Stakes**: His life and his family's

If you're looking to write a grab-em-by-the-throat-must-binge-the-next-epi TV pilot (and why wouldn't you be?), *Ozark* is one to emulate. It's like if *Breaking Bad* started in the middle of Season 2. While the pilot tosses its heroes into the deep end without a life jacket in sight, it balances its twisty plot with conflict-driven character dynamics and life-changing reveals. The show puts its leads into a pressure cooker, where dealing with their marital strife is a life-or-death matter.

Marty Byrde is a relatable everyman hero, a penny-pinching Walter White. Instead of chemistry, Marty's superpower is the way he handles a spreadsheet. He's like the Sherlock Holmes of accounting. When it comes to 401Ks and tax deductions, he can see the Matrix! He's always 10 steps ahead of everyone.

The pilot serves as a "how we ended up in the Ozarks" story. Yet it doesn't put us into the new world where the show will take place (or introduce us to that new world's characters) until its final moments, and even then it only offers a tantalizing glimpse. This pilot spends its time setting up the dangerous world of money laundering and the main characters who are already riding a trainwreck of dysfunction. In the end, we're left with a mission impossible that Marty and family will have to complete... or else!

OPENING IMAGE (0 – 2): The show begins with a voice-over style *opening pitch*. It's actually the pitch Marty gives to prospective clients in his wealth management business, spoken over a flash-forward montage of what Marty's life will look like in the season and series to come. He's hiding money in the wee hours in the deepest woods of the Ozarks.

THEME STATED (2): Marty ends the voice over with: "Patience. Frugality. Sacrifice. Money is a measure of a man's choices." Marty is a man who measures his whole life by money. This episode will poke holes in that philosophy, and the series will put everything he believes to the test.

SET-UP (3-12): At Marty's office in Chicago, we see him pitching a young couple on his wealth management services. But Marty's checked out. He's secretly watching a sex tape of sorts showing a couple in a hotel room. His partner, Bruce Liddell, steps in and closes the deal with the young couple in a very "car salesman" way. These guys are sneaky and morally suspect. Marty's business is doing great, but he seems to get zero joy out of it. Visiting their potential new offices, he's more worried about heating expenses than the huge space and the stunning view. Bruce asks him, "When was the last time you were truly happy?" Bruce enjoys his money, he's a bit reckless, but he has a plan for happiness: The Ozarks! He lays out how he's going to spend his fortune and hands Marty a brochure of the place, reeling off its virtues. Marty pockets it. (The brochure will be important later.) At home and at a dinner scene, Marty has more *things that need fixing*. His constant concern over money leads to a rather soulless family life. He won't even give his daughter $10 to donate for a sick friend. While watching TV that night, Marty secretly eyes the sex tape and we realize his supportive wife, Wendy, is the woman in the video. He won't say anything to her. This relationship is on dangerous ground and neither side is talking to each other about it.

CATALYST (12): Marty sneaks out of the house in the wee hours and picks up a street hooker. He doesn't want sex, instead he bares his heart to the prostitute in the way he couldn't to his wife. He's been faithful and can't believe his wife would betray him, given the wonderful life he's afforded her (yeah, it's all about money for Marty). That's when the phone call comes! It's from Bruce. Del is in town. Marty needs to get over to a trucking office that's key to their business right away.

DEBATE (13-21): Turns out Marty is money laundering for the cartel. And there's a big problem: someone's been stealing and the ever-dangerous cartel enforcer Del is there to sniff out who and shut it down. He gathers everyone in a cramped office and paces around intimidating Marty and Bruce and two truckers and a secretary who work for the trucking company. It's a tense shakedown and as it continues, it feels more and more like someone's going to pay the ultimate price.

BREAK INTO 2 (21-22): While everyone else cowers, Marty decides to make a stand. His superpower is his smooth-talking and thinking-on-his-feet nature, coming up with takes on situations that no one else can see. He points out all the angles to Del, calling him on this "intimidation audit" and reminding Del he needs them and how this whole shakedown is ridiculous. Marty's slick pitch doesn't work. Del shoots the secretary, just to show just how psychotic he is. Marty is in a battle for survival!

B STORY: There's no B Story moment here, as the story chooses to stick in the tense life-or-death scene, but Marty's relationship with his family will be an ongoing runner throughout the series. In this episode, his wife's affair is the major B Story. Set up in the opening scenes, it will come into focus after the Midpoint. Other family beats come into play in flashbacks: happy moments of family life that play out when Marty thinks he's about to die. Despite his sense of betrayal, it's ultimately the thought of his family being killed which pushes Marty to battle for survival—and forces him to compromise with the adulterous Wendy in the back half of this pilot and the series.

FUN & GAMES (22 - 29): Del kills the two truckers as Bruce reveals he stole the $8 million from the cartel over the past three years. He swears Marty didn't know as Del shoots him. Marty's out of options as he scrambles for time asking if he can say goodbye to his kids and pulling out his phone. But when Del hints Marty's wife Wendy will also have to be executed, Marty realizes the *stakes* are bigger. Using the Ozarks brochure that was in his pocket like some Second City improv-skit inspirational seed, Marty spins a tale about moving out of Chicago to start up a big money-laundering operation in the Ozarks. It's a complete lie and Del suspects it, but Marty does his magic and talks him into it by making him an offer he can't refuse: promising to launder $500 million in 5 years.

MIDPOINT (29-30): Del takes the bait but calls Marty's bluff with an ultimatum: Marty must get his missing $8 mil in cash and head off to set up shop in the Ozarks in 48 hours. *Ticking clock* alert! The

Midpoint *crosses A & B Stories*. While Marty may have wanted to leave Wendy in the beginning, he's now trapped with her and must deal with her infidelity (and this fractured marriage) throughout the first season.

BAD GUYS CLOSE IN (29-30): Marty breaks the news to Wendy. Wendy already knows about all his shady business and is complicit in it, but still pushes back about dropping everything and running. Marty, using his gift to "tell it like it is," convinces her there's no other choice. While she deals with the kids' frantic protests, Marty sets out to get $8 million from his bank accounts. The banks give him grief, but again Marty uses his brains and knowledge of banking and finance to run circles around the bank employees. Wendy is still looking for a way out. She heads to a luxurious apartment to secretly meet up with Gary aka the man she's been sleeping with aka "Sugarwood" (the episode's title). Together, they scheme to ditch Marty and escape this predicament. Meanwhile, Marty talks to a detective who made the secret sex tape in the first place and even checks in on the possibilities of going into hiding. As he does, he gets a notification that Wendy has emptied their bank accounts. She's making a run for it!

ALL IS LOST (39-40): Wendy returns to Gary's apartment. Bad news: Del is waiting for her with Gary. Out front, an angry Marty arrives to confront Wendy. As he marches toward the building, Gary's body crashes onto the street, presumably having been thrown by Del from the balcony high above.

DARK NIGHT OF THE SOUL (40): Marty drives away but gets a call from Del and Wendy. It's both a threat and a weird form of family therapy as Wendy sits in shame and Del discusses what to do with Wendy, given her affair and her willingness to run. Del gives Marty an opportunity to decide Wendy's fate. Offscreen, he chooses to save her, which we realize when Wendy returns home. Marty and Wendy sit together in stunned silence. They have no choice now but to continue to the Ozarks.

BREAK INTO 3 (44): Back at the bank, Marty works through some hurdles to get his money. When he goes to deliver the $8 million to Del, Del tells him to go to the Ozarks and launder all of it. Del doesn't believe this was Marty's original plan, so he's putting him to the test. If Marty fails, Del will now kill all of Marty's family. This is an expansion on the original goal and the stakes, which will take a multi-episode plan to solve. Marty accepts the challenge. This is also a Break into Series, ending the immediate conflict of the episode and accepting a bigger, wider combination of goal and conflict, i.e., the Fun & Games of the series itself! The new conflict could almost be stated as a logline to the series: a fish-out-of-water family fight to launder $8 million with a ticking clock, life-or-death stakes, and fracturing personal relationships— all while making their home in the new world of the Ozarks.

FINALE (49-52): The immediate conflict resolved, the family packs up and drives off in this wrap-up Finale, getting us to the next episode and seeding some B Story moments. The pilot takes time to seed one more runner story here, as we learn that Marty's partner Bruce was actually working with the feds and was going to snitch on Del and the operation. The introduction of FBI characters add another layer of tension to the Byrdes' mission and will act as foils in the episodes to come.

FINAL IMAGE (52-54): From a birds-eye view reminiscent of that car-driving shot in *The Shining*, the family's van cruises through the wild Ozarks. The show ends with Marty pulling over to the side of the road and ducking away in the thick woods… where he breaks down and cries, the weight of all this pressure finally getting to him. Then the family joins him and they all stare out at their picturesque new home—The Ozarks—where opportunity and seasons' worth of trouble awaits.

Let the games begin!

> *Stranger Things*: "Chapter One: The Vanishing of Will Byers"
> **Written by**: The Duffer Brothers
> **Franchise Type**: Dude with a Season-Long Problem (with touches of Blast from the Past)
> **The World**: Hawkins — a 1980s nostalgic small town with Spielbergian flair and homages
> **Episode Genre**: Whydunit
> **Platform**: Netflix
> **TV Genre**: Hour-Long Drama
> **Story DNA**:
> - **Hero**: Hopper & Joyce — Hopper the disinterested town sheriff; Joyce, the frazzled and overburdened mom
> - **Goal**: To figure out what happened to the missing kid, Will Byers
> - **Obstacle**: The mystery of what happened to Will
> - **Stakes**: Will they ever see the boy again?

Stranger Things' plot feels like a movie. Of course, a movie only gets about 25 minutes for an Act 1 and only has to set up enough story for 2 hours or less. This pilot digs deeper by expanding its ensemble and elevating characters to full-featured main players, embodying them with flaws and needs and broken compasses and transformational journeys. Ensemble shows that give near equal weight to several characters often break story separately for each character. Typically, in pilots, one character might get more of a nudge into the spotlight than the others. The *Stranger Things'* pilot is like this. Sheriff Hopper and desperate mom Joyce get the most beats. But all of the characters get thorough introductions and have through-lines, and usually get a whiff of change. If you have an equally weighted ensemble and want to break each story thread separately, crack each thread's Story DNA and logline.

The *Stranger Things'* pilot can be grouped into 4 main stories:

1. Hopper & Joyce — A desperate mom enlists a disinterested sheriff to help find her missing son.

Beginning: Joyce discovers her son never came home the night before. After some investigation, she approaches the town sheriff, Hopper, for help. Hop is sort of lazy and doesn't seem too worried, but Joyce's panic lights a fire under him.

Middle: Hopper and Joyce search. Hopper finds evidence that the boy might be in danger.

End: Hopper organizes a search party and hits the woods. We learn Hopper had a kid himself who died. This is personal. At home, Joyce discovers her son's disappearance may be related to something otherworldly.

This is the primary storyline of the episode. It occupies the major single beats and drives the *Save the Cat!* beat sheet's spine.

2. The *D&D* Crew — After their friend goes missing, a crew of kids begins to suspect something nefarious and sets out to find him.

Beginning: Good friends play *Dungeons & Dragons* in a basement. Mike's mom breaks up the game. On the way home, Will ends up in a terrifying encounter with a monster that seems ripped straight from the game (or a nearby Mad Science lab!) and goes missing.

Middle: Will's mom is frantically looking for him and the crew is alerted. The town sheriff, Hopper, comes to school to interview them, and they begin to think this is serious.

End: The kids sneak out to search for their missing friend. Instead of finding him, they find the mysterious Eleven.

This is the second biggest thread and gets almost as much time as the first. The big difference is it's mostly Set-Up beats. The *D&D* crew get the main focus in the opening beats but then fade and are mostly blended into the multi-scene beats later. The boys don't take definitive action until Act 3 when they join the hunt. They end with a *whiff of change* by meeting up with the enigmatic Eleven, which immediately pays off in the second episode.

3. Eleven — A mysterious girl with telekinetic abilities escapes a secret lab and tries to hide in a diner with a friendly cook as dangerous forces hunt her down.

Beginning: A secret lab has a cryptic accident, apparently un-leashing a monster. The scientists begin to search for a girl who has seemingly escaped.

Middle: The diner owner catches the escaped girl sneaking food. Who is she?

End: The diner owner calls in a social worker, but surprise! It's the lab employees. They kill the owner (yep, they're bad guys) and chase Eleven, who uses some telekinetic *Carrie*-like powers to escape. Bad Guys Close In and she takes off! In the last scene, she runs into the *D&D* crew.

The Eleven storyline moves hyperfast and gets some real twists and turns. It ultimately collides with the crew's storyline, where it will merge and play out in the episodes to come.

4. Nancy & Steve — There's not a lot in the way of a logline here. This story thread is more an intro to the duo as teenage Nancy tries to further her relationship with her boyfriend, Steve, despite the whole town being on alert due to Will's mysterious disappearance.

Beginning: We meet Nancy. She's in that "new relationship" mode in a very high-school way. Nancy & Steve meet up at school and organize a date.

Middle: The date gets quashed because Will's gone missing. The town is on alert and Nancy's parents won't let her leave the house.

End: Steve sneaks over and the two have a secret encounter in Nancy's bedroom. Nancy is beginning to really fall for this guy.

The Nancy & Steve storyline is blended into the multi-scene beats. The couple gets a few big scenes setting up their relationship and some general character psychology. Their relationship will pay off in a big way later on down the season.

Remember, if it's not in the pilot, it's not in the show. If you're writing a series that has several main characters who play a huge part, you need to kickstart them in the pilot. In *Stranger Things*, several character-specific threads are being juggled at once. Each is affected by the overall "happening" in Hawkins, but the characters react differently and are motivated by separate goals. In this episode, the Hop & Joyce story takes up the most real estate and gets the most single-scene beats, while the other stories blend into the multi-scene beats.

OPENING IMAGE (1-2): A mysterious horror beat sets the tone. In a high-tech lab, a fleeing scientist is taken by some unseen monster. It's important to set the table here with a horror beat. There's not a ton of sci-fi horror in this pilot episode, but the pilot is a promise. It's a contract of the types of things people will see in Season 1. This is a show with monsters and spooky mad science. Starting the series with this quicker teaser lays the groundwork. Labs! Monsters! Scares! Much like the movies it emulates, the opening scene gives a taste of monster-ey, sci-fi-ey stuff and gives the show some space to introduce the huge ensemble of characters and story threads in their ordinary world... before things get *Stranger*.

SET-UP (2-7): It's the 1980s and our kid-crew is amid a 10-hour *Dungeons & Dragons'* sesh. It's pure nostalgia lifted straight from the Set-Up of *E.T.* In the game, Demogorgon (an infamous *Dungeons & Dragon's* monster) attacks the party and there's a critical die-roll that skips off the table. As the boys search for the lost die and its result, Mike's mom breaks up the game. It's so *E.T.*, there's even left-over pizza. We get a quick glimpse of Michael's teenage sister, Nancy, who is on the phone—such a John Hughesian teenager in the 80s! She wants no part of the crew. The kids hop on their bikes as Mike ominously tells Will that the Demogorgon "got him" (in the game that is, but we know it's coming!). The boys ride off into the night. Will ends up alone and has an horrific encounter with the monster from the teaser. The monster takes him. We get a title sequence with some straight-up Atari sound FX. The next morning, we meet Joyce, who is frazzled and late for work and can't find her keys. In her search, she realizes (along with her older son, Jonathan) that Will didn't come home. It's no big deal... yet... he probably slept over at Mike's.

CATALYST (11): Joyce calls Mike's house and discovers that Will left there for home late last night. No one's seen him since.

In general, a Catalyst happens "to" the main character. Since I'm deeming the Joyce/Hopper story as the A Story in *Stranger Things* Episode 1 (it has the most beats and character range), this is the spot where Joyce discovers this is no ordinary day. To use one of the nostalgic inspirations for *Stranger Things* as an example, *Jaws* begins with an opening "kill scene," but it's not until the sheriff is called to check on a body that washes up on the beach that the hero's story is triggered. Same here.

DEBATE (11-19): The Debate section shows some ripples in the pond as everyone reacts to the news that Will is missing. Most notably, we're introduced to Hopper, the disinterested town sheriff. Arriving in his office, he finds Joyce waiting. Hopper provides the "cooler head" to Joyce's panicked mom. He's not too shaken by the whole thing, but Joyce's fear ultimately penetrates his slackerness.

BREAK INTO 2 (19): Joyce says, "Find my son, Hop! Find him!" The hunt for the missing Will Byers begins.

FUN & GAMES (19-29): This beat mostly focuses on the hunt, while blending in the other character threads. We're back with the kids at school checking out a new ham radio (a set-up for a later episode, reminding us that some set-ups in a pilot don't pay off in this episode—and every inch of your pilot should be servicing some kind of payoff). The ham radio scene is just background for a visit by Hopper, who questions the boys about Will and the night before. The kids view everything as a quest and an adventure. Hopper insists they don't go investigate. Yeah, this guy's never seen *Goonies* or *Monster Squad*. Joyce, on the other hand, is out searching for Will at the fort he's built in the woods. We get a flashback scene with Joyce and Will, deepening the emotional stakes. Joyce tries to get Will's father on the phone, and while she does, the supersecret lab guys monitor her call. Meanwhile, Eleven is hanging at Benny's Burgers magically stopping fans with her brain powers.

B STORY (22-23): The B Story beat comes a little late in this one. Scientists go into the quarantined areas of the building searching for someone. Our central B Story character enters the mix when diner owner Benny finds a girl sneaking food from the burger joint's kitchen (and she's hungry!). While several subthreads are going on, Eleven's has the fullest arc. She's not yet connected to any of our main heroes... but will be soon. Benny tries to figure out what the "11" tattoed on her arm means, and who this mysterious kid is.

MIDPOINT (29): Hopper finds Will's abandoned bike in the woods. Hmm...

BAD GUYS CLOSE IN (30-33): Joyce calls her ex, who is not helping as the cops show up with Will's bike, increasing the dread. Hopper investigates the house. Lots of suspicious stuff. The dog is loose outside. Bullets have been messed with in the garage. And there's this mysterious electrical surge in the house.

ALL IS LOST (33): Hopper finds evidence of a scuffle at Will's house. A rifle is missing. The kid was in danger. This is real!

DARK NIGHT OF THE SOUL (34): A search party is organized as word of missing Will leaks out to the town. This brings repercussions. Nancy isn't allowed to go out for her planned rendezvous with Steve. And the kid crew are on lockdown. Mike, who is the leader of the *D&D* gang, is angry! His friend is missing and he wants to hunt for Will. But his parents won't let him. Meanwhile, the search party heads into the woods in the dark. During their search, a conversation reveals that Hopper has a daughter who died. This is more personal than it first seemed.

BREAK INTO 3 (37): Mike convinces his crew via walkie-talkie to go search for their missing bud. He gears up for adventure, and rides off on his bike. As he does, he spots Steve sneaking into his sister's window.

THEME STATED (37): A late theme is spoken. Referring to the *D&D* game's Demogorgon encounter, Mike says, "He could have cast fireball... but he didn't....He put himself in danger to help the party." Ordinary folks, risking their lives to help their community, neighbors, friends, and family—that's at the heart of *Stranger Things*, Season 1. It's a story of relationships and friendships. It's a theme that fuels the episode and the series going forward.

FINALE (38): Each of the subthreads gets a "finale" of sorts. At the burger joint, Benny has called in a woman from social services with concerns about Eleven. Plot twist: the woman pulls out a gun and shoots him! Eleven uses her abilities to escape, but the bad guys are on her tail. Nancy & Steve are in Nancy's bedroom. He's a bit forward and she wards him off: "My parents are home." But she is falling for him big-time. Joyce gets the mysterious phone call from beyond. It's Will!

FINAL IMAGE (48): We end with the kids in the woods. Rain. Flashlights. Searching. They hear a noise and discover Eleven! It's a crossover of story threads and it bookends the Opening Image (the discovery of Eleven's initial escape). It's also a cliffhanger, where the next episode will immediately pick-up.

Let the games begin!

This Is Us: Series Premiere
Written by: Dan Fogelman
Franchise Type: Trapped Together
The World: Family
Episode Genre: Rites of Passage
Platform: NBC
TV Genre: Hour-Long Drama

For network television, the *This Is Us* pilot does some bold things. It manages four storylines, told at a hyper-fast pace, each hitting all the *Save the Cat!* beats. It introduces each of its central characters (three siblings and their parents) in a unique way that piques curiosity using a time-jumpy structure that would make Quentin Tarantino proud, and it engages the audience in a con-nect-the-dots guessing game while also delivering four compelling and equally developed stories.

This "gimmick" is no mere pilot episode throwaway either. The series uses similar non-linear storytelling techniques and is constantly piecing together connections. It creates mysteries not just with the story but via its time-jumping storytelling, driving viewers to watch the next episode just to find out "how did dad die" or when. Itches that need scratching! That's what it's all about.

If you want to write fast-paced ensemble television where every character is an equal and each gets their own storyline, *This Is Us* is your jam. For this kind of pilot, the best way to break story is to divide and conquer. Craft each individual storyline with either a full beat sheet or at least the pillar beats, and then do a blend beat sheet that mixes the storylines together.

Some tips for breaking multi-threaded stories:

1. Use the Opening and Final Images as bookends to meld your parallel stories together. These beats can represent how the stories work as a unit, tying all your threads in a bow.

2. Your theme should be shared across all stories. It gives cohesion to the overall episode.

3. Come up with Story DNA and loglines for each of your individual threads.

Some threads will crisscross and share beats or even combine for large sections. Here are the four key story threads of the *This Is Us* series' premiere:

1. **The Birth** — Jack & Rebecca — On a young man's birthday, his pregnant wife (with triplets) goes into early labor, and they rush to the hospital where complications force them to take drastic actions.

2. **The Dad** — Randall — On his birthday, a married man locates his biological father and decides to seek him out to finally unburden everything that's been bottled up over the years. It gets the second most weight and hits the *Save the Cat!* beats the hardest of the substories.

3. **The Manny** — Kevin — On his birthday, an actor disappointed with the direction of his silly hit show and the trajectory of his career takes action to force change.

4. **The Date** — Kate — On her birthday, a woman struggling with weight loss meets a charming man who seems to be interested in her, but her own self-consciousness stands in the way.

The Date storyline crisscrosses The Manny storyline. They join together in their Finales.

The quickly paced episode allows each of these subthreads about seven or eight scenes. Many scenes contain multiple *Save the Cat!* beats. You'll see Catalysts roll into Debates and All Is Lost moments dip right into Dark Night of the Soul sadness.

Here's a side-by-side view of the beats of each story thread in the *This Is Us* pilot. It's a convenient way to plan a beat sheet if you're dealing with multi-track storytelling.

	The Birth	The Dad	The Manny	The Date
OPENING IMAGE:	The episode starts with a title card… "This is a fact: According to Wikipedia, the average human being shares his or her birthday with over 18 million other human beings. There is no evidence that sharing the same birthday creates any type of personality or behavioral link between those people. If there is… Wikipedia hasn't discovered it for us yet." The text morphs into the title THIS IS US. The opening text sets a tone and presents a bit of a mystery. Why are we watching these seemingly disparate stories about people with the same birthday all on the same day? What's the connection? Surely that won't be the only connection for the entire series, right? The answer will be revealed through the course of the pilot and confirmed in the Final Image.			
SET-UP	It's everyman Jack's birthday. His verrrrry pregnant wife gives him a "questionably sexy dance" as a gift. These two are fun and loving and on the verge of a new life.	All-business Randall is spending his birthday at the office. It looks like an ordinary day reflecting his responsible and "all business" personality. He's a guy who puts work first.	Actor Kevin is spending his special day with two models he doesn't know. He's an actor on a sitcom and should be on top of the world. But something's off.	Bummed-out Kate is celebrating her birthday stressing over her food urges. There's Post-it notes trying to ward her off cake and other food. This is an ongoing struggle—one she can't even escape on her birthday.

THEME STATED	Each of the episodes shares a single theme. It's best summed up when it's repeated later in the show: "Lemons & lemonade." Each of the stories is about turning a rough patch in life into a positive. Or at least having the intention to do so.			
CATALYST	The water breaks! The babies are coming!	Randall gets an email that cryptically reads: "We found him."	Kevin gets a call to come help his twin sister, just the escape he's looking for. In general, it looks like he's trying to escape this life.	Kate slips on the scale and hurts her ankle. (She calls Kevin.)
DEBATE	They're at the hospital when a different doctor comes in than they expected. They're worried, but the doctor seems wise and kind. He gives them his pitch and bonafides. He's a mentor of sorts, the one who will voice the theme late in the show.	At his kids' soccer game, Randall tells his wife he's hunted down his father. She's a little angry he hid it from her and she asks what he's going to do with the info. He doesn't know.	Kevin and his twin sister both long for something more in life. Kevin cheekily blames the Challenger explosion for setting the course of his life off in the wrong direction.	Kevin arrives to help. Kate works as his assistant and while Kevin and Kate are very close (twins and all), he's a bit self-centered. She needs inspiration and gets some from Kevin. Maybe today will be a day for change.
BREAK INTO 2	The couple decide to proceed with this new doctor. It's onto baby delivering.	Randall reviews some pictures of his discovered dad and makes his move to pay a visit.	Kevin jumps in to filming the day's episode. A scene rubs him the wrong way and he stops and demands a discussion.	Kate recommits to losing weight. She throws some food away. She's gonna do this.

FUN & GAMES	Mom's brought into the delivery room. Jack insists that the doctor keep the babies safe. The doctor bonds with Jack and the labor ensues.	Randall hunts down his father's apartment and knocks on the door.	Kevin and his showrunner debate the direction of his show. His showrunner humiliates him, puts him in his place, and tells him to stick with the script. See! Writers do have the power in TV!!	Kate heads to a Weight Watchers meeting. She is charmed by a new-guy, Toby, and ends up at a restaurant on a date. They're both counting calories so it's sort of sad... but Toby makes it fun. This birthday is looking up after all.
MIDPOINT	The first baby is born but it's a *false victory*. There's trouble with the other two and Jack is kicked out of the delivery room.	His biological father opens the door and Randall gives him the speech he was waiting his whole life to give. Dumping a world of guilt on this stranger. The man then... invites him inside. And he goes!	Kevin and Alan Thicke do a scene that's touching and everything he wants in acting. Maybe he can be The Manny and an artist? But it's a *false victory* when he's asked to do it again with his shirt off.	At home, Toby charms his way inside of Kate's place. It's a bit of a *false victory*. Kate's birthday is looking up, but is she ready for this?
BAD GUYS CLOSE IN	A quick beat of tension as Jack waits for news. This flows right into the doctor's arrival. Rebecca is okay but there's trouble...	His father gives some backstory. This isn't going the way Randall thought... and then Randall invites him home. The family is confused, Randall is confused.	Kevin and his showrunner get into it again. Kevin thinks they nailed the scene but the showrunner insists they need the lighter version.	Inside the house, Kate's nervous about being intimate and self-conscious in general. But she and Toby have a good vibe. And it looks like some romance is in the cards.

ALL IS LOST	...they lost one of the babies. It's heartbreaking. And a true *whiff of death*.	Randall goes to say goodbye and his father tells him he's dying. *Whiff of death*!	Kevin throws a Network-level tantrum in front of everyone. Blaming them, smashing the baby, freaking out Alan Thicke. People record their blow-up. He's about to go viral. His career... *death*.	Kate and Toby are about to kiss when Kevin interrupts. Kate's intimate moment... denied!
DARK NIGHT OF THE SOUL	The doctor sits with Jack and relates a loss he had. Then he gives Jack the big thematic advice about lemons and lemonade. This is advice that Jack will ultimately provide to his own kids and also clue us into tying the pieces of the episode together.	The scene with his dad continues. We see that the grim news is having a deep effect on Randall.	Kate, Kevin, and Toby all watch the video of Kevin's meltdown.	Kate, Kevin, and Toby watch the video. Kate's big date has been tragically interrupted.

BREAK INTO 3	Jack looks at his two surviving babies in the nursery and hears about an infant dropped off at a fire station. A new idea strikes! The scene also clues us in here, for the first time definitively showing that it is 1979.	Randall invites his biological father to stay.	Kevin is reassured by dad's words about "lemon & lemonade." And being we've seen what dad went through to earn those words, we and Kevin get that the future is his to make.	Kate gives Kevin the "lemons & lemonade" prompt. It's advice to Kevin and herself.
FINALE	Jack holds his wife and together they cry. But we know the bold move they're making.	Randall's dad checks out his new room at Randall's house.	Kevin is tucked in. Content. Seemingly more so than at the open. Despite everything. Ah, lemonade!	Kate and Toby kiss. And more...
FINAL IMAGE	We're back in the bedroom where we started, and in the three bassinets are the three children (one adopted)—tying the three modern adults' stories to the flashback story of their parents.			

Let the games begin!

NON-PREMISE PILOTS

Non-premise pilots avoid the origin stories. They're built to give a taste for what an ordinary episode looks and feels like. They're constructed to be perfect examples of what the buyer and viewer will get. But they still have to do all the big introductions of situation, character, theme, etc.—and always sneak in some extra Set-Up. While non-premise pilots are not as in vogue as they once were, if you're doing a sitcom, a procedural, or an animated comedy, you might consider it.

Black-ish: Pilot

Written by: Kenya Barris

Franchise Type: Trapped Together

The World: An African American family who has made it (and the doubts and questions about moving away from their past)

Episode Genre: Institutionalized

Platform: ABC

TV Genre: Half-Hour Single-Camera Comedy

Story DNA:

- **Hero**: Dre — African-American dad who is worried about losing touch with his roots
- **Goal**: "To Keep It Real"
- **Obstacle**: His working environment and his own success (the world he now lives in)
- **Stakes**: His job and his "personal integrity"

Black-ish is another great example of how network television doesn't always play it safe. The series mixes laughs with stories that examine important timely cultural topics. The show's creator, Kenya Barris, brings a fresh voice to one of the oldest of TV genres. For comparison, check out Barris's Netflix show *#BlackAF*, which is very similar in premise, yet different in tone and delivery.

The *Black-ish* pilot really could be an Episode 5, but pilots still have to do that extra duty. The episode introduces all the main players and the overall situation in its teaser, then goes on to tell a story that works thematically as a microcosm of the entire series. Identifying a theme for your series and using it in your pilot is a great way to lay the groundwork for the shows to come.

OPENING IMAGE (1-2): In an *opening pitch* montage, the show's main character, Dre, lays out an elevator pitch for the series through voice-over while comedic scenes illustrate the family, the situation, the strong POV, and the tone. We get a first-hand glimpse of the way Dre perceives this world when a tour bus filled with white tourists pulls up and observes him and his family like they're some unusual wild-life specimens. Dre laments that through their efforts to make it, Black folks have lost a bit of their culture, which has been taken over by the rest of the world and renamed "urban." The opening montage plays like a sizzle reel (in the best way possible). Instead of selling the show to a bunch of executives, the teaser sells the show to the new viewer. It does the duty of an entire premise pilot in 2 minutes, spelling out the situation and hinting of its "newness," performing the heavy-lifting Set-Up-wise, so that the rest of the episode can have the look and feel of an ordinary episode without any additional "pilot Set-Up" burdens. With the introductions out of the way, the rest of the show can now settle into what a nor-mal episode of *Black-ish* looks like. It's non-premise pilot heaven! **(teaser out – 2 min)**

THEME STATED (1): In that opening montage, Dre lays it out: "Only problem is, whatever 'American' it was who had the 'Dream,' probably wasn't Black. And if he was, he should have mentioned the part about how when Brotha's start getting a little money, stuff starts getting a little weird." The tension between "The Dream" and things getting weird is at the heart of *Black-ish*. Dre's struggle to "keep it real" against the trappings of the "American Dream" serves as an internal conflict throughout the series. You could almost list Dre's *broken compass* mantra statements as: "I will never forget my roots. I will always keep it real." This episode also directly leans on Dre's central contradictions, exactly what all great pilots do (even non-premise ones!).

SET-UP (2-7): We open on one of those "getting-ready-for-the-day breakfast scenes" (save me!), but this is not "any other day." A *whiff of change* is already in the air. Dre's marketing firm is going to name a new SVP and he's 100% sure it will be him. Much like we saw in the *Grey's Anatomy* pilot, dropping us into a special day provides urgency and momentum. It's almost a premise-pilot move. It's not a huge situational change in the grand scheme of things (especially given the teaser, which shows they've already "made it") but for a new viewer, it's enough. It feels like an entry point, even if it could be Episode 5 or 6.

CATALYST (4-5): On the drive to school, Dre's son, Andre Jr., tells him he wants to play field hockey. Ouch! This "white sport" hits Dre where it hurts. Andre's school friends also call him "Andy." While the promotion is a big driver in the story, Trapped Together stories are really about dealing with tension from those we're trapped with. This is a classic family show. Andre Jr.'s story gets the main focus (and the big ending!).

DEBATE (5-6): Dre's determined not to let the ride with Andre ruin his big day. As soon as he gets to work, the subtle racism of the office emerges (they even call him "Andy"... hmmm?). Things get worse when he discusses with a goofy white co-worker about how kids should play the sports their dad played. The guy agrees, but then says it wasn't a problem for him because he always wanted to play field hockey like his dad. Ugh! Ultimately, Dre is beginning to question if *he's* the problem. Is his success and the compromises he's made leading his family down the wrong path?

BREAK INTO 2 (7-8): During a company-wide meeting, Dre is, in fact, announced as the SVP... but he's being named the SVP of the new "Urban" division. Not just SVP. This is not good. (**ACT OUT #1 - 8 min**)

B STORY (8): At a dinner scene, Dre's dad immediately makes himself known by pushing on Dre's flaw and emphasizing the show's theme. He congratulates Dre for being named "Head Puppet of the White Man" and then starts questioning Dre's wife, Rainbow, about her fried chicken. (It's baked chicken, and dad questions if "*fried* fried chicken" is "too black" for the family.)

FUN & GAMES (8-14): Dre doesn't want to be the company's first black SVP, he wants to be the first SVP *who happens to be black*. He complains, questioning this world he's invested in. There are also cracks at home. His kids don't even know Obama is the first black president. Pops is casting eye-rolly judgment all the way. Later, Rainbow tells Dre, "You gotta keep it real" and focus. Dre decides to suck it up and make a point at work to represent the person he really wants to be. The next day at the office, the boss chats him up on the big presentation that Dre's working on. The boss makes some tone-deaf suggestions on how to handle the "urban" space. When the boss tells him to "keep it real," it's too much. Dre won't let this stand. He's now convinced his family's issues are a byproduct of his compromises.

MIDPOINT (14-15): Andre Jr. comes home and announces he made the field hockey team! He also declares he knows what to do for his birthday—he wants to have a Bar Mitzvah.

BAD GUYS CLOSE IN (15-16): Dre calls a family meeting. He may have to be urban at work, but at home, they're gonna be Black... not Black-*ish*. Dre announces that Andre Jr. will be having an African Rights of Passage Ceremony. *B Story crosses A Story* and suddenly the family is dragged into Dre's personal crisis. Increased tension ensues!

ALL IS LOST (16): Dre shows an intense Urban promo video, scaring his coworkers. The shocked boss dismisses it with "We're not really doing this right." (**ACT OUT #2 – 16 min**)

DARK NIGHT OF THE SOUL (17-18): At home, Dre has taken it to the next level. He is dressed in traditional African garb. Even his old-school dad thinks it's a bit much. Rainbow's been called by Dre's worried co-workers and hears about the incident at the office. She's hot about it. Dre has been given an ultimatum to decide if the company is a good fit for him. He might get fired. Or quit. It's a *whiff of death*! He's gone from promotion to potential unemployment. Dre talks to Andre Jr. about culture. His son tells him he's unsure of "who he is" and admits field hockey is more about getting close to girls. This is something Dre can relate to.

BREAK INTO 3 (19-20): Dre sits down with his dad and asks him, "When we were younger, how did you keep it real?" Dad says, "I didn't, I kept it honest." Then he drops some Morpheus-like knowledge: "Whatever you do... make sure it's right for you." This advice is just what Dre needs. It spurs him into level-headed action.

FINALE (20-22): In a *synthesis* of old and new worlds, Dre throws his son a Hip Hop Bromitzpha. Keeping it real means admitting you're wrong. Urban can mean hip, cool, and colorful, just like family. The Finale is a wrap-up finale. Since his conflict is mostly internal, once he makes the choice to compromise, the tension falls away. The Finale gives us a fun taste of this compromise in action.

FINAL IMAGE (22): In his SVP of the Urban division office, Dre proudly puts the photo of his family on his desk. But he still doesn't feel urban. He just "feels like a dad willing to do whatever it takes for his family...and isn't that the American dream?" The picture is reminiscent of the scene on the front lawn in the Opening Image, giving us a bookend. There's a *whiff of change*. Maybe Andre can successfully learn to merge his new world with the old one. But it's not complete change. He'll continue to wrestle with the keeping it real aspects of his life in the episodes and seasons to come.

Let the games begin!

Law & Order: Special Victims Unit: "PAYBACK"
Written by: Dick Wolf
Franchise Type: Blank of the Week
The World: Special Victims Unit
Episode Genre: Whydunit
Platform: NBC
TV Genre: Hour-Long Drama
Story DNA:
- **Hero:** Benson & Stabler — cop partners (a little Buddy Love style)
- **Goal:** As with most "case-of-the-week" procedurals, unravel the mystery and find the killer
- **Obstacle:** The mystery at hand (typical detective work problems) and the internal dilemma this case presents

- **Stakes**: Justice. Their job is to deliver justice. When they fail, justice goes unserved.

Law & Order: SVU is an episodic show and its pilot feels like it could easily be Episode 7. But a little less than midway through the first episode, the writer mixes in a character reveal that may have an impact on the overall series. This case is personal and while you can't have every case in an episodic cop show be a personal one, your pilot is a good place to press that button. Pilots need to do more than just deliver great plotting, they need to reveal character enough to earn precious DVR slots. Make 'em personal! Make 'em the *most* personal.

OPENING IMAGE (1 - 2): The title screen specifically states what the SVU unit is; it could be the first slide of a pitch. The graphic will show up every week, doing its job. We know what we're watching and can jump right in. We meet our two heroes, Stabler and Benson, at a rainy crime scene. The first thing they do is introduce themselves to the cop on duty, saying their names and that they're from "sex crimes." The case appears to be an ordinary murder, not specifically in the SVU wheelhouse, until the cop says there's sexual mutilation. This *is* a job for SVU. We get a trademark *Law & Order* DONK-DONK, which means it's time to move on to the Set-Up. **(TEASER OUT – min 2)**

SET-UP (2 - 6): In a walk-and-talk, we get a quick *guided tour* of "the office." We meet all the cop characters that'll be part of the show going forward and get a feel for their traits and attitudes. These characters don't get much time in this episode, but remember: if it's in the show, it's in the pilot! If you have characters that will appear as part of the ensemble, find a way to include them. Here they're used like a chorus when the main heroes are bouncing ideas and reacting to new info. Stabler is going off to court to testify against some offender. In the economic world of pilot writing, he gets the extra scene to establish character (Benson's backstory will get some love later when it directly ties into the A Story). In court, Stabler shows himself as confident, cocky, and perhaps a bit jaded as he tricks a sex-crimes defendant into exposing himself.

CATALYST (6): The driver's license says the victim from the opening scene's name is "Victor Spicer." When the cops run a check against it, they discover that Victor Spicer is actually doing time at Rikers Island. He's alive and well. The dead guy ain't him! So who is their dead guy? Benson and Stabler deal with crimes and murder every day. But this is a special case. A weird one. This twist is what kicks the story into gear.

DEBATE (6-7): The characters debate the mystery's possibilities with their boss. They speculate on what's going on. The Debate emphasizes the due diligence of the team and sets the case up as important and interesting.

BREAK INTO 2 (7 - 8): Benson and Stabler head off to interview the real Mr. Spicer in prison. At an interrogation room in Rikers, Spicer gives them some leads on who the dead guy might be. He says that he sold his license to a man with a baby on Broadway for $100. Ahh! Their first real clue. Now, they're on the hunt!

B STORY (8): The B Story is the relationship between the two partners. Benson has a backstory that makes this case challenging. Stabler has a cold demeanor that will bump up against Benson's internal struggles. Will Benson's cop career survive this case? Will their partnership?

FUN & GAMES (8 -18): The partners are on the case investigating the murder. They head to a diner and find out the victim was last seen giving a cab ride to two women. They go to break the news to his widow. It's a tough moment and we see the impact of the crime and the pain our heroes must deal with each day. (**ACT OUT #1 – 12 min**) The Act Out is not a huge plot-twist cliffhanger. It's a bit of a *stake raiser* as we put human feelings to an otherwise distant crime. The wife reveals the dead guy was a Czech living illegally in the US. The cops show their softer sides with her, adding to their *rooting resumes*. Given his illegal immigrant status, they send his prints to Interpol. Meanwhile, forensics comes back with a red fingernail that broke off the killer's finger during the murder. The killer must be a woman! Benson and Stabler follow some leads and even get some of the other office characters, who will be important to the series, involved in some interrogation, police work, and inter-office flavor.

MIDPOINT (18 - 22): Interpol ID's the victim. He's a Serbian war criminal accused of the rape of 67 women, several who now live in the city. This is where Benson's backstory crosses. She has personal experience with rape. Her boss and partner discuss whether her past will be a problem. It can't be an issue if you work for this unit. Stabler sticks up for her. But Benson will wrestle with an internal question that may have an impact on her career: is she a cop or a human first? Things are personal now. Internal bad guys eat away at Benson. There's a Buddy Love dynamic here too, two characters with opposing POVs need to find a way to handle this "war criminal" case. Stabler thinks it's just a job. Benson would rather jeopardize her career than punish the perpetrators. It's an "I will never..." type dilemma that *broken compasses* are made of. It's the type of stuff that's great for a pilot (even a non-premise one). At the morgue, they discover they're looking for more than one killer, confirming the revenge angle and deepening Benson's internal tension. This case just got more complicated... and personal. (**ACT OUT #2 – min 20**)

THEME STATED (22): "I'm a good cop, Elliot," Benson says. What does it mean to be a good cop? That's what will be tested in this first *SVU* story. The deeper message behind this: can you ignore your personal feelings and ethics and just do the job? Is it even right to fight for justice for a horrible person? Typical of themes, the heavy lifting of this question is carried out by the B Story.

BAD GUYS CLOSE IN (22 - 24): They go back to the war criminal's wife. Now Benson is angry and accusing the wife of knowing exactly what kind of man her husband was. It ends in an ugly screaming match. Benson is off the rails and Stabler scolds her. He warns her that the boss is already worried about her objectivity, and if she takes herself off the case she'll be off the unit. Can she reign in her personal feelings? There aren't a ton of obstacles to finding the killers, so the tension is all generated from the *ticking time* bomb of the two partners and how they'll react once they find the killers. The closer they get, the more our heroes' inner demons begin to surface. We're leading up to a showdown that may change the course of the career of a "good cop." They focus their search on the dead man's rape victims. The first is a woman blinded by the war criminal. Benson tells the frightened woman he's dead. The woman bursts into tears. Shaken by the encounter, Benson throws up afterward. Stabler wonders aloud if he should talk to the boss.

ALL IS LOST (24): The next victim isn't home when they arrive, but they meet a child and realize the boy is likely the product of rape, which puts the boy's mom in prime-suspect territory. This is a real crisis point for Benson.

DARK NIGHT OF THE SOUL (25 - 32): As her partner heads off to deal with some family stuff at his kid's school (a small set-up for future episodes), Benson goes it alone and confronts the suspect about the child and the possible murder. The woman tells her horrible story of the dead man's crimes, which leaves Benson in tears. When she calls to fill in Stabler, he's angry. She shouldn't have visited the woman (a suspect!) and shouldn't have gone behind his back. Benson and her mom talk about the case. The big reveal happens here. Benson was born of rape and sympathizes with the killers in this case. Her mother empathizes with the killer and asks if Benson would have been better off with her own mother in jail. Benson is conflicted. Deep down she'd like to kill the man who raped her mother. The rape is Benson's *shard of glass*. (**ACT OUT #3 – 32 min**). The tense conversation is another character moment Act Out. And also a *stake-raiser*. We know an arrest is coming and the "will she be able to do it" is now at its most questionable point.

BREAK INTO 3 (32 - 34): Benson defends the mom suspect to Stabler, despite knowing she's probably guilty. They decide to check out the next person on the list, a woman who works at a restaurant. She has an alibi, but her hand is injured. She's one of the killers. It's the new piece of information that sets everything in motion!

FINALE (34 - 42):

1. **Gathering the Team** — Stabler lays out the case. They go to get a witness to ID the suspects. Benson is still on the fence, but Stabler wants to bring them in and get a confession.

2. **Execution of the Plan** — Benson arrests the mom but advises her not to talk without a lawyer.

3. **High Tower Surprise** — Stabler goes to arrest the woman in the restaurant, but she grabs a knife and stabs herself. She refuses help and whispers something in Stabler's ear as she's dying.

4. **Dig Down Deep** — They go to interrogate the mom. Something has stirred in Stabler, based on the whisper.

5. **Execution of the New Plan** — The woman gives an intense confession that's a bit made up. It doesn't show pre-meditation. The cops don't press. But the Boss knows what's up. The partners are helping this woman get a lesser charge by fudging their police work and angling for a lesser charge. They used their "get-out-of-jail-free" card, he tells them, and "there's only one in the pack." Benson asks Stabler what the dying woman said to him. He responds, "I just want to be with my family." It calls back to when he was with his family earlier... and now we see, even though Benson was tested throughout the episode, it's really Stabler who is revealed here, and there may even be a little *whiff of change*. Stabler is a "good guy" too, and a "good cop."

FINAL IMAGE (42): A call comes in and Benson answers: "Special Victims Unit"... and the beat goes on. The pilot closes with another wide shot of the office. Metaphoric of another day at work. But with the compromise between the two partners, we know this story has changed things... even if just a little.

Let the games begin!

Rick & Morty: **Pilot**
Written by: Dan Harmon & Justin Roiland
Franchise Type: Buddy Love/Blank of the Week
The World: Sci-Fi Spoofery
Episode Genre: Buddy Love
Platform: Cartoon Network/Hulu
TV Genre: Half-Hour Animated Comedy.
Story DNA:
- **Hero**: Rick & Morty — *Back to the Future*-style Professor & Kid team
- **Goal**: To retrieve mega-seeds from an alien world
- **Obstacle**: The dangers of interdimensional travel and the usual sci-fi threats
- **Stakes**: Rick needs the seeds for an experiment. Everything's life or death to Rick.

The *Rick & Morty* pilot doesn't feel like a first episode. It exudes Season 2-level confidence, delivers on the premise, and knows exactly who its characters are and what makes the show special. The first episode centers on a non-premise plot that isn't about Morty moving in or discovering inter-dimensional time travel. It's not even the first time Rick & Morty meet or go on a wacky adventure. But it does establish the show's *Back to the Future* send-up theme: is it really appropriate for mad scientist Rick to be taking little Morty on dangerous sci-fi adventures?

OPENING IMAGE (1-2): In two darkly funny minutes, the teaser delivers everything we need to know about the show. Morty is yanked out of bed by his drunk Uncle Rick, and whisked onto some two-passenger spaceship. Rick tells him he has a neutrino bomb and he's going to use it to reboot the world. The teaser is a microcosm of the whole series. We get a taste of their relationship and the wacky sci-fi comedy this show will deliver. It could almost be a short-film proof-of-concept of the show. The teaser does 99% of the "pilot work." Now we can just sit back and enjoy the episode... as if it were Episode 7. (**COLD OPEN OUT**)

SET-UP (2-5): It's the old breakfast scene, done *Rick & Morty* style. Morty falls asleep right into his breakfast. It's *things that need fixing* time. Uncle Rick is keeping Morty out all night doing "high concept sci-fi rigamarole." This is the "home" part of setting up their lives. Rick's dismissive of Morty's school (thinks it's for not smart people). Morty's dad is angry about all of Rick's sci-fi hijinks and the effect they're having on Morty. Morty's mom's is a tad defensive of her brother, Rick. The family overall is a bit mundane compared to the wild scene we've seen in the opening. The "work world" is school, where Morty is obsessed with his fellow student, Jessica. Because of his late-night adventures, he can't concentrate on his math test and instead dreams about Jessica and falls asleep during a test. Morty is struggling in school and the stuff he's dealing with on his Rick & Morty adventures isn't helping. Later, Frank, the bully, pulls a knife on Morty, but Rick shows up at school and uses one of his sci-fi weapons to freeze him.

CATALYST (6): Rick needs "mega seeds" from another dimension. Overall, it's a routine mission for this bonkers world. But it serves its purpose as Rick recruits Morty into the mission: Rick is once again dragging Morty into his nonsense!

DEBATE (6-7): Morty doesn't want to leave school. Rick insists, further illustrating the inappropriateness of this relationship that's at the heart of the pilot and the series.

B STORY (7): At mom's veterinarian office, dad and mom chat while mom performs a surgery. Dad wants to put Rick into a nursing home. They debate and we get the feeling that Rick has outstayed his welcome. The argument is a nod to the show's situation… spotlighting the conflict at home.

BREAK INTO 2 (8): Despite Morty's resistance—and because Rick is a horrible human—they leave anyway, stepping through a portal to Dimension 35C. Back at school, the frozen bully Frank shatters into a million bloody pieces. Yes, we're going there. Tonal set-up is critical to pilots and *Rick & Morty* is a master class in setting up a very specific tone. As soon as Rick and Morty reach dimension 35C, they're attacked by a scary monster and we cliffhanger to our first Act Out! **(ACT OUT #1 – 8 min)**

FUN & GAMES (8-12): Rick & Morty are in dimension 35C. They hunt for the special fruit with mega seeds that Rick needs for his research. High concept sci-fi rigamarole ensues and tons of quick gags and fun one-liners hint at the broad sci-fi universe this show will send up. Ultimately, the duo find the mega trees with the mega seeds. Rick convinces Morty to put on grappling shoes to retrieve the seeds, but Morty ends up breaking his legs. Morty wonders aloud if Rick is a monster.

THEME STATED (10:41): "The only influence I can see... is for the first time in his life, Morty has a friend." The thematic question of this first episode is: is Rick a bad influence on Morty? Is Rick the reason Morty is doing badly in school? The show is a deep dive into *Back to the Future*'s relationship between Marty McFly and Doc Brown. Yeah, *Back to the Future* was amazing... but what's really going on there? Should Doc Brown be dragging Marty McFly into dangerous worlds and questionable quantum physics experiments? Is this good for a young boy? Or does friendship make the risks worthwhile? Morty's parents continue to debate the dubious nature of Rick's influence while we see it play out in real time in the other dimension.

MIDPOINT (10-12): The parents get a "we have to talk about Morty" call from the school's vice-principal, as the *A and B Stories cross*. The sci-fi adventure may be life or death, but whether Rick will end up in a nursing home is what really is at stake here.

Meanwhile, Rick goes to another dimension to heal Morty's broken legs. During this offscreen mission, he uses up his interdimensional charger. It's a *false victory* in that, yes, Morty's legs are healed, but this mission has become a lot more complicated.

BAD GUYS CLOSE IN (13-17): Now they're forced to go through interdimensional customs. Rick tells Morty he needs to smuggle the seeds inside his butt. Ouch. Back at home, things are getting more tense when mom and dad realize Morty's having trouble in his classes and Rick has been intercepting calls from the school. Rick & Morty try to sneak the seeds through customs. Rando customs checker guy says Morty has to go through an x-ray machine. Uh-oh. They're busted. Rick and Morty run for it. A chase ensues! They're cornered as Rick tries to open a portal to escape back home. And just as things seem at their worst... (**ACT OUT #2 – 16 min**)

ALL IS LOST (17): ...the dimensional portal opens and they escape back to Morty's school cafeteria—only to run into mom and dad!! Which is scarier and more threatening to the duo's relationship than any sci-fi threats. The sci-fi stuff from the Opening Image is "galaxy-level stakes," but the relationship with Morty's parents has the real drama here. And for that reason, it's this mom and dad face-off that heralds the All Is Lost, as opposed to facing death in some bizarre off-world dimension (which in this show is generally shrugged off). The *whiff of death* is the end of Rick & Morty's relationship. After all, they're the title characters. Take out that ampersand and there's no show!

DARK NIGHT OF THE SOUL (17-18): A weighty conversation ensues. The parents have decided to move Rick into a nursing home. They can't put up with his negative influence on Morty.

BREAK INTO 3 (18): When dad tells Morty he has a learning disability, it presents an opportunity for Rick.

FINALE (18-21): Rick claims their adventures have helped Morty. Turns out Morty knows all kinds of math stuff. He knows Pi and the laws of thermodynamics, learned during their wacky inter-dimensional hijinks. The parents' minds are completely blown. They decide to keep Rick around. Once they're gone, Rick reveals it's the mega seeds dissolving in Morty's rectal cavity that are making him smart (temporarily). This show really isn't about the happy ending. It darkly thumbs its nose to such things. Rick is true to his monstrous ways. No cute wrap-up, just setting the tone for the dark comedy to come.

FINAL IMAGE (21-22): Rick gives a speech about how the two of them are up against the world. They're the only friends they've got. As Morty writhes in pain from the seeds inside, Rick goes into a litany of how it's Rick & Morty forever. It's a *whiff of change... stated*. A Buddy Love, indeed.

Let the games begin!

What We Do in the Shadows: **Pilot**
> **Written by:** Jermaine Clement
> **Based on the film written by:** Jermaine Clement and
> Taika Waititi
> **Created by:** Jermaine Clement
> **Franchise Type:** Trapped Together
> **The World:** Vampires living on Staten Island
> **Episode Genre:** Dudes with Problems
> **Platform:** FX
> **TV Genre:** Half-Hour Single-Camera Comedy
> **Story DNA:**
>> • **Hero:** The Staten Island vampires
>> • **Goal:** Prepare for the coming of the Baron
>> • **Obstacle:** Each other, their own incompetence,
>> and the current state they're living in
>> • **Stakes:** The Baron's ruthless judgement. If he's
>> disappointed in them, it could end in disaster.

What We Do in the Shadows could be pitched as *The Office* with vampires. It's about a "family" of bloodsuckers who live together in a ramshackle house in Staten Island. While the series is filled with horror tropes and plots, the real drama comes from the recurring tension of this makeshift family forced to work together eternally in spite of their eccentric and conflicting personalities. Trapped Together indeed!

The pilot begins with the characters already deeply entrenched in their Trapped Together situation. The show jumps right into the lived-in character dynamics and group tension. Like many non-premise pilots, it still throws a change grenade into the status quo. The pilot introduces a new character who literally challenges the ordinary life of our heroes. The situation kicks off a series of season-long dilemmas, but ultimately the show is about keeping the family intact despite the threats that come their way.

OPENING IMAGE (0-2): "It's nightfall," Guillermo, our everyman vampire familiar, says as he prepares for the triumphant awakening of his boss, Nandor. The coffin is stuck. It's a microcosm of the series. *What We Do in the Shadows* undercuts the Bram Stoker gothic tropes with the boring mundane reality of modern living and flawed personalities. Guillermo talks right to the camera in that mockumentary style we've seen in recent classics like *The Office*, *Parks & Rec*, and *Modern Family*. It's a different take on the *opening pitch*, using the documentary crew (and we, the viewers) as the show's window characters. Guillermo and the vampires will speak directly to us through a series of cutaway interviews giving us the *guided tour* of their home, their lives, the history of vampires, and the challenges of their very undead existence. During his on-camera, Guillermo dumps a bunch of exposition about his duties and his own hopes and frustrations. Guillermo's 10-year anniversary of being a familiar is coming up and he thinks his master is going to celebrate by turning him into a vampire. Guillermo has been dreaming of this day. The teaser sequence ends with Nandor, a tall, imposing vampire, rising supernaturally from his coffin as Guillermo watches in awe. Guillermo stares right down the barrel of the camera, giddy with excitement, and chimes, "Very cool, master. Very scary."

SET-UP (2-4): It's almost a breakfast scene without the bacon and eggs, as the just awakened vampire crew gathers and Nandor announces that they have received a letter. The Set-Up mixes in more direct interviews where characters introduce themselves, spill their backstories, and let us in on their feelings about their housemates. Nandor the Relentless is a bit Vlad the Impaler with a goofy side. Nadjla and Laszlo are a pair of married vampires. Nadjla is nostalgic for the old days of flings with humans and wild love affairs. Laszlo is a tad pretentious, tracing back to his noble roots. They're all past their prime and have settled into an ordinary, embarrassing Staten Island life where they get on each other's last nerve while longing for their glory days of murder and debauchery. They're as dysfunctional and frustrated as any family, as evidenced when Nandor scolds them for hygiene issues in the cells where they keep the prisoners they feast on. He complains about some "half-drunk" victims, i.e., they were half-drunk of their blood. If you're gonna drink, drink all your victim's blood. The vampires hiss at each other—it's their bloodsucker way of clapping back.

THEME STATED (4): In Nadjla's interview, she states the theme of the series: "The problems with living with other vampires are the vampires I have chosen to stay with." Learning to tolerate and appreciate their fellow undead housemates and their drab Staten Island existence provides both the core internal conflict and the lesson that needs to be learned throughout the show.

CATALYST (5): Finally, Nandor reads the letter. Baron Afanas, an ancient and revered vampire from the Old Country, is coming for a visit. He'll be there tomorrow!

DEBATE (5-10): This surprise guest is not good news. For one, the Baron thinks our heroes came to the new world and conquered. Instead, they're just bored and lame. The Baron is old school (really really really old school) and thinks vampires should rule the world. If he sees our Staten Islanders' docile living habits, he might kill or punish them. Their comfy life is now threatened. To make matters worse, both Nadjla and Laszlo confess they've had wild sexual affairs with the Baron, which may throw a wrench in their already iffy marriage. Nandor is worried about preparing a proper welcome for this highly lauded and royal monster. They need to send appropriate transportation to get the Baron's coffin from the boat to the house (they decide against the carriage pulled by black alligators and instead go practical with a dark van). Also, their crummy house isn't fit for such a lord of evil. They'll have to hurry to ready the place for the Baron's arrival.

BREAK INTO 2 (10): As usual, they task Guillermo with most of the grunt work, including finding virgin sacrifices for the Baron's welcome Blood Feast. They also decide to keep the big visitor a secret from their other annoying housemate, Colin, a vampire who preys on victims by boring them and absorbing their energy. He's despised and so annoying he even drains vampires of their energy. But Colin overhears them. He's sure to ruin everything! He always does. **(ACT OUT #1 - 10 min)**

B STORY (10): It's time to go to work. We follow Guillermo as he explains his typical chores: cleaning up dead bodies, boarding windows in the attic to block the sun for their new guest of honor, etc. Guillermo has dreamed of being a vampire ever since he was a little boy and saw Antonio Banderas in *Interview with a Vampire*. He can't wait to grow fangs of his own and he's convinced tonight is the night! The B Story reflects the overall theme of family dysfunction. Guillermo idolizes his vampire bosses, but they treat him horribly and constantly disappoint. The ups and downs of appreciating the people we're stuck with is what the series is all about.

FUN & GAMES (11-17): Guillermo hunts the virgins. It's not hard; he crashes a group of live-action role players (LARPers) and invites them to come over to the house later that evening. That night, we follow Nadjla and Laszlo and learn how vampiring in Staten Island isn't all it's cracked up to be. They're quickly made fun of for their old-fashioned clothes and told to "go back to your own country!" When Laszlo returns home, Nadjla hangs back. A small runner story is introduced when Nadjla stalks a human that she believes is a reincarnated long-lost lover. Meanwhile, Nandor and Guillermo shop in a craft store collecting items to decorate for the big arrival. Nandor considers getting glitter to glue on himself so he can sparkle like the vampires in the *Twilight* movies. He also buys lots of crape-eeee paper (aka crepe paper). We also see how Nandor disrespects Guillermo despite all the familiar's hard work. Back home, the group prepares a basement chamber for the Blood Feast. But it turns out Colin is already there. Instead of messing with Colin, they decide to go with the attic. They'll have to move the stairmaster, but it's better than dealing with Colin.

MIDPOINT (17-18): The group claims the Baron's coffin at the shadowy docks. His arrival is a *raising of the stakes*. Things just got real. Soon he will arise and everything will change. *Crossing with the B Story*, Guillermo muses that the Baron is probably there to see him turn into a vampire. Huge disappointment is on the horizon! **(ACT OUT #2 - 18 min)**

BAD GUYS CLOSE IN (18-21): Nadja should be preparing for the Blood Feast but instead is obsessing over her presumably reincarnated lover. She introduces herself to the man she's been stalking and has an awkward interaction. She groans and moans and hisses at him in primal lust. She wants to have an affair with him but is conflicted—after all, she's married. Finally, she turns into a bat and flies off, leaving the man very confused. Back at the house, the LARPers arrive and are a bit weirded out by all the questions about their virgin-ness and even witness an escaping victim crawling out from a cell. Guillermo explains it away as vampire LARPing stuff and ushers them into the house to prepare for the feast.

ALL IS LOST (21-24): The Staten Island vampires gather in the attic and stand around the Baron's coffin ready to greet him. The Baron awakens and he immediately attacks an old lady familiar, killing her. Nandor chuckles, while Guillermo goes pale wondering if he's next. The Baron speaks in an ancient language. He's actually terrifying, more Nosferatu than Bela Lugosi. The group immediately turns on each other, blaming each other for their junky house and their unbecoming lack of vampiric dominance. The Baron demands silence and scolds them for allowing centuries to pass without conquering the new world!

DARK NIGHT OF THE SOUL (24): The group realizes how screwed they are and laments the crepe paper and other preparations. The Baron says that the world of vampires is now focused on coming to the new world and he's there to lead the charge.

BREAK INTO 3 (25): Needing to slumber, the Baron returns to his coffin, proclaiming that when he arises they'll rule Staten Island. Nandor states the obvious: "If they don't conquer the new world, he's going to kill us... again." It's a Break into Series. Conquering Staten Island is a big task—and there are only a couple minutes left in this pilot. That new goal will kick into gear in Episode 2 and carry on throughout the season. **(ACT OUT #3 - 25 min)**

FINALE (25-27): We close with a wrap-up Finale that ties up some loose ends. As a consolation, the housemates decide to feast on the virgins. Unfortunately, Colin has gotten to them first and he's bored the LARPers to sleep. The vampires determine the LARPers now have no nutritional value. Back in Nandor's chamber, Nandor realizes Guillermo is glum. But Nandor hasn't forgotten the anniversary. Nandor gives him a reward for his years of service. Guillermo undoes his collar readying for the life-changing bite he's always dreamed about. Instead, Nandor presents him with a crafty glitter portrait of Guillermo as a vampire. Nandor tells his familiar he deserves the gift for his two years of service. Guillermo, disappointed beyond belief, corrects him, "10 years of service." Nandor closes his coffin, ending the conversation.

FINAL IMAGE (27): In the attic, one of the boards Guillermo attached to the windows to block out the sun falls off... a beam of light shines down on the Baron's coffin. It's not enough to kill the Baron, but it's enough to once again remind us that despite their vampire trappings, these Staten Island vampires are a bit bargain-bin.

Let the games begin!

EXERCISES

There are so many pilots of all types streaming everywhere, you can dive into a long and deep education about TV writing like you never could in the days before the streaming wars. Additionally, you can discover pilot scripts out there in glorious PDF. So google up some of your favorite pilot screenplays or take notes while watching!

1. Find the pilots of your favorite shows. Choose ones with comparable *Save the Cat!* genres, parallel platforms and audiences—ones that feel like cousins to your own show.

2. Do *Save the Cat!* breakdowns for as many pilots as you can. Pay particular attention to Act Outs, whiffs of change, and things like opening pitches and guided tours, along with how the writers use the show's theme to make the episode personal.

PART 3

BOARDS, OUTLINES & PITCHES, OH MY!

🐾 BUILDING THE BOARD

Walk into any writers' room in Hollywood and what do you see? Go ahead, I'll wait.

What, too lazy to find a real writers' room?

Sheesh. Slackers.

Okay, just google "TV Writers Room."

Do an image search.

Ignore those bleary-eyed weirdos. They're writers. Nobody cares about them.

Look at those walls.

See the boards? All the boards? Most are just the boring type with index cards tacked on 'em. But you'll see dry-erase ones, ones with countless Post-it notes, and some with fancy magnets.

The board has been a key component of *Save the Cat!* since Blake Snyder saved his very first British Shorthair.

Turns out, TV writers are board geeks. And for you, building the board is the next step to turn your *Save the Cat!* beat sheet into your awesome TV pilot.

Just the way the pros do it!

GO SHOPPING

You're going to need index cards. Find the 3"x5" kind that come in packs of 100 or more. I get them for a dollar at my grocery store. The multi-colored ones are fun if you want to track B Stories or character threads, but plain vanilla works too. Any kind of card that comes in large packs, so you have lots to rip up or throw into the bonfire like sacrifices to the story gods. Shameless plug: *Save the Cat!* offers amazing pre-printed story cards (see page 221 for examples).

You'll probably want to pick up a big corkboard too or if you're cheap like me, you can lay them out on the floor and stand over them like Godzilla writing his autobiography on teeny tiny billboards. It's important to see all of the cards spread out in front of you—a corkboard is aces for this. And it's what Vince Gilligan and Shonda Rhimes and Aaron Sorkin use. The story gods!

You can also go high-tech. You can use any software that can represent index cards or word processor tables or even spreadsheets. *Save the Cat!* has its own software that does a killer job and comes with a bunch of other *Cat!*-riffic functions.

But there's something special about the old-fashioned cards. You can carry them around and jot notes on the subway or while you're standing in line at the Starbucks or in between commercials (aka act breaks) of *The Walking Dead*. It can be productive to get away from those inescapable screens. A different look or feel can help activate dormant brain juices. There's something about the tactile nature of cards and thumbtacks and corkboards that gets us out of ruts and inspires. It's the same reason many writers like to hand-write first drafts of scripts or novels.

WHADDYA WRITE ON THESE CARDS?

Cards are small. This is a feature, not a bug. It forces you to summarize your beats and not get lost in the weeds of all the nitty-gritty details.

At the top, describe the location. Use screenwriting notation (INT. for Inside/Interior and EXT. for Outside/Exterior). Beneath that, put a quick blurb of what happens in the scene.

EXAMPLE:

```
EXT. HILL - DAY

Jack and Jill get in a fight at the top of the hill.
Jack pushes Jill down the hill.
```

Sometimes it's useful to add little bits of emotion on the card.

INT. LAW OFFICE - DAY

Saul realizes he left his cellphone at the crime scene.
Oh crap!!

If you find yourself describing multiple twists and turns on a single card or writing dialogue exchanges or sketching in every beat of a fight, you've crossed into The Screenplay Zone. Turn back! Quick! Save that for the scriptwriting phase!

Don't go beyond two or three sentences. One sentence is perfectly fine. Keeping your descriptions brief has another advantage. It makes the card more disposable. It's a lot easier to tear up a single goofy card with a few words on it than five pages of carefully written screenplay gold.

At this stage, the more willing you are to throw a card away the better. If the story math doesn't add up, something may need to get ripped up. It's where the term "killing your darlings" comes from. Sometimes just demolishing a single card is all you'll need for the floodgates to open. The more you can see your cards as expendable, the better your imagination will flow.

Let your cards flow. Use shorthand or just jot down: "THE BIG CHASE SCENE" or "THEY KISS!" or "THE MANDALORIAN CAPTURES HIS BOUNTY!"

Try to keep it fun and don't get too hung up on rules or wording or overthinking. If you get a wacky idea, put it in. You can always tear it up later.

Or put it in... the bucket.

THE BUCKET

In the corner of your board, away from your main story, carve out a special section called the bucket.

The bucket is where you dump any rando idea that doesn't fit yet. Any wild thought, gag, line of the dialogue, set design, story idea, or scene goes right into the bucket. (In the *Save the Cat!* software, it's called the Litter Box.)

On *The Simpsons*, the writers are constantly thinking about wild gags and instead of tossing them, they put them in the bucket. So if they come up with "BALLOON ANIMAL DOG," they'll eventually go through these cards and use the little gag showing Krusty petting the Balloon Animal Dog like Blofeld in a James Bond movie with that loud annoying skreeeech sound.

The bucket allows you to leave that creativity door open without getting derailed from what's important: breaking story. Take your zany jokes and clever gags, write them on a card, put them in the bucket, and move on.

The bucket can also be used as a recycle bin. Instead of ripping your cards up, pin them in the bucket. It'll make the hard act of dumping a scene feel less difficult.

BUILDING THE BEAST (Err... BOARD)

Before you break out the cards, make sure you have a rock-solid *Save the Cat!* beat sheet that you've vetted and crosschecked and shown to your online writing pals. If there's anything questionable in your beat sheet, don't go to the cards.

Think you're ready?

Can't think of any ways to improve your beat sheet?

Okay, then, break out the cards and thumbtacks and let's look at the 6 steps to building your own board.

STEP 1: START WITH THE SINGLE-SCENE BEATS

For each single-scene beat, create one card. Translating single scenes onto an individual card should be a no-brainer and a good way to get in the groove.

When you're done, you'll have cards for the following beats:
1. Opening Image
2. Theme Stated
3. Catalyst
4. Break into 2
5. Midpoint
6. All Is Lost
7. Break into 3
8. Final Image

Put a big shiny star on these cards or reserve these beats for one of those fancy-colored cards (if you have a multi-color pack). These cards are special. When you're stuck, they'll be the ones you'll move around. When you're completely blocked, they'll be the ones you tear to shreds to give yourself maximum freedom to reinvent your story.

Woo-hoo!

You already have eight cards done! If you're writing a 30-minute pilot... you're about halfway there!

STEP 2: BREAK OUT YOUR ACTS!

If you have an hour-long show, take four cards out and write Act 1, Act 2, Act 3, Act 4. These are the row headers for your board. While the far left of each row is your row headers, the far right card in each row is for your Act Outs. Even though I suggest you don't worry too much about commercial breaks, using a cliffhanger strategy is a great way to satisfy the most important thing in TV: *what happens next?* These Act Outs serve as a double-down on making sure your show hits this very important step.

Your first two cards are easy to place. Put the Opening Image card immediately after the Act 1 card. Put the Final Image card at the end of the last act row (leaving room for an act's worth of cards).

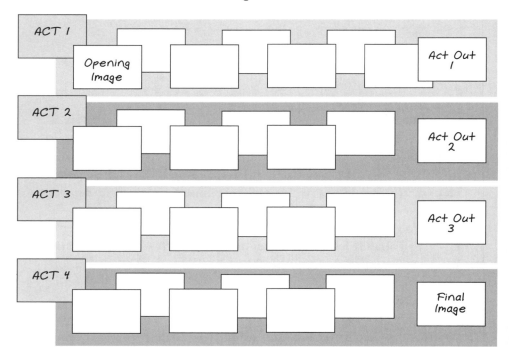

If you have a half-hour show, do the same but just write out three acts. It's a bit arbitrary. I've found 3 works better than 2. But there's wiggle room. For now, run with 3.

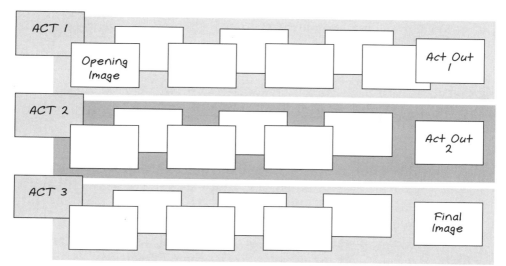

STEP 3: FIND YOUR ACT OUTS

With the cards you have left, find your Act Outs. They'll be in your single-scene beats. Because TV is an itinerary, you get *lots* of wiggle room here. Maybe too much. If you were being a purist, your board would look something like this:

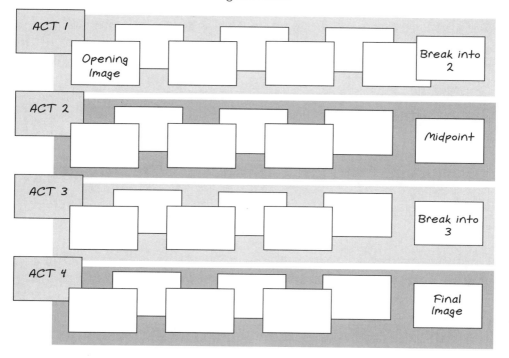

That's the most common set-up.

And it's great.

But TV is wonky.

There are other options. Wonkier ones.

First, don't think of your rows as acts at all, think of them as the stuff between the commercial breaks or sequences or mini-stories. As we've seen, some shows have long Set-Ups, some have super short Finales. Itineraries, remember!

At this point, throw caution to the wind and just block your show out for the best possible pacing and tension. The goal is hitting all your beats, but for each card you place, do what you can to keep the audience asking, "What will happen next?"

One way to do that is to hit those Act Outs hard! The single-scene beats are the best place to find your most awesome cliffhangers.

For an hour-long, you're probably looking at the Catalyst or the Break into 2 for the first Act Out. For the second Act Out, it's going to be your Break into 2 or your Midpoint. For your 3rd Act Out, it's going to be your All Is Lost or your Break into 3.

HOUR-LONG ACT OUT OPTIONS

Break into 2 for Act 1, and for Act 2 it could be your Midpoint or All Is Lost or even your Break into 3. In half-hours, it really depends on how you want to handle that Act 3. If you go with your Midpoint for an Act 2 Out, it means you'll have to squeeze all the other beats into the Act 3 sequence. If you go with Break into 3, you'll have some real estate to do a lengthy (for a half-hour, at least) Act 3 row. You, the showrunner of your own pilot, choose where you spend the time in your story for maximum impact.

HALF-HOUR-LONG ACT OUT OPTIONS

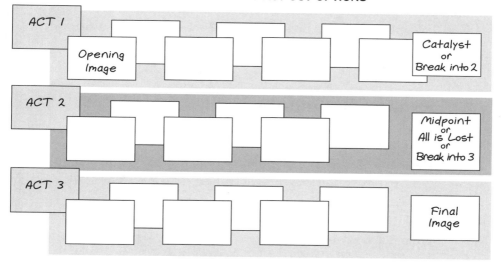

Try to pick the best cliffhanger or *Duh-duh-duhhhh* moments for your Act Outs.

They might be plot twists or huge character gut punches.

Usually, these jump out at you right away.

Again, you'll find the Act Outs in the single-scene beats. And remember: pick the ones that will make your audience ask... *What happens next?*

STEP 4: THE OTHER CARDS

Remember, there's a lot of wiggle room and wonkiness here, but it's better to be strict than to be too loose. So assuming an hour-long pilot script is 50-60 pages and the average beat is around 2 minutes, let's make an educated guess that you'll need 26 total cards for your hour-long pilot. Pilots tend to run a little long in the writing stage; it's very normal to have a 40-minute story run 50-ish pages in pilot land (some even spill to 60 or 65; they'll get edited down in development and possibly in post-production).

Transcribe your multi-scene beats to whatever cards are left over. Remember: multi-scene beats likely mean multiple cards. One Fun & Games section or Bad Guy Close In section will translate to several cards for the Board.

Here's some guidance for the number of cards per multi-scene beat.

OF CARDS FOR AN HOUR-LONG

Single-Scene Cards: 7

Set-Up + Theme Stated: 2-5 cards

Debate: 1-4 cards

B Story (and other sub threads) + Fun & Games: 3-6 cards

Bad Guys Close In: 3-6 cards

Dark Night of the Soul: 1-4 cards

Finale: 2-6 cards

Total Cards: 22-32 (26 on average)

Again, it's TV, so there's wiggle room. It's an itinerary. You get to decide what section gets an extra card or two. Just don't go too far, and try to land about 26 cards total.

OF CARDS FOR A HALF-HOUR-LONG

Single-Scene Cards: 7

Set-Up + Theme Stated: 1-2 cards

Debate: 1-2 cards

B Story + Fun & Games: 1-3 cards

Bad Guys Close In: 1-2 cards

Dark Night of the Soul: 1-2 cards

Finale: 1-3 cards

Total Cards: 12-17 cards (14 on average)

In the half-hour show, almost half your cards are already taken up by single-scene beats. This is why a lot of half-hours might combine beats into one scene—they tell stories at a hyper-fast pace. It wouldn't be out of the question to have an Opening Image and a Set-Up and a Catalyst all in the same scene. You might get one Fun & Games scene total. Things move really fast.

STEP 5: FILL OUT THOSE ACT ROWS

As a guideline for our hour-longs, here is a recommended card breakdown :

HOUR-LONG CARDS PER ACT

ACT 1: 6-10 cards

ACT 2: 5-8 cards

ACT 3: 5-8 cards

ACT 4: 5-8 cards

Why does Act 1 get extra cards? For starters, if you have a cold open or a teaser, I'm lumping it into Act 1. (You could separate teaser and tags into their own separate rows if you choose.) Teaser aside, first acts are almost always the longest acts in TV. This is both practical and good business. On the practical side, it gives you time for character and world set-up, and to fire up the plot and hit a good strong first Act Out that has the audience caring about your hero... and dying to know what happens next. Having them hooked by the end of that first act is mission-critical to your pilot. You may sell an agent or producer on that alone!

On the business side, it gives you extra time to hook the audience, so they don't give up on the show when they get to the commercials, which hit them faster and more furious toward the end of the episode. It's easy to punt on a show in the middle of the Set-Up, much harder after you stuck through 30 minutes of plot twists and want to know who the killer is or if the hero will win the day.

Here's the way a Board might fill out:

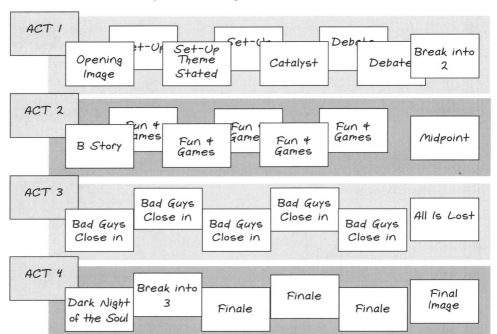

Note all those Fun & Games and Bad Guys Close In beats could be blended with B Story beats for this episode. That gives room for 1-2 cards in each section.

Our half-hour will have around 14 cards.

HALF-HOUR-LONG CARDS PER ACT
ACT 1: 4-8 cards
ACT 2: 3-6 cards
ACT 3: 3-6 cards

The three-act split gives you a few options. Here are a couple of samples of where your beats might land.

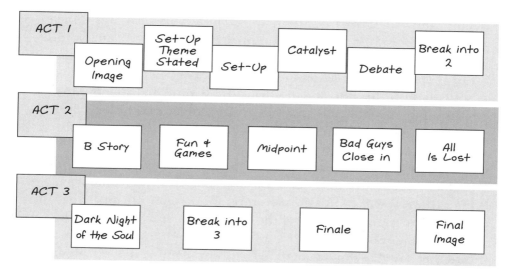

Or one with a Break into 3 row 2 Act Out:

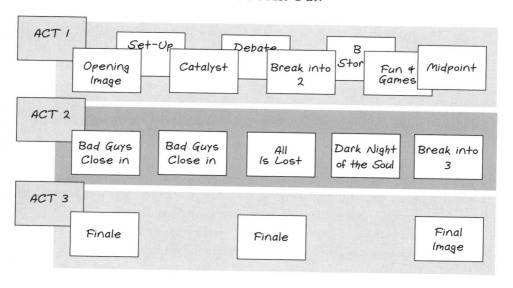

STEP 6: MIX, MATCH, COLLAPSE

Step back and look at your Board.

If you have too many cards in one row, do some reshuffling. Slide your Act Outs around or break out a fresh card and come up with a new cliffhanger or emotional gut punch to try and keep things roughly balanced. Make a point to hit those Act Outs with strong *Duh-Duh-Duhhhh* moments. These water-cooler moments need room to breathe and resonate. If all your eyeball-popping beats are bunched together, you run the risk of having long dull stretches that give the viewer a chance to flip over to *The Bachelorette*. Oh, the horror!

If you have too many cards, it's time to collapse. Usually, the problem lies in the multi-scene cards (especially if you come from the writing worlds of novels or features, where Fun & Games, Bad Guys Close In, and Finales get the bulk of your story). Collapsing scenes means taking multiple cards and reimagining them as one card that does the work of both. This is why opening pitches are so prevalent. Instead of spending three cards on Set-Up, an opening pitch might get away with all that work with just one card. Then you have two extra cards to give to the Fun & Games or the Bad Guys Close In or the Finale!

If you have too few cards—less than 20 in your hour-long or less than 10 in your half-hour show—you'll end up with longer and slower-paced scenes. If you have too many beats in general—over 16 for a half-hour or over 32 for an hour-long—either you'll have a rapidly paced story with a bunch of 1-minute scenes or you'll need to condense. Each card is around two pages of teleplay (or 2 minutes of run time). New writers struggle to execute succinct scenes in three pages or less, let alone two. So be cautious not to cheat too much in the name of hyper-fast pacing or undisciplined beat sheeting. Pay attention to how many cards you've thumbtacked up on your board; review and condense or expand as needed.

Don't kick your problems to the script phase either. Be strict on yourself now. It's better to solve these problems in the cards. It's much harder when you have an 85-page script that needs to be cut down under 65 pages. Keep your cards around that 24-28 sweet spot in your hour-long and 12-16 cards in your half-hour stories. Wrestle your board into shape. Make tough decisions. Do it now, before you get to script. Fill up that bucket!

BONUS STEP: CONFLICT AND EMOTIONAL CHANGES

There are two more things to add to each of your cards. In the lower left-hand corner put a line for the following:

```
THE BIG SCENE!

+/-

<>
```

The **<>** is the spot for the **conflict** of the scene. Remembering our Story DNA, conflict results from a hero trying to achieve a goal with an obstacle in the way. That's what you put in this spot: Scene Hero, Goal, Obstacle!

Scenes are mini-stories where there's always something at stake.

Important note: the hero's goal or obstacle in a scene or card is not necessarily the same as the pilot Story DNA you originally set (though it very well might be). It's often a sub-goal. Additionally, there might be B Story scenes or non-POV scenes where the hero of the scene is not the hero of the movie. These scenes will have their own heroes with their own goals.

Raiders of the Lost Ark has the following Story DNA:

HERO: Indiana Jones — swashbuckling archeologist

GOAL: Get the Ark of the Covenant!

OBSTACLE: The mystery of the Ark's whereabouts + Nazis who are also searching for it

STAKES: The Ark can be used to win WW2.

In one of the first scenes on Indy's quest, he goes to Marion

Ravenwood's bar and tries to get the headpiece that will lead him to the Lost Ark of the Covenant. In that scene, acquiring the headpiece is Indy's goal and he needs to overcome a huge obstacle: his rocky personal history with Marion and her long-simmering hurt and anger toward him. She might be the hardest person in the world to convince.

The Scene DNA might be:

HERO: Indiana Jones

GOAL: Get the headpiece from Marion.

OBSTACLE: Marion doesn't want to help him.

STAKES: He needs it to find the Ark of the Covenant.

It's a sub-goal of the higher-level Story DNA, and the tactics he'll take to work around the obstacle are obviously different than those he'll take later with the evil Nazis!

But where are the stakes?

The +/- on the index cards represents the **emotional change** in the scene. All scenes must have an emotional change. In every scene, something is at stake.

Scenes that don't change something are cuttable!

Think about it. If nothing changes, why can't we just skip that part?

If I told you that a certain chapter in a book had zero impact on the story, what's the point? Skip it. Or cut it.

These are typically beats of pure exposition.

Boooooring.

Instead, find a place to blend exposition into moments that propel your story forward. There's an old saying in sitcoms, "Put your exposition into jokes!" You need to find a way to fold your exposition into scenes that have plot, that have change.

Many writers like to whine (I'm the whiniest writer ever): These non-emotional change scenes are vital for "character development" or "introducing someone."

Stop. Don't. I've been there. I've created fun, carefully crafted character development scenes that were critical to your hero's rooting resume and helping the audience get on board with the flaws and needs.

They're the first scenes the powers-that-be cut after test screenings or when they need to get their 50-minute edit to 44.

Why those scenes? Because they can.

You can cut exposition and character development and still have a functioning story. It'll be less deep, more confusing, less good... but it'll work.

Your job as a TV writer is to make every scene uncuttable!

One way to ensure change is to make sure you have established it at the card stage.

Next to that +/-, pencil what's at stake in the scene emotionally.

Let's look at a card (using the *Save the Cat!* pre-printed story cards).

INT. BAR - NIGHT

Indiana Jones goes to get the headpiece from Marion, but she just wants to talk about the past and kicks him out of her bar.

+ / –   Emotional start (Hopeful he can get the headpiece!)
Emotional End (Doubtful she'll ever give it to him)

> <   Scene Hero (Indiana Jones) Goal (Get the headpiece from Marion) Obstacle (Marion hates him)

Here are some cards I made for the pilot of *Black-ish*:

INT. CAR - DAY

Despite doubts of not "keeping it real." Dre is intent on maintaining a positive attitude on the day of his big promotion... but as he drives his son to school, Andre Jr. tells him he's playing field hockey instead of basketball.

+ / - Emotional start (Optimistic about his day/life)
       Emotional End (Pessimistic about his day/life)

> < Scene Hero (Dre) Goal (Stay positive)
       Obstacle (His son's plans)

INT. MARKETING OFFICE - DAY

Dre endures the usual tone-deaf co-workers at work... and hears that the boss is making a big announcement today. (Yep! He's getting promoted!)

+ / - Emotional start (Negative about his day)
       Emotional End (Yes! He's getting promoted)

> < Scene Hero (Dre) Goal (Regain his positivity)
       Obstacle (Tone-deaf co-workers)

> INT. CONFERENCE ROOM - DAY
>
> Dre goes to the meeting to hear about his promotion and once again endures the co-workers... then gets the bad news: he's being promoted to SVP of the Urban Devision. Ruh-Roh! This isn't good.
>
> +/− Emotional start (Excited to get promoted)
> Emotional End (The rug pulled out from under him)
> > < Scene Hero (Dre) Goal (Get promoted)
> Obstacle (The lack of respect he gets at work)

If you don't have conflict or emotional change or a hero, FIND THEM. Make it work. Be strict now. It might change your story a bit. It might even force you to move some cards around. So be it! Everything's disposable. Change means improvement.

FINALIZING YOUR BOARD

The most important thing is balance. You don't want to end up with one row that has eight cards and another with two. The beauty of the board is that you'll be able to see at a glance if one of your rows is running too long or too short.

You should ultimately be able to read through your board without making changes or getting that icky feeling that it's not working. If something's off, get in there, tear up cards, change Act Outs, cut out sub-threads.

Do the work. They're only index cards.

PITCH IT OUT

Now it's time to read the cards out loud. If you have a friend you can call, try using the cards to pitch the story. It's a great way to see if you have a real story or just a jumble of ideas. Make sure all the scenes have cause and effect. Is the character making logical and active choices along the way? Is there enough conflict? Is it fun?

IF ALL ELSE FAILS... GO BACK TO THE BEAT SHEET

If for some reason things just don't work... or you get a bit stuck, take what you've got back into the *Save the Cat!* beat sheet. Sometimes your board decisions will reveal new issues or new paths to take that pull the rug out from all your rock-solid planning. Sometimes it totally undercuts your Story DNA. It's okay. You're making things better. Writing is rewriting. Thinking is good. So is revision. It's how you get to awesomeness.

EXERCISES

- Start building your board. (Write one card for each single-scene beat.) They're the easiest.

- Next dive into the multi-scene beats. Each of the beats may have more than one card.

- Organize your cards into rows based on your TV acts.

- Designate a space on your board for your bucket.

- Find strong Act Outs to end each of your acts and place those cards on your board.

- Finish your board so you can see all the cards, then dig in and make sure they work.

- Consult your bucket. Anything worth saving?

- Once all your cards are on the board, fill in conflicts (< >) and emotional changes (+/-) on each card.

- Now, call up a buddy and walk them through your story.

CHECK YOURSELF

- Are you using too many cards? Limit yourself to at most 18 for your half-hour and 30 for your hour-long. Be strict! Collapse or remove scenes that aren't needed.

- Are your act rows generally balanced? No row should vary by more than two or three cards. The first act is usually the longer one.

- Does each card seemingly lead to the next?

- Are your Act Outs strong cliffhangers or emotional character moments?

- Do you have conflicts (< >) for each card?

- Do you have emotional turns (+ /-) for each card?

🐾 OWNING THE OUTLINE

Many writers go right from the board to scripting. The board gets you 90% there. Typically in TV there's one more step: the outline.

The outline is a semi-standardized document that you'll probably be writing when you get your first job on a big TV show. It bridges the gap between writers' room work and the actual script. On in-production shows, it's normally the first "for review" document that gets sent to the network or streaming channel bigwigs.

This last extra step forces you to stop painting your story in high-level brushstrokes and start laying out how scenes will actually play.

For example, instead of saying:

"Jerry and Elaine argue."

You'll describe what we see:

"Jerry accuses Elaine of stealing his toothbrush. Toothbrush thief! Elaine can't take it. She squeezes all his toothpaste out onto the floor and storms out. Jerry leans down to clean up the mess and sees his toothbrush under the sofa."

Now's the time to put a little voice in it, add a little oomph, and describe the way the actual scenes will unspool. TV outlines resemble scripts without dialogue, laying out all the scene headings and describing the action. You can throw a line or two of dialogue in the action paragraphs in quotes or italics, but don't use screenplay dialogue format. And don't attempt to dig into all the detail of a script or use all the "white space" that screenplay format might use.

It's not a script.

It's script-ish.

An outline for an hour-long show runs about 12-15 pages. Anything over 18 is too long. Anything under 5 pages is a bit short. Outlines typically run 1-2 pages per every 5 pages of script. But it's your call; it's your process. You're writing on spec here. Be the showrunner of yourself. You do you.

Some writers use outlines like first drafts, putting them into their screenwriting software and quickly visualizing their script. They'll add detail and white space and dialogue later. In these cases, the outline is actually the first cut of a script that will be rewritten and expanded into the final screenplay. Other writers start with the blank page and use the outline as a reference.

Make the outline detailed enough so that you can send it to your screenwriting pals for feedback but not so detailed that people can't read it over their lunch break.

Here's an example I worked up using the *Stranger Things'* pilot (it's not the real outline, it's just a quick reverse-engineered model) to give you an idea of level-of-detail and format:

EXT. HAWKINS LAB - NIGHT

In the dark woods, a large industrial building looms like a forgotten fortress.

SUPERIMPOSE: "HAWKINS NATIONAL LABORATORY"

INT. LAB - CORRIDOR - NIGHT

We creep toward a large steel door. Lights
ominously flicker.

BOOM! The door bursts open. A SCIENTIST rush-
es out. Fleeing for his life. He races for
the elevator. Smashes the button. A sound
comes from above. A growl. His eyes widen.
And just as he's about to get away - WHOOSH!
He's sucked into the ceiling. Screaming.
Flailing. Kicking. The elevator doors shut.

EXT. SUBURBS - NIGHT

Sprinklers, bikes in driveways. It's the 1980s
and this is the stuff of *E.T.* and *Explorers*.

INT. BASEMENT - NIGHT

Four 12-year-olds sit around a table playing a game of *Dungeons & Dragons*. MIKE, LUCAS, DUSTIN, WILL. Mike, the Dungeon Master, describes a new monster - reminiscent of what we just saw in the lab. The Demogorgon. Zoinks! This is one scary beast. The boys choose to have their game characters run away. But Will decides to divert the creature with a fireball. Mike rolls a twenty-sider. The critical roll slides off the table and as the boys rush to find the die —

The basement door swings open spilling a shaft of light down the steps. It's MIKE'S MOM. She breaks up the game. It's a school night and she kicks the boys out of the house.

INT. KITCHEN - NIGHT

They shuffle off. Dustin asks if anyone wants the leftover pizza. When no one claims it, he takes it upstairs.

INT. BEDROOM - NIGHT

Dustin peeks in a room where Mike's sister, NANCY(16), is on the phone with her boyfriend STEVE. He offers her the pizza but she just rolls her eyes and shuts the door. Denied!

EXT. MIKE'S HOUSE - NIGHT

The kids climb onto their bikes to head home. Will approaches Mike and tells him — "It was a seven...the Demorgorgon got me." Will pedals off into the dark night.

```
EXT. SUBURBAN STREETS - NIGHT

The boys decide to race home. Winner gets a
comicbook. Will toasts Dustin. Finds himself
way in front of the rest. He pedals ahead
onto a forest road.

EXT. FOREST ROAD - NIGHT

Will bikes alone. It's dark and desolate. He
cruises past a large steel fence. A sign on
it says: "HAWKINS NATIONAL LABORATORY — NO
TRESPASSING."

Suddenly, his bike headlight flickers. He
peers ahead and looming over him is a LARGE
OMINOUS FIGURE.

At the sight of it, he veers out of control
and falls off the road.
```

The above sample shorthands about 10 pages of actual screen-play—all in about two pages. You could boost the action a bit, but try not to mix in too much dialogue. A couple lines here and there are great for flavor and to get you in the rhythm of the story, but hold back from writing much more. Again, force yourself to format your dialogue like prose instead of screenplay dialogue to help keep you from diving into full-blown conversations. There will be time for that later—the outline is about high-level story mechanics, not scene execution.

EXERCISE

- Using your board as a reference, open your favorite screen-writing software or word processor, and begin to write your outline.

- Once done, get feedback from friends. Ask them if any parts were confusing or unclear.

- Adjust your outline based on feedback.

CHECK YOURSELF

- Does your outline translate to roughly 1-2 pages per every 5 estimated final script pages? Does it total 12-15 pages for an hour-long? 6-8 for a half-hour?

- Does the story translate into playable scenes that will be scriptable?

- Is the potential for the series obvious from your pilot outline?

- Is the world clear?

- Do the scenes make the reader ask, "What happens next?"

🐾 PERFECTING YOUR PITCH

During the summer and early fall, studios and producers bring writers in to hear verbal pitches on shows. This is called Pitch Season (clever, huh?)! The chosen few get developed and some of those will get made into pilots during... you guessed it... Pilot Season!

The reality is that this is the old-school model. In the modern world of Netflix, Disney+, and HBO Max, TV shows are bought and sold every day.

Live every day it's Pitch Season!

One thing that hasn't changed is that studios and producers like the malleability of pitches because they offer obvious opportunities for collaboration. You're pitching a medical drama... suddenly it becomes a lawyer show. You have a show with a strong teenage male lead... boom! It's a talking dog show for AppleTV. Script submissions are a bit colder: you send an email, they read, they respond with a yes or usually a no. There's no wiggle room. It's just "Here's the thing, you in?"

Pitches are conversations and invitations to play. They invite the buyers in to join the fun.

That said, until you've proven yourself in some epic way (selling a script, getting staffed, winning an Oscar®), it's best to keep churning out those pilot scripts. Early in your writing journey, scripts are still the best way to get your work into the right hands and prove you've got chops. Once you land an agent or a manager or just so happen to hit a producer or studio exec at the right time with the right project, you're gonna need to pitch your awesome shows.

THE (NOT SO) TOP-SECRET PITCH FORMAT TEMPLATE

Years ago, when I was prepping my first TV pitch, my manager opened up the secret vault hidden behind the ceiling-high stack of printed scripts. There he shared with me the company's super-secret "Pitch Format Template."

Shhhh. Don't tell anyone.

I was in the club.

Trade secrets!

Huzzah!

A few years later, I was generating another pitch with a totally different producer and they sent me their own eyes-only "pitch format template."

"Shhhh. Don't share this," they said as I botched the secret handshake.

After I lost that one to the ravages of hard drives past, I googled it and found pretty much the exact same thing everywhere. I even found old documents where the big studios had their own "preferred format docs" they'd send out.

I'm gonna tell all. So much for the secret.

There's more good news. You've been Mr. Miyagi-ed. If you've been following along and doing the exercises at the end of each of the preceding chapters, you've already got everything you need to work up your own breezy quick-to-read memo or conversational verbal pitch.

So get ready to "wax the car" and "paint the fence."

A PITCH DOCUMENT IS NOT A SHOW BIBLE

A **show bible** is a document that describes world, character, backstory, tone, and more that can be used as a reference for new writers, producers, directors, executives, cast, etc. Show bibles can be anywhere from 20 pages to 100.

That's not a pitch document.

The **pitch document** is "bible-lite." It contains a lot of the same information as the show bible, but its intended audience is completely different. Show bibles are for people working on in-production shows to use as a reference when they have questions; the pitch is for high-level execs to read over lunch.

The pitch document has just enough information for someone to get the gist of what they might be buying, but not such a deep dive that they know the favorite peanut butter of the lead character (Jiffy, btw, it's always Jiffy).

THE TELEVISION PITCH TEMPLATE

A pitch document should generally be 5-10 pages long. I usually aim for 8 pages. Don't go over 10.

There should be 7 sections to your pitch. And here they are:

SECTION 1 – WHY YOU? or HOW YOU THOUGHT OF THIS IDEA (1/2 - 1 page)

Get personal. Describe why your original idea and you are a perfect match. This is that spot where you drop your heartfelt history—why you love this world, why the story's broad themes or characters speak uniquely to you. One way to start is to simply say "The reason I thought of this story is because..." It might be a personal story. It might be a documentary you watched or a blog you read or a job you worked at. It might be a story about how a similar piece of entertainment changed your life. Whatever specific thing roped you in is likely going to hook someone else. Get personal and get specific. In TV, the execution of the idea is as important as the idea itself. It's your idea and you are that execution. Tell them why.

Keep it short. Keep it in your voice. Then bring this section home with some natural transition into...

SECTION 2 – WHAT'S THE BIG IDEA? (1- 2 pages)

Stating your logline and format and genre upfront is a bit of a spoiler, but it will give your buyers a framework. It also provides a safety net. One of the worst things that can happen during your pitch is that you spend 10 minutes pitching your carefully crafted hour-long drama and they think you're pitching a half-hour comedy. But if you state all the basics early on—when your audience is most attentive!—your pitches can frame the rest of your show idea and self-correct along the way. And, best of all, if your pitch goes completely off the rails, they know the most important stuff. Maybe that'll be enough.

Your logline should have the following elements: world, main character (or characters), franchise type (stated in your own organic language), genre, show format.

The Good Place is a half-hour single-cam comedy about a morally questionable girl who finds herself in a perfect afterlife designed for only "the good people," but soon realizes she's there by mistake and decides to become a good person to earn a legitimate spot—all the while keeping the error under wraps.

The Mandalorian is an hour-long sci-fi action drama about a bounty hunter who lives by a strict moral code in a seedy corner of the *Star Wars* universe, and faces a crisis of conscience after not killing one of his marks. He struggles to continue his bounty-hunting ways while protecting the creature he was meant to kill.

It's similar to the story logline we discussed in our Story DNA chapter. If your Season 1 or series is heavily serialized, you might even be able to lean heavily into that model and use the first season's Story DNA as a basis for your one-liner. But remember a series is not necessarily a story, so the pilot might not have all the elements of your series' Story DNA. The goal of a series' logline is to get your audience to see the potential of the series to generate weekly Story DNA. Describe enough of your world + franchise type + character(s) so the potential for recurring Hero/Goal/Obstacle/Stakes is apparent.

SECTION 2A (OPTIONAL) – THE TONE (1/2 page)

Tone is hard to describe. Do your best to put it in words, like "broad comedy" or "gritty drama" or "dramedy with laughs and tears." I find it most effective to break out comparables in this section of the pitch: "It's like *Guardians of the Galaxy*. Laugh out loud humor, real stakes, but characters that pull at the heart too."

Is the show gritty and real or heightened and fun? Is it Christopher Nolan's *Batman* or the CW's *The Flash*?

When I pitch, I don't usually give the tone its own section. I like to mix the tone in with the high-level pitch (that opening logline section) or sometimes squeeze it into the description of the world when rattling off your franchise type. I find if the exec understands the tone as I trot out characters and season trajectory, that tone can help color the details of their mental picture.

But it's important to be clear, and it's not the worst idea to give tone its own section of the pitch, especially if you have a quirky story or one where the tone is not obvious from the subject matter.

SECTION 3 – THE SYNOPSIS (THE WORLD & FRANCHISE TYPE) (1-2 pages)

Describe what makes your world so fresh and interesting. Hint at the depth and the complexity and how your world will intrigue an audience and provide a perfect backdrop for storytelling. If you're pitching a world-building story, this is what you've been waiting for. If you're pitching a relationship-first story like *This Is Us* or Netflix's *Love*, you may want to hint at the backdrop but save your real firepower for the character section (coming up next!).

This section is also where you want to sneak in the franchise type by communicating how it creates conflict. The franchise type is the one-two punch of your show and demonstrates how your interesting, fresh world can be adapted into a weekly television powerhouse. It's a window into turning a world into a story machine.

SECTION 4 – THEMES & WHY NOW (1/2-1 page)

Describe what your series is *really* about. What are the deeper themes it explores and why is it relevant at this moment, right now, in human history?

Keep this brief. It's the executive summary. There'll be plenty of time to go into details and depth in the next few sections.

SECTION 5 – THE CHARACTERS (1-3 pages)

Outline your top 5-10 characters in order of importance and describe each in 1-3 quick paragraphs. Specify what makes them unique and interesting, how they're relatable (high-level rooting resume material), what their needs and their wants and their flaws are, so we understand the internal struggle they'll be facing throughout the show. After that, detail their key relationships: who are their friends, love interests, rivals, confidants, etc. Summarize their overall season arc as it relates to their flaws and interpersonal relationships.

Characters can get a little dry without context. Do your best to frame these sections by telling stories. Give each character a pithy season arc synopsis that allows you to tie in the various attributes you need. Describe where your characters start, where they're going, and all the struggles they'll face in between. Keep in mind that the next sections of the pitch are all about the pilot and the Season 1 story, so be brief here, don't be redundant or go overboard so that the next section (Section 6) isn't needed.

Stay away from casting suggestions in your document, but be ready with them. Sometimes it's the first question that comes up and dropping the perfect choices can go a long way of showing you have your finger on the pulse of your story... and the business.

SECTION 6 – THE PILOT (1-2 pages)

Give the broad strokes of your pilot.

BROAD. STROKES.

This is not where you drop an entire *Save the Cat!* beat sheet. Give the Set-Up and Catalyst and hit the Midpoint and some of the big turns. Leave everything loose on specific details. Relate the pilot's story as if you were telling a friend what happened on a show they missed the night before. Give 'em all the cool stuff. The exciting stuff. The stuff that makes them wanna see your show.

Additionally, because you've pitched characters, you can skimp on anything you've already laid out, sticking to the plot a little more in this section... but not entirely. The execs will want to see that you can visualize character psychology and backstory. Keep this short. 1-2 pages. This is just the pilot; there's still a whole season to pitch.

SECTION 7 – SEASON 1 AND BEYOND (1-2 pages)

In even broader strokes, discuss where the season will go. This is where your pillar beats come into play. A quick overview of those beats is exactly what you need. Paint a picture of the overall trajectory. Mix in what an average show will look like. If your story is more episodic, discuss what some episodes might be and how they fit into the big picture, giving enough information so your audience can project the show in its entirety without hearing a rundown of several episodes.

You may want to touch on where future seasons can go, but keep it high-level and loose. A couple of sentences or short paragraphs is all you need. Don't break out your *Save the Cat!* beat sheet for Season 2. Let's get Season 1 up and running before we go crazy.

MAKE THE TEMPLATE YOURS

There are no rules!

While the template works great, feel free to shuffle parts around. For example, if you write up a big character section, maybe you can go light on some of the character-specific info in your pilot's Set-Up and move quickly to the plot. Or if you create a big world-building data dump, you won't need to describe the nooks and crannies of your world when you lay out your Season 1 outline. Make the template work for your series while being cautious to avoid redundancy.

Sometimes I open my pitch with the pilot or Season 1 synopsis and, since all the main characters are introduced there, I pepper the character section with quick logline style breakdowns of each of my heroes—focusing on their internal conflicts or rooting-resume stuff that might be beyond the scope of the other parts of the template.

Do what makes sense.

Do what flows

Do what's right for your pitch.

THE TEMPLATE IS NOT AN IRS FORM

There are a bunch of situations where you could be asked to submit a **paper pitch**. You could be a new writer submitting to an agent or a producer, you could be dropping a paper pitch to a producer after doing a verbal, you could be developing something with a producer. Whatever the situation, less is usually more. Do enough to put your show's best foot forward and sell that show!

Do whatever it takes!

In the words of Alec Baldwin in *Glengarry Glen Ross*: "Coffee's for closers! And ABC, always be closing."

Every document you submit is an opportunity to further a relationship, win a job, sell a script, and sell yourself. Most writers hate spending time on outlines and pitches and non-script stuff—if you can be the one that rocks it, you might have a leg-up on all those other complainers!

Make a pitch that's you on a plate. Make it interesting, fast, and fun. Use it as an opportunity to demonstrate all the things that make you a unique writer.

JUST TELL THE STORY

Translate your beat sheets and story engines into a pitch that doesn't show its foundational elements. Don't specifically say your show is a Trapped Together. Instead, describe the story engine in simple terms: the hero is trapped in a DMV every day with an oddball cast of characters and even odder customers, blah, blah, blah. Don't just drop your *Save the Cat!* beat sheet in the pilot or season breakdown section, remove all of your beat sheet headings (FUN & GAMES, ALL IS LOST and BREAK INTO 2 or 3) and massage your beat sheet into pithy fun-to-read prose. Put it in words your best friend and Grandma can ride with.

VERBAL PITCHES

TV writers rarely do paper pitches, i.e., submit a pitch document for review and evaluation. In fact, the above template was originally created as a guide for verbal pitches, not written ones. Generally, the verbal pitch should be about 15-20 minutes. Again, there are no rules. Mine tend to go 25-30, and while I've never been told that I'm going too long, I am. I had one recently that was 35 minutes and right as I rolled into the big finale, the execs had to interrupt to take a call (ugh!). There are practical reasons for keeping these things under 30 minutes. Execs keep their schedules tight. If you have a 45-minute pitch and there's a lot of pre-pitch chatter, you might run against some hard deadline. Writer, beware!

It's also hard to hold someone's attention with a verbal pitch for more than 25 minutes.

If you're pitching a cable series and you need to discuss interconnected storylines or possibly multiple seasons, it's okay if the pitch is a little longer, but try to never exceed 25-30 minutes of just you talking about the show.

Creating a pitch is real work. First, you have to do all the drudgery of a paper pitch: figure out your world and story engine, demonstrate why you're the best writer for it, break your season and pilot, etc, etc. Once you have everything written down, you still have to learn how to say the pitch and memorize it.

PRACTICING YOUR PITCH

I usually start by reading from the page. My first several attempts involve saying the pitch out loud and fixing the rough spots. The act of speaking aloud will force you to wordsmith and even inspire you to come up with new ideas, or at least new ways to present.

Once I have the basics down, I practice when I'm driving. My commutes are usually 25-40 minutes, which gives me time to say my entire pitch to my steering wheel 2-3 times a day. I find that if you do something else (driving, playing golf, MMA, whatever) while rehearsing, it takes you out of overthinking it and getting stuck or throwing in lots of "ummms" and "uhhhhs."

You don't want it to sound memorized. I try not to word-smith it to the point I'm doing it verbatim. In fact, sometimes I'll just rehearse the short form of the beats (the prompts and the transitions), so I'm remembering the order of things and the important topics. It's a bit like stand-up comedy; you go up there with an ordered list of the topics and then you riff.

Usually, after my steering wheel has heard my pitch a few times, I pitch over the phone to bored friends or pitch it out to my very bored wife or very attentive dog (he loves the treats).

Lately, I've been scheduling Zoom calls with writer friends a couple of days before my actual pitch. It's not a huge ask for friends—much easier than giving notes on a script—so they're usually game. Having a live body listening changes things up, so be ready for that. It's a great way to ease some nerves (pitching to friends is almost as nerve-wrackingly awkward as the real deal) and friends can help find those blind spots you haven't noticed.

IT'S A CONVERSATION

The more you can engage your audience in a back and forth—where they're adding to the story and making conclusions about the series potential—the better.

You have to do your homework, break your story, and practice your beats, but strive to have a conversation, not give a presentation. Show the buyers you're someone who is collaborative and enthusiastic, and you'll be way ahead of the game.

DELIVERING YOUR PITCH

If you're pitching to multiple studios or people, you'll get better as you go. If there's any flexibility in schedule, it's smart to save the "best bets" for later. Get your "unlikely buyers" out of the way first. Use them for practice. I'll go out to LA on a Tuesday and stink it up for the first couple of days and then by Friday I'll finally be ready to go! And then it ends...

(In reality, it never goes as it seems. The "unlikely buyers" tend to be the ones who surprise me with their interest, so ya never know.)

Remember, there are no rules.

And that can be a good thing.

You're the expert on your pitch. Most people just go the all-verbal route, pure and simple. Others go in with look-books or slideshows or sizzle reels or concept art. Keep in mind that these Hollywood folks are used to seeing the coolest of the cool in art and sizzle reels and presentations. Use visual aids if they help clarify, but know they probably won't "dazzle." In fact, they may have the opposite effect. If your illustration isn't as good as the one J.J. Abrams and the Russo Brothers just showed them, you may get unfairly judged. I tend to keep my pitches purely verbal when I'm face to face, but if it's a Zoom pitch I'll throw together a PowerPoint to fill the online awkwardness. And when I'm doing a pure phone pitch (the worst—try not to do it!), I'll usually send a look-book ahead and try to keep my pitch short.

The weirdest part about pitching is getting into it. Usually, that's where the "why I'm the person to write the script" part transitions to:

"FADE IN -- A BIKER BAR FOR STUFFED ANIMALS..."

There comes a point where you stop talking about your favorite flavor of LaCroix (Key Lime, btw) and start saying, "Sooo, I heard you love talking dog musicals..."

Practice that part too, so you'll be able to segue seamlessly into your pitch. You're really driving and they don't have a lot of time. If your small talk goes on for too long, they might just clap their hands and say "Let's do it!" But if not, you'll be the one in charge of making the move from small talk to pitch. Know when to pivot.

PLAN FOR QUESTIONS

Immediately after a pitch, execs always ask a few pointed questions. (It's their job, so unless time is really rushed, you'll always get one or two.) I've done many a great pitch then botched the Q&A part. Make a list of the hardest questions you think they'll ask and come up with good answers. Be assured; the questions you don't want them to ask will be the ones they ask. Every time. So come up with good answers; they don't have to be perfect answers, but they need to be good enough for the exce to feel "this person has a handle on this material and can overcome obstacles." Be honest with yourself. If your pitch is about a world that's a little too similar to a current show, you need to tackle that head-on and have an answer why it's different. If your new show feels more like a movie than a TV show, that's what they're going to stick on. Going in and hoping they won't ask the tricky question you know is on everyone's mind is not a strategy. Plan for those questions. Your answers might literally be the difference between a sale and a pass.

You can't really control what happens during the pitch. Sometimes the audience is not interested, sometimes they're combative, sometimes the fire alarm goes off just when you're about to reveal the big twist (true story). You can control everything you're bringing into the room: your story, your pitch, your answers to their questions. Prep, then just let it fly. Leave the room knowing you couldn't have prepared any better. Take stock of things you might change about your preparation (or even your pitch) in the future. Use the moment to evolve, then move on.

Also, know that pass/fail isn't the only goal here. Committing to a TV show is a huge thing for a studio. Your pitch is an opportunity to show just how competent you are. Your delivery, creativity, and preparation might lead you to other work or, at the very least, future pitch meetings.

NERVES!

Here's a secret: everyone hates pitching. Writers are mostly introverts. The idea of being the center of attention and doing a performance in front of a room full of disinterested execs is the polar opposite of the sit-on-the-couch-alone-for-hours act of writing.

I remember the first time I pitched. I had fancy artwork—a pirate ship!—that I held tightly chest high. My hands shook, really really bad. I think the development execs thought I was trying to imply the motion of the boat. I couldn't even hide my hands in my pockets because holding this board was part of my pitch.

I still get nerves. I still have butterflies. The best advice I can give is to prepare. The more nervous you are, the more you should prepare. Preparation is a channel for all that anxiety.

The other comfort I can give is the people you'll be pitching to generally are cool and empathetic and get that what we're doing is really difficult.

And just know, you're not the only one that gets nervous. We all do. Everyone of us. It's part of the fun. Just make sure you put in the homework and I promise you'll do fine.

EXERCISES

- Write out the pitch document for your show. If you've been following along with the process, you'll have more than enough material to fill out each section of the template. The template has everything you'll need going forward.

- Try pitching your show verbally, even if it's just the logline or the pilot. Pitching is a skill. It needs to be nurtured. If you're in a writers' group, suggest a pitch night. Start small. Five-minute, high-level pitches. Critique each other. It's a great way to get over the awkwardness, to find your pitching voice, and it can help you work out high-level story issues.

CHECK YOURSELF

- Do you have a compelling reason why you're the best writer for this particular show?

- Is this show relevant to our current times?

- Do you have a logline that pitches the show and acts as a safety net for skimmers and interruptions?

- Have you conveyed compelling main characters with flaws, broken compasses, and rooting resumes?

- Does your pitch give a feel for the tone of the show?

- Is it clear how your pilot sets up the show's world and its situation?

- Do you represent the potential for the first season and beyond?

🐾 SO YOU STILL WANNA BE A TV WRITER?

So, you're one of those.

I still haven't scared you off.

With the work, the challenge, the terrifying pitch meetings.

Okay, cool.

You still have questions. The same ones everyone has:

How do I get a TV job?

How do I find an agent or a manager?

How do I get my pilot script in the soft supple hands of Greg Berlanti?

I've never heard a great answer to any of these questions.

Ever.

And you won't find one here. Sorry.

There's a problem with those questions.

Imagine asking a bazillion-dollar Powerball winner, "How did you do it?" They may answer "find a lucky sweater" or "only buy at liquor stores" or "use those magic numbers from the TV show *Lost*."

There is no typical TV career path.

Assuming you have oodles of talent, it's a bit like being an Olympic athlete.

Imagine being a great pole vaulter. The best. Talent is a must, of course. But you need opportunities, too. You'll need the right mentors and supporters to recognize your pole-vaulting talents along the way and guide you to the places where you can improve and have a legitimate shot. You'll need sponsors and money and healthy relationships to endure the time and sacrifice you'll be putting into chasing your dreams before they ever pay off. And after you have all that lined up, you'll still have to train for years and hope bad luck doesn't strike (injury, canceled Olympic games, or the committee eliminating your sport). And that's just to be in the game.

Because when you're in the game, things really get interesting.

I once heard Rodney Dangerfield quoted as saying to be a stand-up comic you need to "be a tank. You need to be able to plow through the boneheads and obstacles that get in your way."

And that's the best answer. That's something you can control. It'll take time. It'll take struggle. Through study and experimentation and bullheaded determination, you can hone your voice, hone your craft, build your confidence, and educate yourself to the level of expert—ready to make decisions that point you in the right direction without putting too much weight in one decision or one path. But if you keep trying and work smart making steps toward achieving your goals, you'll get there.

Follow your own *unbroken* compass. There will be serious gut punches along the way. It's part of the process.

KEEP WRITING SCRIPTS

Scripts! Scripts! Scripts! You'll probably write a dozen scripts before you're either good enough or lucky enough to get anyone to pay even a lick of attention. My very first script did great in a contest! My sixth was optioned. Writing was easy! I was so wrong. I didn't make any money or sell anything until my 10th or 11th when I was 4-5 years in! And still, I had a long way to go.

You'll learn a lot about the craft along the way but also about yourself and what you want to write. It's going to take time. Get on it. Get 10 scripts out.

Even professionals have to be tenacious about creating their own opportunities, so much so that the one key trait I see in pros isn't talent… it's persistence. They have a motor that doesn't stop. If you ask them "What are you up to?" their real answer would take about three hours to lay it all out.

I've heard of managers who require their new clients to do two features and two pilots a year. That's *after* you get the manager. They know that the most important thing is the material. You can write yourself out of anything. Keep cranking out the words. One day opportunity will match your effort. What you're doing might not pay off for years. So ya gotta keep at it.

KEEP BUILDING YOUR TRIBE

Networking, yuck.

I've never networked.

So gross.

But I make an effort to participate in things that are aligned with my interest and goals. Simply, if it sounds like fun, I do it! If someone asks me to be a guest on their podcast, I'm there! Someone wants to build a team to do a 48-hour film, I'm your guy. Be in a play! Sure, I love the community. Come speak to our writers' conference. Is there free food?

Don't think of networking as some weird nightclub where you're eyeing up potential power players to slide in and start small talk. Networking is just saying "yes" to things it would be easier to say "no" to, things that are good for the soul. The stuff you're glad you went to after the fact. Any of these moments might be the twists and turns in your story down the road. It's why no one has good answers to the "how to break-in" questions—these meet-ups and connections are so rando, you just have to put yourself out there.

For some, it's classes or schools. For others, it's writers' groups. Take improv classes. Go to talks by producers. Go to the Austin Writers Conference. Make a podcast. I made many of my first contacts volunteering to hold the boom on independent films. Keep saying "yes" to opportunities to join or mingle with creative people in ways that interest you. It's not networking. It's getting off the couch. It's chasing your bliss. Chase it hard. But chase it in ways that you meet people and get curious about other creative things.

Cast a wide net, take some time to get away from the computer, and go live a creative life.

SHOULD I MOVE TO LA?

Eventually, for sure.

But maybe not yet.

Yes, TV is a room gig. And the rooms are in LA.

Everyone's tolerance for risk and adventure and change is different. You have to plan for the long haul. That means knowing what kind of life you want to lead.

I've known just as many people that moved to LA as soon as they got the chance, flaming out and ultimately giving up their TV writing dreams, as those who didn't make the jump and eventually found some success working a day job and writing scripts at night.

There are lots of advantages to being in LA. Everything is about meeting people. Any way you can increase your circle of creative types who work in the business can increase your odds. Living in LA will increase the odds of that exponentially.

But there's still the timing thing. You need scripts. You need craft. You need confidence. You need to be that tank Rodney Dangerfield talked about.

Some people just have a genetic makeup that they can stay focused while making a new life in a new place.

Others might have reasons they can never move. Or might just feel really comfortable with life where they're at.

The landscape of TV is evolving fast. By the time you're ready, the landscape could change. Zoom writers' rooms might be the norm. YouTube-distributed owner-created shows might be on the rise. Or selling pilots to content-starved streamers might open the gates wide.

Or not...

Moving to LA is a question you have to figure out for yourself. You know you. Making the move isn't going to open all the doors. Be sure you're ready. And when you are, go kick some doors open.

DON'T FORGET TO MAKE STUFF

More and more, short films, fictional podcasts, and web series are getting bought up and adapted for TV and film.

That's not to say don't write your pilots. Write your pilots!!

But mix in the "making stuff" too. Turn one of your scripts into a YouTube web series (like *Insecure* or *Broad City*, which both had their roots in web series) or a fictionalized podcast (like *Homecoming*), or make a short-film prototype of your series (*It's Always Sunny in Philadelphia*).

It's good for your soul—and your craft! Instead of being a wannabe, separate yourself from the pack by being a doer, a creator. It'll give you confidence when you find yourself in front of agents and producers. You can execute. You've done things they may not have done. It'll give you a special sheen.

Don't spend too much of your own money on this stuff. Choose things that you can get your arms around —if you're doing big fantasy and sci-fi stuff, maybe go the graphic novel route or shoot a 2-minute short-film prototype. Try a fictional podcast instead of trying to produce an entire season of a TV show.

Make stuff. Get it out there. Feed your soul. Keep your eye on the prize.

It'll make you a better writer, a better creator, and a better person.

Here's a funny thing...

I've Miyagi-ed you again.

Fictional podcasts, comic books, web series, and book series can be developed using the exact same methods as have been laid out here for your TV series.

You're ready.

Don't wait for the TV gods to find you. Go. Do the thing.

AND NOW... THE TAG

At the end of *The Marvelous Mrs. Maisel* pilot, Midge asks Lenny Bruce about his rough career in comedy, "Do you love it?"

Any writer's journey is filled with buckets of failure, disappointment, and rejections.

This week alone, I had two different big-time pitches I spent weeks working on shot down. I had a producer give tough notes on a project. I had a studio say "meh" to a long list of potential loglines for new TV shows.

Ouchie.

Every one of those rejections was a body blow. Every one of those opportunities was something I was wildly excited about. I worked hard to land. I dreamed of the possibilities.

In a quick flurry of emails, hopes can get dashed. Days go from good to soul-crushing.

Producers will ghost you. Agents will block you. Studios will pass and pass and pass and pass and pass and make you do a free rewrite and pass and pass.

Do I love it?

Emphatic "Yes."

Because on those same days... I write on a new project. I give notes on an edit of a film. I crank out a new page. I take meetings that open new doors. I teach students. I learn something new. I get better.

Every day an imperfect writer becomes less imperfect.

Ultimately through all the ups-and-downs, you realize there's not really a specific destination to be reached.

It's just more journey.

We're not all going to be Aaron Sorkin.

But right now, he's battling it too. He's fighting the fight. And the fight is interesting. It's fun. It gets you up in the morning and keeps you up at night.

If ya love it, ya just love it.

And the best way to combat frustration is not to wait around for anybody or anything.

The only rule of such an aimless journey is to keep walking.

Don't stand still.

With each step, you'll be closer to less imperfect.

Go write your next pilot. Create your next show.

It's gonna be awesome.

ACKNOWLEDGEMENTS

As much as I'd like to say this book is "me on a plate," it has lots of sous chefs. Thanks to Pete Barnstrom for all the spontaneous on-line *Save the Cat!* conversations we've had over the last two decades in the way mad scientists test their weird regeneration formulas. Huge thanks to Bradley Paul for being my insider about what goes down inside TV writers' rooms and their super-secret processes. Thanks to Chris Mueller, who let me bend his ear on many afternoon phone conversations and enthusiastically contributed to some of my favorite new insights in this book. Also to Jimmy George and Bob Rose, my *Thundergrunt* podcast compadres who enjoy cracking a movie's Fun & Games and Midpoint as much as I do. Thanks to all my students over the years—you have no idea how valuable it's been to work with you and have a place to discuss and try out ideas... ideas that now have a home in this book.

Thanks to Amy, Luke, and George... who let me binge watch pilot episodes of shows over and over and over. You can have the remote back now.

Mega shoutouts to Jason Kolinsky and all the other *Save the Cat!* peeps who have kept the lights on in the *Cat!* offices. Thanks for all the work you do spreading the *Cat!* philosophy to new writers every day.

And a huge high-five to layout artist Gina Mansfield, who turned my words into an actual book and suffered through all my last-minute ideas with unending grace and professionalism.

And biggest thanks of all to "King Cat" BJ Markel, who has always remembered me over the years and suggested I write this very book. BJ not only loaned his expert eye to these pages, but also had key suggestions and inspirations along the way. Thanks for giving me the chance to be part of this whole *Save the Cat!* thing. I'm truly honored.

And lastly, thanks to Blake.

It was great co-writing with you again, after all these years.

Thanks for everything.

I hope I made you proud.

Let's finish that talking car movie next...

ABOUT THE AUTHOR

Jamie Nash has written and sold almost every type of story under the sun, including the horror films *Exists*, *V/H/S/2*, *The Night Watchmen*, *Altered*, and *Lovely Molly*, and the family films *Santa Hunters* and *Tiny Christmas*. He has written the Middle Grade novels *Bunk!* and *The 44 Rules of Amateur Sleuthing* and the sci-fi novel *Nomad*. Jamie knows what it's like to make a living as a writer. When he's not writing and selling work, he teaches screenwriting at the Maryland Institute College of the Arts (MICA) and co-hosts the podcast *Writers/Blockbusters*. Jamie lives in Maryland with his wife, son, and a talking dog.